HOPELESSNESS

HOPELESSNESS
Developmental, Cultural, and Clinical Realms

Edited by
Salman Akhtar
and Mary Kay O'Neil

LONDON AND NEW YORK

First published 2015 by Karnac Books Ltd.

Published 2018 by Routledge
2 Park Square, Milton Park, Abingdon, Oxon OX14 4RN
711 Third Avenue, New York, NY 10017, USA

Routledge is an imprint of the Taylor & Francis Group, an informa business

Copyright © 2015 to Salman Akhtar and Mary Kay O'Neil for the edited collection, and to the individual authors for their contributions.

The rights of the contributors to be identified as the authors of this work have been asserted in accordance with §§ 77 and 78 of the Copyright Design and Patents Act 1988.

All rights reserved. No part of this book may be reprinted or reproduced or utilised in any form or by any electronic, mechanical, or other means, now known or hereafter invented, including photocopying and recording, or in any information storage or retrieval system, without permission in writing from the publishers.

Notice:
Product or corporate names may be trademarks or registered trademarks, and are used only for identification and explanation without intent to infringe.

British Library Cataloguing in Publication Data

A C.I.P. for this book is available from the British Library

ISBN-13: 9781782202585 (pbk)

Typeset by V Publishing Solutions Pvt Ltd., Chennai, India

To
our children
Kabir and Nishat
David, Eric, Adam, and Sarah
enduring and endearing barriers to hopelessness

CONTENTS

ACKNOWLEDGEMENTS ix

ABOUT THE EDITORS AND CONTRIBUTORS xi

INTRODUCTION xvii

PROLOGUE

CHAPTER ONE
Hope and hopelessness: an introductory overview 3
Salman Akhtar

PART I: DEVELOPMENTAL REALM

CHAPTER TWO
The encounter with hopelessness in childhood 23
Ann Smolen

CHAPTER THREE
Adolescent hope and hopelessness 43
Rose A. Vasta

CHAPTER FOUR
Hopelessness and midlife
Jon P. Ellman
57

PART II: CULTURAL REALM

CHAPTER FIVE
Literary depictions of hopelessness: a short story, a novel, and a poem
Eve Holwell
85

CHAPTER SIX
The illusion of a future: hopelessness in contemporary cinema
Sylvia Chong
107

PART III: CLINICAL REALM

CHAPTER SEVEN
From hopelessness to despair
Jeanne Bailey
139

CHAPTER EIGHT
On the edge of hopelessness and despair: an uncertain landscape
Judi B. Kobrick
153

CHAPTER NINE
Hope and hopelessness in the couple relationship
Sarah Fels Usher
165

CHAPTER TEN
Hopelessness in the countertransference
Dhwani Shah
181

EPILOGUE

CHAPTER ELEVEN
The hopelessness and helplessness dyad: a concluding commentary
Mary Kay O'Neil
203

REFERENCES 215

INDEX 229

ACKNOWLEDGEMENTS

We are deeply grateful to the distinguished colleagues who contributed to this volume. We appreciate their effort, their sacrifice of time, and their patience with our requirements, reminders, and requests for revisions. We are also thankful to Jan Wright for her skillful help in preparing the manuscript of this book and to Fred Lowy for his supportive comments. Oliver Rathbone and Kate Pearce of Karnac Books gave unerring support of this project and shepherded it through various phases of publication. To both of them, our sincere thanks.

ABOUT THE EDITORS AND CONTRIBUTORS

Salman Akhtar, MD, is professor of psychiatry at Jefferson Medical College and a training and supervising analyst at the Psychoanalytic Center of Philadelphia. He has served on the editorial boards of all the three major psychoanalytic journals, namely, the *International Journal of Psychoanalysis*, the *Journal of the American Psychoanalytic Association*, and the *Psychoanalytic Quarterly*. His more than 300 publications include sixteen books—*Broken Structures* (1992), *Quest for Answers* (1995), *Inner Torment* (1999), *Immigration and Identity* (1999), *New Clinical Realms* (2003), *Objects of Our Desire* (2005), *Regarding Others* (2007), *Turning Points in Dynamic Psychotherapy* (2009), *The Damaged Core* (2009), *Comprehensive Dictionary of Psychoanalysis* (2009), *Immigration and Acculturation* (2011), *Matters of Life and Death* (2011), *The Book of Emotions* (2012), *Psychoanalytic Listening* (2013), *Good Stuff* (2013), and *Sources of Suffering* (2014)—as well as forty-two edited or co-edited volumes in psychiatry and psychoanalysis. Dr. Akhtar has delivered many prestigious addresses and lectures including, most recently, the inaugural address at the first IPA-Asia Congress in Beijing, China (2010). Dr. Akhtar is the recipient of the *Journal of the American Psychoanalytic Association*'s Best Paper of the Year Award (1995), the Margaret Mahler Literature Prize (1996), the American Society of Psychoanalytic

Physicians' Sigmund Freud Award (2000), the American Psychoanalytic Association's Edith Sabshin Award (2000), the American College of Psychoanalysts' Laughlin Award (2003), Columbia University's Robert Liebert Award for Distinguished Contributions to Applied Psychoanalysis (2004), the American Psychiatric Association's Kun Po Soo Award (2004), the Irma Bland Award for being the Outstanding Teacher of Psychiatric Residents in the country (2005), and the Nancy Roeske Award (2012). Most recently, he received the Sigourney Award (2013), which is the most prestigious honor in the field of psychoanalysis. Dr. Akhtar is an internationally sought speaker and teacher, and his books have been translated in many languages, including German, Turkish, and Romanian. His interests are wide and he has served as the film review editor for the *International Journal of Psychoanalysis*, and is currently serving as the book review editor for the *International Journal of Applied Psychoanalytic Studies*. He has published seven collections of poetry and serves as a scholar-in-residence at the Inter-Act Theatre Company in Philadelphia.

Jeanne Bailey, MD, is a training and supervising analyst at the Minnesota Psychoanalytic Institute and has been its director for the past two years. She graduated from the Institute for Psychoanalysis in Chicago, Illinois and practiced in Chicago for over ten years. She then moved to Minnesota and became one of the founding members of the Minnesota Psychoanalytic Institute. Dr. Bailey continues to teach courses there on transference and countertransference, object relations theory, and models of depression. She also conducts a fifteen-week continuous case conference each year. Her activities in national-level seminars include clinical presentations on the mother–daughter relationship with Paula Bernstein, on grief with Salman Akhtar, and on female sexuality with Nancy Kulish. Her review of the book *Play and Playfulness* was published in the *American Journal of Psychoanalysis* in December of 2012 and her concluding commentary appeared in the edited volume titled *Guilt: Origins, Manifestations, and Management* (2013). Dr. Bailey coordinates and teaches a psychodynamic psychotherapy three year seminar for psychiatry residents at Hennepin County Medical Center and has received awards for Teacher of the Year, and for Exceptional Community Service. She maintains a private practice of psychiatry, psychotherapy, and psychoanalysis in Minneapolis, MN.

ABOUT THE EDITORS AND CONTRIBUTORS

Sylvia Shin Huey Chong, PhD, is an associate professor in English and American studies at the University of Virginia, where she also directs the Asian Pacific American studies program. She received her doctorate in rhetoric from the University of California, Berkeley, an MA in education from Stanford University, and a BA in English from Swarthmore College. Her recent book, *The Oriental Obscene: Violence and Racial Fantasies in the Vietnam Era* (Duke University Press, 2012), uses psychoanalytic and Deleuzian film theory to investigate the fantasies of trauma and violence which animate mass media representations of the Vietnam War and also frame racial politics at large during the 1960s–80s. She has also written articles and book chapters on the filmmakers Samuel Peckinpah, Oliver Stone, and Michael Cimino, on the Virginia Tech massacre, and on Asian American cultural studies and American Orientalism. She was a recipient of an American Psychoanalytic Association fellowship in 2012–2013, and also held a Woodrow Wilson Career Enhancement fellowship in 2007–2008. Her current research focuses on issues of racial masquerade, assimilation, and performance, analyzed through the intersection of social science and cinema in the mid-twentieth century, with a side interest in the development (and critique) of social psychology and psychoanalysis to study racial minorities and foreign cultures during this period.

Jon P. Ellman, MD, is a training and supervising analyst at the Canadian Institute of Psychoanalysis, in Montreal. He is the former director of the English Division of this Institute and served as the chair of its Curriculum Committee. He was also the director of the national Canadian Institute of Psychoanalysis and of the Midlife Unit at the Montreal General Hospital. He is an assistant professor of psychiatry, McGill University School of Medicine, Montreal.

Eve Holwell was born and raised in New York City. She attended Yale University, graduating in 2005, with a degree in humanities. She wrote her senior thesis on Edmund Burke's and Thomas Carlyle's works on the French Revolution. Later, she was involved in curriculum development at the University of California in Merced, and then returned to New York City for further studies at Columbia University. There, she wrote a series of papers on ethical issues surrounding egg donation with Robert Klitzman, director of the master's program in bioethics. She is currently a rising third year medical student at Jefferson Medical College in Philadelphia and has recently published "Three Literary Characters in Search of Revenge" in the book, *Revenge: Origins, Manifestations, and Management* (Aronson, 2014).

Judi B. Kobrick, PhD, is a founding member and president of the Toronto Institute for Contemporary Psychoanalysis, where she also serves as a faculty member and a supervising analyst. She is the past president of the Toronto Psychoanalytic Society and Institute and remains on its teaching faculty. Dr. Kobrick is a consulting psychologist and past director of the eating disorders program at the Credit Valley Hospital, and maintains a private practice of psychoanalysis and psychotherapy in Toronto.

Mary Kay O'Neil, PhD, is a supervising and training psychoanalyst who has recently moved from Montreal back to Toronto, where she is in private practice. She is the past director of the Canadian Institute of Psychoanalysis (Quebec, English) and a North American representative on the board of the International Psychoanalytical Association. In addition, she has served on a number of IPA committees, including the publication committee and ethics committees at the local, national, and international levels, and on the editorial board of the *International Journal of Psychoanalysis*. Dr. O'Neil received a PhD from the University of Toronto, where she was an assistant professor in the Department of Psychiatry. She completed her psychoanalytic training at the Toronto Institute of Psychoanalysis and is a registered psychologist in both Quebec and Ontario. The author of *The Unsung Psychoanalyst: The Quiet Influence of Ruth Easser*, she has co-authored/edited five other books and has contributed numerous professional journal articles as well as chapters and book reviews. Her publications and research include studies of depression and young adult development, emotional needs of sole support mothers, post termination analytic contact, and psychoanalytic ethics. Her research activities have been funded by foundations in Toronto and Montreal.

Dwani Shah, MD, is a clinical associate faculty member in the Department of Psychiatry at the University of Pennsylvania School of Medicine and an attending staff psychiatrist at Princeton University's Counseling and Psychological Services. He did his residency in psychiatry at the University of Pennsylvania, School of Medicine, where he also served as chief resident. Later, he completed a fellowship in the treatment of resistant mood disorders at the same institution, and then trained at the Psychoanalytic Center of Philadelphia. He is the recipient of several awards, including the University of Pennsylvania's PENN Pearls Teaching Award for Excellence in Clinical Medical Education, the University of Pennsylvania Residency Education's Psychodynamic Psychotherapy Award, and the Laughlin Merit Award for professional achievement. He has published papers on diverse topics, including neuroscience, mood disorders, and psychotherapy. Dr. Shah maintains a private practice of psychiatry, psychotherapy, and psychoanalysis in Princeton, NJ.

Ann Smolen, PhD, is a supervising and training analyst in child, adolescent, and adult psychoanalysis at the Psychoanalytic Center of Philadelphia. Dr. Smolen graduated summa cum laude from Bryn Mawr College and received her master's degree in social work from Bryn Mawr College School of Social Work and Social Research. She received her doctorate in philosophy from the Clinical Social Work Institute in Washington, DC. Her first profession was as a member of the New York City Ballet. Dr. Smolen has won several national awards for her clinical work, and has presented her clinical work both nationally and internationally. Dr. Smolen has published several articles including *Boys Only! No Mothers Allowed*, published in the *International Journal of Psychoanalysis* and translated into three languages. Dr. Smolen is the author of *Mothering Without a Home: Representations of Attachment Behaviors in Homeless Mothers and Children* (Aronson, 2013). She maintains a private practice in child, adolescent, and adult psychotherapy and psychoanalysis in Ardmore, PA.

Sarah Fels Usher, PhD, CPsych, is a psychologist and psychoanalyst in private practice in Toronto. She did her undergraduate studies at McGill University in Montreal, and her doctoral degree at York University in Toronto. Dr. Usher received her psychoanalytic training at the Toronto Institute of Psychoanalysis. She is past president of the Toronto Psychoanalytic Society and former secretary of the Canadian Psychoanalytic Society. She is the founding director of the Fundamental Psychoanalytic Perspectives Program at the Toronto Psychoanalytic Society and serves on the faculty of the Toronto

Institute of Psychoanalysis. She is also the book review editor of the *Canadian Journal of Psychoanalysis/Revue Canadienne de Psychanalyse*. Dr. Usher is the author of *What is This Thing Called Love? A Guide to Psychoanalytic Psychotherapy with Couples* (Routledge, 2008) and *Introduction to Psychodynamic Psychotherapy Technique*, the second edition of which has recently been released (Routledge, 2013).

Rose Vasta, PhD, FIPA, is a training and supervising psychoanalyst of the Canadian Psychoanalytic Institute, a member of the Western Branch of the Canadian Psychoanalytic Society, the current director of the Vancouver Psychoanalytic Institute and an assistant clinical professor in the Island Medical Program of the University of British Columbia. Dr. Vasta received the Miguel Prados Essay Prize from the Canadian Psychoanalytic Society in 2011 for her paper "Bion's Negative Grid". She maintains a private practice of psychoanalysis and psychotherapy in Victoria, British Columbia, treating both adults and adolescents.

INTRODUCTION

According to ancient Greek myth, when Pandora's Box was opened, all emotions escaped but one. The emotion that refused to leave, after each passion was spent and all sorrow spilled, was hope. Indeed, hope is the most reliable sustainer of life. It offers the promise of something good in the future, contributes to resilience, and keeps one going. All this is agreed upon. Our daydreams, fables, literature, and anthems celebrate the fruitfulness of retaining hope in adverse circumstances. Hope holds our hand when evening descends into night and when dawn appears to be too far away.

Sadly, such is not always the case. There are circumstances when hope, the silent fountainhead of life, dries up. Dreams dissipate, expectation turns gloomy, and the pockets of psyche contain no coins of optimism. It is this dark terrain of hopelessness that our book seeks to map out. The book opens with a broad overview of the nature, developmental origins, and technical implications of hope and hopelessness. And, it closes with a thoughtful summary, synthesis, and critique of the intervening essays; this summary forges theoretically and technically significant links between the experiences of helplessness and hopelessness. Sandwiched between these opening and closing commentaries are nine essays which address the ontogenetic trajectory, phenomenological variations, cultural and literary portrayals, and clinical ramifications of sustained hopelessness. Together, these essays provide an opportunity for the readers to enrich their knowledge base, deepen their empathy with patients struggling with despair, and sharpen their therapeutic skills in this painful realm of clinical practice.

PROLOGUE

CHAPTER ONE

Hope and hopelessness: an introductory overview

Salman Akhtar

All individuals who seek psychotherapy or psychoanalysis do so because they harbor the hope of sorting things out, improving their lives, and overcoming this or that problem. The extent, intensity, and tenor of the sentiment might vary but the fact that hope is what drives them to seek treatment remains certain. This hope can be realistic (e.g., of becoming able to mourn early losses and of accepting what current life does offer in the form of possibilities and gratifications) or pathological (e.g., of reversing time, growing up all over again, bringing dead people alive). And, this hope can be conscious (e.g., of actualizing one's wishes) or unconscious (e.g., of finding development-facilitating objects). It is, therefore, of profound importance to empathize with, discern, uphold, and, at some point, interpretively handle (if necessary) the hope that has brought the patient to the therapist's threshold. The same applies to the pallor or absence of hope. In other words, hope and hopelessness warrant comparable interest from the analyst: recognition, curiosity, exploration, validation, reconstruction, and interpretive resolution. Both poles of this spectrum—hope and hopelessness—are of pertinence to our work. Yet, outside of general psychiatric practice, these issues have received scant attention.

In this chapter, I aim to fill this lacuna. I will begin my discourse with bringing together the scattered psychoanalytic literature on hope and add some of my own views to it. Then I will survey the psychoanalytic literature on the experience of hopelessness and provide a fresh perspective from my own side. I will challenge the reflexive tendency to regard hope as healthy and hopelessness as morbid, demonstrating that both hope and hopelessness have adaptive and pathological variants. I will then delineate the technical implications of the foregoing conceptualizations and conclude with some observations regarding populations that are especially vulnerable to hopelessness and also regarding the existential despair that is the inevitable legacy of our tragically violent world.

Normal and pathological hope

There is a long-held tendency in psychoanalysis to regard optimism in exceedingly positive terms. This tendency was set into motion by Freud's (1917b) well-known correlation of "confidence in success" with being mother's "undisputed darling" (p. 156) and by Abraham's (1924) linking "imperturbable optimism" (p. 399) with an overly gratifying oral phase. Glover (1925) repeated that profound oral gratification leads to an "excess of optimism which is not lessened by reality experience" (p. 136). Benedek's (1938) upbeat notion of "confident expectation" and Erikson's (1950) normative concept of "basic trust" were similarly anchored in satisfactory outcomes of the infantile-appeal cycle, that is, the infant's expression of need—his gratification by the mother—the infant's return to quiescence. Other contributors (French, 1945; French & Wheeler, 1963; Menninger, 1959) also focused on the positive aspects of hope and optimism.

This positive emphasis on hope found a novel twist in Winnicott's (1956) seminal paper, titled "The Antisocial Tendency". Winnicott observed that hope, even when expressed through pathological behavior, is essentially healthy and adaptive. He declared that "the antisocial act is an expression of hope" (p. 309) insofar as it seeks redress an early environmental deprivation. The individual, by behaving in a provocative manner, forces the environment to attend to him. Viewed in this manner, antisocial tendency is a desperate manifestation of the hope that someone will listen and do something to change the situation. Winnicott went on to state that stealing and destructiveness are always present in the antisocial tendency, though one or the other might be more marked in a given case.

> By *one* trend the child is looking for something, somewhere, and failing to find it seeks elsewhere, when hopeful. By the *other* the child is seeking that amount of environmental stability which will stand the strain resulting from impulsive behavior. This is a search for an environmental provision that has been lost. (p. 310, italics in the original)

The individual who steals is not looking for the stolen object but is seeking a person over whom he could have such unlimited rights. Similarly, destructiveness towards someone is coupled with the hope of being accepted by that person. This "nuisance value" (p. 311) is an essential aspect of the antisocial tendency that seeks repeatedly to test the environment's containing capacity and resilience.[1]

Khan (1966) extended Winnicott's ideas to certain narcissistic and schizoid individuals who seemed uncannily capable of creating special and exciting experiences for themselves, experiences from which they nonetheless withdrew and which left them basically unchanged. It is as if they had hoped for something but did not find it. Casement (1991) related "unconscious hope" to repetition compulsion through which unconscious conflicts continue to generate attempts at solutions which do not actually work. At the same time, patients do contribute in various ways, and "hopefully" (p. 301), to finding the clinical setting needed by them.

In an exception to the "classical" and British independent positive perspective on hope, Angel (1934) noted that optimism can at times be a defensive development.[2] She described five patients with chronic, unrealistic hope of a magical event (*Wunderglauben*) to improve their lots. She traced the origin of three female patients' undue hopefulness to a denial of their lacking a penis and associated feelings of inferiority. Angel offered a different explanation for undue optimism in two male patients. They had been prematurely and painfully deprived of their infantile omnipotence and were seeking its restoration by a fantasied regressive oneness with their mothers. Their optimism contained the hope of such longings being realized. Angel's conceptualization reflected the phallocentrism of psychoanalytic theorizing of her times. The fact most likely is that the latter dynamic applied to her female patients as well.

Over the sixty years following Angel's significant paper, only a few contributions commented upon the defensive functions of excessive optimism. First, Searles (1977) noted that realistic hope needs to be distinguished from "unconscious denial-based, unrealistic hopefulness" (p. 484). The former emanates from a successful integration of prior disappointments. The latter results from an "essentially manic repression of loss and despair" (p. 483). In contrast to healthy hopefulness, which is a source of support and gratification for oneself and others, excessive hope serves sadomasochistic aims. Searles outlined two connections between such inordinate hope and sadism:

> First, one of the more formidable ways of being sadistic toward the other person is to engender hope, followed by disappointment, in him over and over. Second, the presenting of a hopeful demeanor under some circumstances can constitute, in itself, a form of sadism toward the other person, for it can be expressing, implicitly and subtly, cruel demands upon him to fulfill the hopes written upon one's face. (p. 485)

Following Searles's contribution, Amati-Mehler and Argentieri (1989) described two cases in which "pathological hope" (p. 300) represented "the last and unique possible tie with the primary object, [which] giving up would mean the definite downfall of illusion and the admission that it is really, truly lost" (p. 302). Likewise, Potamianou (1992) asserted that excessive hope can serve as a character armor that keeps reality at a distance. In normal and neurotic conditions, hope sustains a link with the good object and makes waiting bearable. In borderline conditions, however, hope serves as an expression of the patient's narcissistic self-sufficiency; waiting is made bearable only by recourse to infantile omnipotence. For such individuals, the present has only secondary importance. They can tolerate almost any current suffering in the hope that future rewards will make it all worthwhile. Potamianou emphasized that excessive hope, besides fueling (and being fueled by) narcissism, strengthens and prolongs the hidden masochistic suffering of these individuals.

It is in this context that I described "someday ..." fantasies (Akhtar, 1991, 1994, 1996). These pertain to the feeling which almost all individuals have that a day will come when most of their problems will be solved and they will be at peace. Under normal circumstances such belief is attached to realistic goals, permits some sense of humor, and sustains ambition. But under pathological circumstances, the "someday ..." fantasy becomes tenacious, imbued with powerful defensive motives, and a servant of regressive, narcissistic, and masochistic aims. Patients vary greatly in the extent to which they provide details of their hopes from "someday ...." Often they feel puzzled, uncomfortable, ashamed, and even angry upon being asked to elaborate on their "someday." This is especially so if they are asked what would happen *after* "someday." It is as if "someday," like God, is not to be questioned. Some patients use metaphors and/or visual images to convey the essence of "someday ...," while others remain silent about it. Frequently, the analyst has to fill in the blanks and surmise the nature of their expectations from "someday ...." In either case, it is the affective texture of "someday ..." that seems its most important feature. Basically, "someday" refers to a time when one would be completely peaceful and conflict-free. Everything would be available, or nothing would be needed. Motor activity would either be unnecessary or effortless. Even thinking would not be required. There would be no aggression from within or from outside. Needless to say, such a universe is also oblivious to the inconvenient considerations of the incest taboo and the anxieties and compromises consequent upon the oedipal situation.

A complex set of psychodynamic mechanisms helps maintain the structural integrity of "someday ...": (i) denial and negation of sectors of reality that challenge it, (ii) splitting-off of those self and object representations that mobilize conflict and aggression, (iii) a defensively-motivated feeling of inauthenticity (Gediman, 1985) in those areas of personality where a healthier, more realistic, compromise formation level of mentality and functioning has been achieved, and (iv) a temporal displacement, from past to future, of a preverbal state of blissful unity with the "all good" mother of the symbiotic phase (Mahler, Pine, & Bergman, 1975). The speculation that this fantasy, at its core, contains a longing for a luxurious (and retrospectively idealized) symbiotic phase gains strength from the inactivity, timelessness, wordlessness, thoughtlessness, unexcited bliss, and absence of needs implicit in "someday ...." This genetic backdrop is supported by my observation that individuals who tenaciously cling to "someday ..." had often been suddenly "dropped" from maternal attention during their second year of life (at times due to major external events, e.g., birth of a sibling, prolonged maternal hospitalization). However, other factors including early parent or sibling loss, intense castration anxiety, and problematic oedipal scenarios also play a role in the genesis of the "someday ..." fantasy. Boys who were excessively close to their mothers, especially if they also had weak or absent fathers, might continue to believe that "someday ..." their oedipal triumph could actually be consummated; Chasseguet-Smirgel's (1984) delineation of "perverse character" is pertinent in this context. Girls who were "dropped" by their mothers and valiantly rescued by their fathers persist in the hope of "someday ..." finding an all good mother–father combination in adult life.

Mention also needs to be made of Boris's (1976) contribution which juxtaposed hope with desire, noting the frequently antagonistic relationship that exists between them. Delving deeply into this phenomenological realm, Boris declared the following:

> Desire is sensual; hope is not. Desire arises from the cyclic, appetitive passions of the body; hope appears to arise from preconceptions of how things should be. Desire seeks gratification and surcease—it is kinetic; hope is possessive and potential. Desire likes the here-and-now, the definite, the actual; hope likes the yet-to-be, the changeable, the ambiguous. When thwarted, desire tends to retreat, we call it "regress," to its last best success, while hope goes forward beyond even a lifetime or outwards beyond the confines of probability. Desire, frustrated, gives rise to rage and jealousy; hope—to outrage, and to envy and spite and revenge. When renounced, each, however, gives over to sadness; but desire changes it object while hope changes over to desire. (p. 149)

In sum, the psychoanalytic literature on hope can be grouped into three broad categories emphasizing (i) its normative, healthy aspects whereby hope acts as a restraint against the urgency of desire and, in doing so, undergirds sublimation and effort, (ii) its adaptive role in seeking redress, including that through pathological behavior, of early environmental loss, and (iii) its deployment as a defense against early loss and defective object constancy as well as its covert narcissistic and masochistic aims. The nuanced portrayal that emerges from this is that hope can be normal and manifest through healthy aspirations, exist as a subterranean dynamic in outrageousness, and, at times, serve defensive and pathological functions. Similar complexity is to be found in regard to hopelessness.

Normal and pathological hopelessness

Psychoanalytic literature directly pertaining to hopelessness is truly meager. The word "hopelessness" appears all of two times in the entire corpus of Freud's work (Guttman, Jones, & Parrish, 1980)[3] and the PEP web offers only six papers with "hopelessness" in their titles over the 115-year history of psychoanalysis. The reasons for this paucity are unclear. Perhaps the darkness of despair leads the observer to recoil from it. Or, the clinical population with greater and sustained hopelessness ends up with general psychiatrists more often than with psychoanalysts. Or, the encounter with true hopelessness propels adjunct, unusual or even "heroic" interventions that the practitioner is averse to putting down on paper. Regardless of etiology, the lack of psychoanalytic literature on hopelessness appears a significant finding in itself.

That being said, the phenomenon of hopelessness first received attention from Spitz (1946, 1960) and Bowlby (1958, 1960, 1961), who observed infants and their reactions to separation from their mothers. They stressed that infants have attachments to their mothers that are independent of "orality" and physiological needs. Upon separating from their mothers, infants at first protest (e.g., crying loudly, looking eagerly for signs of her return), then display increasing hopelessness and despair, and finally resign themselves to the situation and become unenthusiastic about later attachments. Frequent and long separations from mother (e.g., due to her illness or hospitalization), especially when coupled with unreliable replacements, intensify feelings of hopelessness and turn it into a core feature of personality to which the individual can readily regress under need-frustrating circumstances.

An additional viewpoint to this formulation was provided by Kelman (1945), who declared that a love-deprived child constructs an idealized self that is (in imagination) need-free and/or completely able to meet his own needs by the methods of withdrawal, cleverness, or clinging. Since these maneuvers frequently fail, the individual is riddled with dissatisfaction, depression, feelings of doom, chronic hopelessness, and a sense of psychic deadness. The futile striving to eradicate childhood feelings of defectiveness (e.g., "I am not loved because something is wrong with me") and achieve a peaceful existence in which one feels loved results in feelings of utter hopelessness and doom. One feels lost, meaningless, and emotionally dead.

> These patients often complain that they are dead ... [and] ... feel that their relationships are dead. They are limited, rigid and controlled. Although they feel that they can move wherever they please, they still feel completely bounded. They suffer from monotony, boredom, and a feeling of ennui. Each day, each feeling, each act seems like the one before and the one after. Nothing changes. Everything is static and dead. (Kelman, 1945, p. 432)

Schmale (1964) distinguished between "helplessness" and "hopelessness." The former reflects a loss of ego autonomy due to the inability to receive a desired gratification from an important other person. The latter reflects a loss of ego autonomy due to one's own inability to provide oneself with gratification. With a deep anchor in child developmental observations, Schmale proposed that the affect of helplessness occurs first at the end of the oral phase when there is a dawning awareness of being separate from one's mother. Along with this comes the realization of dependence upon her. Now, if the maternal availability (for provision of ego support, gratification of wishes, meeting of developmental needs) is inconsistent, "confident expectation" (Benedek, 1938) fails to develop and the seeds of vulnerability for helplessness (i.e., being unable to draw others to help) are sowed.

Schmale went on to state that the affect of hopelessness occurs first during the phallic phase where there is increased awareness of sexual wishes on the one hand and strict incest prohibition on the other. It is the inability, at this state, to provide gratification to oneself that lays down the groundwork for future experiences of hopelessness. Schmale allowed for thinking that some hopelessness might actually be salutary for personality growth.

> The experiencing of the feelings of hopelessness in relation to unfulfilled aspirations, if not too overwhelming or too quickly defended against, leads to a giving up of fantasied wishes. Such giving up is basic to the acceptance of a more realistic sense of self as well as to a more appropriate and realistic awareness of the object world .... A change in psychic self may be necessary to meet and maintain ego autonomy over the ever-pressing instinctual drives and the bodily and external objects. In order to remain reality-oriented and psychically as well as somatically healthy, such changes in self representation are repeatedly required as man grows, explores, achieves, ages, and declines. (p. 308)[4]

The shift from fantasized perfection and desired gratification of prohibited wishes to reality-oriented self perception and achievable pursuits enunciated by Schmale has unmistakable echoes of Klein's (1935) proposal of the "depressive position" in development. Unlike the earlier "paranoid position" characterized by disowning of aggression, retention of a "purified pleasure ego" (Freud, 1915c), omnipotence, greed, envy, and smug certainty, "depressive position" implies the recognition of one's (real and fantasized) destructiveness towards love objects, humility, cognitive flexibility, sadness, gratitude, and reparative longing. Moreover, the nature of hope also changes with this developmental achievement. In "paranoid position," the hope is one of perfection and purity. In "depressive position," the hope is one of relatedness and love. In Klein's (1957) own words:

> This hope is based on the growing unconscious knowledge that the internal and external object is not as bad as it was felt to be in its split-off aspects. Through mitigation of hatred by love, the object improves in the infant's mind. It is no longer so strongly felt to have been destroyed in the past and the danger of its being destroyed in the future is lessened .... The internal object acquires a restraining and self-preservative attitude. (p. 196)

Thus, in Klein's formulation, real hope emerges only after false (i.e., idealized) hope has been given up and when love predominates over hate in the internal psychic economy of the child. In other words, a certain "normal" hopelessness is essential for psychic growth; the germ of this idea seems inherent in Freud's (1911b) distinction between "pleasure principle" and "reality principle" whereby the hope of gratification, in order to be safe and therefore more satisfying, has to give up its urgency in the moment.

The experience of hopelessness also drew the attention of Miller (1985), and Amati-Mehler and Argentieri (1989). Miller described chronic hopelessness in the setting of pathological narcissism. The narcissistic person cannot experience a feeling of being loved; he derides it as mere "admiration" or based upon others not knowing him well-enough. He cannot love himself either. As a result, he feels perpetually hopeless to connect with others and with his own self. There is also the sense that one can never vent the pent-up rage within oneself since this rage is against the caregivers (past and present) upon whom one feels dependent. Amati-Mehler and Argentieri (1989) emphasized that the way of chronic hopelessness is paved by inward clinging to the pathological hope that "what is past or lost forever can still be provided and restored" (p. 300).

> There is no alternative intermediary space between how "it was" and how "it should be"; pathological hope cancels realistic hope and gives way to hopelessness. Real chances available in life are dismissed, or rather not recognized, because they do not fit the rigid mold that illusion pretends to realize. Capacity to feel and experience oneself as occupying a dynamic-spatial-temporal dimension, in relation to others too, enhances difficult symbolic tension to make it possible to think, to discriminate fantasy from reality and personage from person, and thus to organize boundaries of mental representation linked with intrapsychic and interpersonal separation processes. What distinguishes the case we observed instead is a situation in which a very tenuous ridge divides illusion from disillusion: experiences of painful separation cannot be denied nor can they be accepted; there's an eternal present in which loss is furiously felt, but the "drama" which *has already irreparably happened* is not recognized or realized as such. (p. 300, italics in the original)

Putting all the foregoing material together, I can envision five vertices to conceptualize the experience of hopelessness. These include the following.

- *Normal versus pathological hopelessness,* with the former emanating from the renunciation of infantile omnipotence and aiding personality development, and the latter clinging to that very omnipotence and fueling fixation on unrealistic goals.
- *Focal versus generalized hopelessness,* with the former pertaining to the dawning sense that certain specific aims will not be realized and the latter to not finding any aspect of life gratifying and meaningful.
- *Situational versus characterological hopelessness,* with the former ensuing largely from contemporary environmental barriers to gratification and the latter emanating from the internalization of an early, severely disappointing, environment.
- *Melancholic versus militant hopelessness,* with the former expressing a wish to give up on this world out of a sense of existential fatigue, and

the latter representing a relentless attack upon others with the knife of loud despair.
- *Pleading versus resistant hopelessness*, with the former serving as a desperate method to pull the caregiver close so as to receive love and attention and the latter to render the caregiver helpless by keeping him away from the horrible infantile trauma that is being repudiated by the preoccupation with the present moment.

Such conceptualization prepares us to consider the technical measures needed to help patients with the anguish of pathological hope and pathological hopelessness.

Technical implications

From the foregoing discourse, it is clear that pathological hope is a defense against the unbearable experience of hopelessness. The individual who tenaciously clings to inordinate optimism (regardless of whether it is manifested through fierce ambition, flailing search, or futile waiting) is, at his psychic base, unable and unwilling to accept the devastating loss of love and support experienced during childhood. He cannot bear hopelessness that lurks just below the surface of his excessive hope. This dynamic becomes evident gradually as the treatment proceeds. More striking is the converse of it, that is, the slow unearthing of pathological hope under the manifest surface of intense hopelessness. Individuals who insistently and constantly declare themselves to be hopeless turn out to be harboring (however secretly) manic expectations of total reversal of their childhood trauma. Considered this way, pathological hope and pathological hopelessness appear to be twins: maladaptive responses to the inability to tolerate normal hopelessness and sustain normal hope. Both pathological hope and pathological hopelessness are seen in the setting of severe childhood frustrations, even though the patients tend to repeat rather than recall the (actual and fantasized) relational scenarios consequent upon such trauma.

Treatment of these individuals must rest upon the general principles of handling psychic trauma outlined in psychoanalytic literature as well as upon certain specific interventions vis-à-vis pathological hope and hopelessness. Surveying the literature on the former aspect, I have recently (Akhtar, 2014a) delineated the following twelve features of technique: (i) welcoming attitude, (ii) prolonged holding, (iii) flexible framework, (iv) validation of trauma, (v) belief in the principle of multiple function, (vi) sensitivity to nonverbal communication, (vii) enhancement of verbalization, (viii) creation of a transitional space, (ix) attunement to the patient's fluctuating psychostructural organization, (x) utilization of developmental interventions, (xi) facilitation of mourning and, (xii) management of countertransference. All these principles apply to the treatment of patients with pathological hope and chronic hopelessness.

In addition, such patients require certain specific interventions. For instance, after establishing an atmosphere of trust and security and after ample use of "affirmative interventions" (Killingmo, 1989),[5] the analyst must help the patient unmask what underlies his waiting attitude. This will pave the way for the two of them to squarely face the idealization inherent in "someday" fantasies. For instance, to a patient who after four years of analytic work continued to complain bitterly about the ineffectiveness of psychoanalysis vis-à-vis his short stature (a disguised but closed version of his actual complaint), I once responded by saying, "You know, the pained disbelief in your voice and the intensity with which you berate me about this issue makes me wonder if you really believe that analysis could or should lead you to become taller. Do you?" The patient was taken aback but, after some hesitation, did acknowledge that all along he had believed that he might become taller as a result of our work. Similarly, to a patient who constantly wept and expressed profound hopelessness, I said, "What exactly are you hopeless about?" And, at another occasion, I said, "If you are too certain that nothing will come out of this treatment, how are we to understand your coming so regularly and for such a long time for your sessions?" In both instances, the patient's initial reaction was to brush my questions aside but, after further confrontation and questioning, the patient began to see the split-off and unrealistic hope that underlay her vociferous pessimism.

Once such omnipotent expectations from analysis are brought to the surface, the analyst can help the patient bring forth the narcissistic and masochistic gratifications derived from these fantasies, which keep the patient's existence in a grand, suffering limbo. He might now point out to the patient the illusory nature of his "someday" fantasy. However, even during this phase, the analyst must remain respectful of the patient's psychic "soft spots" and be affectively and conceptually prepared to oscillate between affirmative interventions, when thwarted growth needs and ego deficits seem to dictate the transference demands, and interpretive interventions, when more traditional conflict-based transference is in the forefront. Such "oscillations in strategy" (Killingmo, 1989, p. 75) would necessitate a conceptual freedom on the analyst's part to view the patient's idealization as both a thwarted developmental need and a pathological defense—that is, a psychic configuration requiring both empathic and interpretive handling.

Failing to engage the patient in such an interpretive undertaking, the analyst must be prepared to rupture the patient's inordinate hope. Clearly, many analysts would question the need ever to rupture the patient's excessive hope. They would suggest that simply understanding its origins and functions and letting the usual analytic approach take its course would lead to the transformation of such fantasies. This does happen in milder cases. However, in those stubbornly fixated on "someday" fantasies, it comes down to "having to state that neither analysis nor analyst [is an] omnipotent rescuer, as the patients in their illusion needed to believe" (Amati-Mehler & Argentieri, 1989, p. 301). With those endlessly lamenting a long-dead parent, the analyst might have to literally confirm the irreversibility of the situation. A less dramatic, but essentially similar, example is of the patient who "kept crying and saying, 'I can't help it,' and the analyst [who] said: 'I am afraid I can't help it either'" (Amati-Mehler & Argentieri, 1989, p. 296).

Such interventions can be subsumed under the broad rubric of "optimal disillusionment" (Gedo & Goldberg, 1973), which requires that the analysand learn to give up magical thinking. They are neither conventional nor risk-free. They disrupt the transference dynamics and can be traumatic to the patient. Indeed, when their "dosage" or timing is inappropriate—and this may not be entirely predictable—the resulting despair and psychic pain might lead the patient to become seriously suicidal. This puts the analysis to a most severe test. Temporary departures from neutrality might now become unavoidable and adjunct; stabilizing measures might have to be deployed. On the other hand, interventions of this sort might constitute a turning point of the analytic process in less complicated circumstances, provided, of course, the analyst's "holding functions" are in place, and the effects of such an intervention can be analyzed. Rupture of pathological hope is a necessary precondition for mourning that is otherwise blocked in these patients. At the same time, the analyst: "... must convey to the patient not only the direction he wants to patient to move in, but also confidence that the movement is inherent in the patient, which means that what the uncured patient wants is indeed a representation, however distorted, of what the cured patient will get" (Friedman, 1969, p. 150).

In other words, the analyst must make sure that the consequence of his intervention is not a transition from pathological hope to hopelessness but one from pathological hope to realistic hope. This movement is facilitated if the analyst has faith in the patient's capacity in this regard, a proposition reflecting Loewald's (1960) outlining of the childhood need to identify with one's growth potential as seen in the eyes of one's parents.

In cases where pathological hopelessness is on the surface, unrealistic hope lurks underneath. According to Miller (1985):

> The depressed patient harbors the secret hope that he will be re-united or merged with the eternal, omnipotent object (to some, death). It is one of the things which he does not say and which he does not let himself become aware of consciously. The expression of hopelessness about himself is a way of expressing this hope indirectly while at the same time keeping it out of conscious awareness. By repetitively expressing hopelessness about himself—his worth, his abilities, his being able to change, etc.—he prevents himself from experiencing the true hopelessness of attaining this state of paradise .... The other crucial aspect of this understanding of depression and of the expression of hopelessness is the way in which is it used in the attack on the object. (p. 75)

In such cases, interventions must focus upon validation of the patient's anguish, reconstruction of the lack of love during childhood, and the masochistic dependence upon the internalized "dead mother" (Green, 1980). If the patient shows a militant quality to hopelessness in the clinical situation and the analyst feels himself to be a target of sadism, then that too has to be interpreted. However, the risk in doing so is to increase the patient's guilt which, in turn, can preclude his internalization of the analyst's kindness and concern. The tetrad of (i) repudiated horror (about how negligent and coldly cruel one's parents were), (ii) the distorted self-assessment of parental "gaslighting" (Barton & Whitehead, 1969), (iii) the hatred consequent upon early deprivation, and (iv) the pervasive guilt over this hatred as well as over one's existence, impedes recognizing, accepting, and assimilating the goodness offered by the analyst. Needless to add that throughout this work, the analyst must be highly vigilant toward his own emotional experience. Within transference, the analyst is invested by these patients with the task of preserving an illusion. This puts pressure on the analyst. On the one hand, there is temptation to actively rescue the patient. On the other hand, there is the allure of quickly showing the patient that his expectations are unrealistic and serve defensive aims. Cloaked in the guise of therapeutic zeal, hasty attempts of this sort often emanate from the analyst's own unresolved narcissism and infantile omnipotence. "The determinedly optimistic therapist coerces ... his patients into experiencing the depression which he is too threatened to feel within himself" (Searles, 1977, p. 483). Clearly, both extremes (rescue and rejection) are to be avoided. In this context, the issue of the analyst's own hope is pertinent (see also Mitchell, 1993).[6] While he does envision an ego more free of conflicts in the patient's future, his hope must not become unrealistic. An analyst-analysand collusion around waiting for an omnipotent solution for the patient's suffering is a certain recipe for an interminable analysis.

Concluding remarks

In this contribution, I have elucidated the developmental foundations of hope and hopelessness. On a phenomenological and psychodynamic level, I have delineated the normal (adaptive and growth-promoting) and pathological (maladaptive and fixation-fueling) variants of both hope and hopelessness. I have emphasized that the experience of both hope and hopelessness (the latter in limited, focal, and phase-appropriate dosages) is necessary for healthy personality development. After laying down such a foundation, I have delineated the technical strategies necessary in the treatment of pathologically optimistic and pathologically hopeless patients.

Now, before closing, I wish to touch upon two other areas. The first pertains to special populations that might be more vulnerable to a sense of hopelessness in life. The second pertains to the avoidance of hopelessness in a world replete with hunger, uneven distribution of resources, oppression, and war. As far as special populations with greater vulnerability to hopelessness is concerned, those afflicted with serious poverty come to mind first along with those who are politically oppressed, socially disenfranchised, and otherwise disadvantaged.

Children who grew up in homes where their basic needs could not be met and where a "climate of defeated parents" (Symonds, 1968, p. 16) prevailed often carry profound, even if covert[7] hopelessness in their hearts. The sense of there being no escape from the soul-crushing realities of their environment gets internalized over time and dooms the ego's capacities for hope, patience, and sustained effort. Crowded living arrangements, often associated with poverty, over-expose the child to the vagaries of adult behavior and this, in turn, adds to disillusionment. Severe sociopolitical oppression, restriction of movement and travel, segregation along racial lines, and apartheid-like governmental policies contribute to feeling helpless and hopeless; those subject to such circumstances find little reason for optimism and become fatalistic.

The effect of old age and infirmity on hope and hopelessness also deserve consideration. To be sure, it is the collective economy of good internal objects that regulates the capacity for optimism in life; nonetheless, the increasing loss of bodily and cognitive functions during old age often erodes this inner confidence. Semel (1990) writes about the prevalence of themes of hopelessness in the treatment of older patients and Lax (2008), in an especially poignant paper titled, "Becoming Really Old: the Indignities," has elucidated the everyday struggle of the elderly to retain hope and not succumb to hopelessness.

Finally, there is the much broader question of how to maintain hope for mankind in a world rife with ethnic conflicts, territorial aggressions, genocides, and the ever-present threat of nuclear Armageddon (Slochower, 1984). Certainly, political praxis, including that which is psychoanalytically informed (Varvin & Volkan, 2005; Volkan, 1999, 2004, 2006), can be of assistance in making the circumstances less dire and disarmament agreements can reduce the threat to life on our planet. In the end, however, it is the fierce preservation and celebration of goodness which already exists in this world—in the form of altruism, courage, freedom, democracy, poetry, art, and love—that strengthen our hope and make our hopelessness bearable.

Notes

1. Winnicott (1960, 1963) reiterated this conceptualization a number of times and it seems to undergird his technical approach to patients in general.

2. Nearly 200 years before this, Voltaire (1759) had declared optimism to be "a mania for maintaining that all is well when things are going badly" (p. 54).
3. This is striking in the light of a deep pessimistic bent to Freud's view of mankind, the "strange feelings of inferiority" (Jones, 1955, p. 3) he suffered from, his "punishing conscience" (Gay, 1988, p. 140), and his remarkable insights (Freud, 1917e) into the problem of melancholia.
4. Freud's (1914c) statement regarding the importance of retaining the capacity for love speaks to the same point. He said, "A strong egoism is a protection against falling ill, but in the last resort we must begin to love in order to not fall ill, and we are bound to fall ill if, in consequence of frustration, we are unable to love" (p. 85).
5. Such interventions are composed of an "objectifying element," which conveys the sense to the patient that the therapist can feel what it is to be in the former's shoes, a "justifying element," which introduces a cause-and-effect relationship, and an "accepting element," which imparts a historical context to the current distress by including the mention of similar experiences from the patient's childhood. Affirmative interventions often necessitate that the analyst deliberately restrict the scope of his communication, yet such superficiality paradoxically prepares the ground for unmasking interpretive interventions.
6. The question of the analyst's hope remains open, with some analysts (Bion, 1967; Boris, 1976) suggesting that he approach the patient without preconceived aspirations, and other analysts (Hoffman, 1992; Loewald, 1960) advocating the importance of analysts' optimism for the progress of treatment.
7. The occasional hedonism of their adult lifestyle during adulthood reflects what Boris (1976) has described as the "fundamental antagonism between hope and demise" (p. 141); possession of hope acts as a restraint against desire and loss of hope results in a burgeoning of desire.

PART I

Developmental Realm

CHAPTER TWO

The encounter with hopelessness in childhood

Ann Smolen

Georgie, Rose, Lizzie, Anita, Sara, and Helen are just six children of the many whom I have had the privilege to work with, and get to know over the years. They each, in their own way, exemplify what it may feel like to experience hopelessness and shared that terrifying emotion with me, yet simultaneously they all exhibited hope as they forged their way forward. The hope was always present, even in the worst of times. "Such hopelessness is, of course, not the loss of hope itself. It is the losing of hope for one's hope" (Boris, 1976, p. 141). But before I delve deeper into the realm of hopelessness during childhood, let me introduce you to the children I have just mentioned.

Georgie lay in an orphanage crib flat on his back for the first nine months of his life. When his adoptive father came to fetch him from across the ocean, he was not able to sit up or roll over, staring with empty eyes, opened wide, toward his hands held palms up seemingly searching.

Rose, an eleven-year-old girl with the bluest of eyes and hair like Rapunzel, could no longer walk or speak. She needed to be dressed and fed by her parents and developed a chronic gagging reflex. She kept a tissue covering her mouth as she lay mute on my couch.

Lizzie, a sweet three-and-a-half-year-old girl, refused to even entertain the idea of potty training. She had undergone multiple intrusive medical interventions to alleviate severe constipation and was terrified to defecate and urinate. She seemed to want to remain an infant, terrified to grow up, her rage always threatening to erupt, but only communicated through her body.

Anita, a beautiful and gifted seven-year-old girl, was academically years ahead of her peers. She had difficulty making and keeping friends and withdrew into her books. She too was terrified of the world and enraged by her own and others' limitations.

Sara, age two and a half, spent her first two years living on the street, her mother unable to look at her, for she only saw an image of herself staring back, and she hated what she saw. Sara sat alone in the corner of the daycare unable to connect or engage with anyone.

Helen was diagnosed with Asperger's as a school-aged child. At sixteen, she came to me asking for an analysis with the hope of one day having a friend. Helen often felt her life was not worth living.

A quick survey of literature

Spitz (1946) shocked the medical community with his videos of "hopeless" children. He formulated the term "anaclitic depression" to describe infants after six months of age who experienced prolonged separations from their primary caregiver and developed symptoms of weeping, apathy, inactivity, withdrawal, sleep problems, weight loss, and developmental regressions. In addition, feelings of loneliness, helplessness, and fear of abandonment are now understood to be a part of the syndrome. If adequate mothering is re-established within a reasonable time period, the infant is expected to recover. Spitz (1965) also described this as an "emotional deficiency disease." The occurrence of an anaclitic depression was linked by Spitz to the "developmental milestone of the mother's becoming a consistent and recognized object for the infant" (Wagonfeld & Emde, 1982, p. 66). "Anaclitic" means "leaning upon," and in anaclitic depression the infant becomes depressed because the mother is not experienced as available to lean upon. Anaclitic depression is related to the establishment of an object tie. Spitz emphasized that the children who develop anaclitic depressions are those who had once developed satisfactory object ties. A good object attachment must first be established in order for its loss to be mourned.

Many of the babies that Spitz observed died. I believe that those infants experienced hopelessness. Without hope there is no will to live and we die. In the Greek myth of Pandora's Box, Zeus put hope at the very bottom beneath all the evils in the world. Under greed, vanity, envy, and slander lay hope. "Sometimes, hope for the right thing can be reached only through an immersion in prolonged and harrowing dread" (Mitchell, 1993, p. 228). The babies that Spitz observed had become hopeless.

Later observers confirmed what Spitz had noted. Erikson (1950) spoke of the loss of maternal love as a cause of anaclitic depression, which he described as a "chronic state of mourning." He further speculated that infants and young children who suffer from the loss of the libidinal object during the second half of the first year might experience a depressive undercurrent for life. Bowlby (1960) wrote of the effect of maternal loss on the developing infant and observed the sequence of protest, despair, and detachment behaviors from prolonged separation. Mahler (1968) understood anaclitic depression in terms of separation-individuation. She stated that after six months, once a symbiotic relationship with the mother has been established, she is no longer transposable, and her loss produces an anaclitic depression in the infant.

Erikson (1950) and Winnicott (1956) wrote further about hope in relation to children. Erikson connected the ideas of hope and hopelessness to a *basic sense of trust* and a *basic sense of mistrust* that developmentally occurs in early infancy. If the infant's psychological and physical needs are met within reason, he learns to trust, and within this trust lies hope. Erikson viewed hope as progressive and growth enhancing, not regressive. Winnicott, in his 1996 work with acting-out adolescent boys, understood their difficult behaviors as an expression of hope. Winnicott too viewed hope as constructive and progressive. Winnicott saw regression as a vital characteristic of the therapeutic process.

Besides these early writings, there is very little in the psychoanalytic literature about hope and hopelessness. Boris (1976) and Mitchell (1993) are among the few who have explored this topic. Boris stated: "If one searches the literature hope itself is nowhere to be seen. This is no accident. Psychoanalysis is primarily a theory concerning desire and its vicissitudes" (p. 139). He conceived of hope as a psychological space where the self may find a new beginning. In Boris's theory, hope must first be given up within the analytic experience, in order to experience despair. In Boris's mind, only then can one truly experience desire. Mitchell (1993) pointed out that psychoanalytic theory has approached hope from two opposing angles. The more traditional view regards hope as essentially progressive and facilitating of richer experiences. The opposing viewpoint is that hope, especially when excessive, is regressive and obstructs maturation and gets in the way of enjoying one's life experiences.

The children

The following clinical vignettes demonstrate how hopelessness and hope are represented and communicated within the psychoanalytic treatments of six children.

Georgie

At nine months old, he was developmentally more like a three-month-old infant and deteriorating quickly. He could not hear due to untreated ear infections, did not smile, and stiffened when held. His adoptive father was horrified as this was not the infant son he had fantasized holding in his arms, but he could not turn around and fly back across the world without him or he would feel like a murderer. Once in the States with his adoptive parents, Georgie quickly caught up developmentally. His hearing returned to normal, he developed an infectious smile, and he became a very energetic toddler and preschooler. However, by kindergarten, Georgie began to exhibit some disturbing behaviors that caused his private school to recommend psychological testing. Georgie was unable to maintain friendships, urinated on the floor, hoarded food, ran out impulsively into parking lots and, as his father put it, refused to listen or be affectionate with his father.

I have written about Georgie elsewhere (Smolen, 2009), but here I wish to focus on one small portion of Georgie's treatment. I imagine that as an infant Georgie felt annihilation anxiety—or as Winnicott (1987) poetically described it—like "falling and falling and falling." I assume that that feeling is as close to hopelessness as one can get without dying. Georgie was an imaginative and creative little boy always engaging me in elaborate and sometimes convoluted dramas. Together we were many characters. What was strange and different about Georgie's imaginative play was that we were never human. Sometimes we were two marbles, or matchbox cars, or magnetic sticks, or magic markers. We were never living figures such as animals or dolls from my dollhouse. A few months into his analysis, Georgie told me that he was never born, never had a mother, and in fact had evolved from a bug. Shortly after this interchange, Georgie began to play with a small toy transformer that transformed from a bicycle into a boy. The only problem with this toy was it was extremely fragile and would fall apart easily. Georgie named it "Fragile" as he cupped it tenderly in his hands telling me over and over how difficult it is to not fall apart, how very fragile he felt and so very broken. Georgie's sessions were first thing in the morning before school. He would run up my stairs eager to begin where he had ended the day before, but first would curl into the fetal position in front of the heater, warming himself as he tenderly held onto Fragile. As we sat together in front of the heater, I imagined him as an infant in a barren hospital ward, cold and alone.

Georgie and I confronted many intrapsychic conflicts, and worked on several areas where he had become stuck developmentally; however, most problematic was Georgie's relationship with his father. After much deliberation, Georgie's father began to attend one of his sessions each week. The following vignette is from that first triadic session.

I was quite anxious about bringing Georgie's father (Herb) into the treatment. I was concerned that he might feel criticized by me. I somehow wanted to help both of them view their conflicts without causing Herb to feel incompetent. This first joint session was filled with tension. Herb was immediately intrusive into Georgie's play, asking questions that demanded a correct answer. Georgie regressed to his very first interaction in the playroom and began to play basketball. Herb commented on all correctly thrown balls. Finally Georgie told his dad that he did not wish to be watched.

G: Don't look at me!
DAD: Are you worried I will judge you? I love you. Does it feel like I don't love you?
[Georgie becomes very silly and falls to the floor.]
A: Um, Georgie has become very silly. I'm wondering if something feels uncomfortable? Dad, what do you think about these silly feelings Georgie is having right now?
[Georgie hides.]

D: I see he is hiding now. [He jumps out of his hiding place with a loud "Boo!"]

A: I'm thinking that maybe you don't want Dad to look at you and you do want Dad to look at you all at the same time. Something got uncomfortable and you told Dad not to look, then the silly feelings came, then the hiding feelings. But you jumped up with a loud "Boo" and a big smile. I think you want Dad to look and not look.

[Georgie agrees and puts his head down, visibly upset and begging his father to leave the room.]

G: I don't want you here. It feels very bad.

D: But, Georgie, I want to be part of your life. I want to know what you do in here.

G: It doesn't mean you aren't part of my life if you don't come in here. I don't want you here. Please leave.

Herb refused to leave, so Georgie ran out of the playroom and out of my waiting room. Herb ran after and carried him back, allowing him to come alone with me but he was angry. Once upstairs and safe in the playroom, Georgie was quite agitated and explained that his dad "is the busiest man in the world and does not know how to play." I wondered if we could work together to help Dad learn how to play. Georgie gathered up Fragile, and, cupping it in his hand tenderly, carried it down to the waiting room and explained to his father why Fragile had to be handled with care. Dad came back into the playroom where Georgie destroyed Fragile, and he and Georgie, head-to-head, gently and carefully put him back together. Later that afternoon, I processed the session with Herb who was moved by my interpretation of "Fragile." Herb opened up and spoke at length about his own painful childhood experiences and spoke of his identification with his young son. Georgie was showing his father, through his play, how broken and helpless he has felt, and at times continues to feel, but he can be put back together and he can be a human boy, if handled with care. Georgie was full of "hope."

Rose

Rose, an eleven year old extremely bright and beautiful girl, was referred to me with a diagnosis of conversion disorder. She was no longer able to eat solid food, could not speak or walk without heavily leaning on a parent, and even stated that she had lost cognitive function. For example, when her mother asked her to use a spoon in order to eat her ice cream, she responded that she no longer knew what a spoon was.

The first time I met with Rose, her father practically carried her into my office and laid her down on my analytic couch. I pulled my chair away from behind the couch to sit facing her. Rose appeared extremely distressed with a towel pressed against her mouth as she chronically gagged and spit saliva. After telling Rose what I knew about her condition and acknowledging her parents' frustration and worry, I suggested we write a story together. I was seeing Rose every day so for the first week she dictated the narrative and I typed. Rose quickly grew tired of my slow typing skills; by the second week she was sitting up in a chair and typing the story as I sat beside her, commenting on the drama that unfolded. The following is what Rose dictated to me in her first session:

> Setting: An orphanage 100,000 years in the future.
> Main character: Five-year-old girl with long blue curly hair and beautiful violet eyes. She has no name. Her parents gave her away. They kept her older brother and sister. She was two years old when she was given away to the orphanage. Robots operate her orphanage. The children are the only humans in the orphanage. There is no love.
> This is a world in the sky. They live on the clouds.
> When they leave the orphanage they go to the government and are given a name. They do not leave the orphanage until age fifty, but they live until age 1000.
> In this world you can't be sick. When you are born, you are given all of the medicine in the world in a vaccine. But if the government doesn't like you, they kill you. They throw them off the clouds. The government doesn't know that you don't die when thrown from the clouds. Instead you fall into the past. You fall into now.
> The only way you can get thrown off the clouds is if you are different from everyone else.
> The ending: The reason why we have all different people NOW is from the different children thrown off the clouds into NOW.
> Her parents gave her away because she was different. They didn't want to be sad when she was thrown from the clouds. It is

really bad. They were only thinking of themselves, not her. They were thinking of their other children.

She is different because she is super smart. That is how they knew she was different. When she was two she could read and write and had a huge vocabulary.

Over the next fourteen months, Rose continued to write *her* story. The main character (Different) experienced jealousy, envy, sadness, rage, physical illness, and injury; she fell in love with her teacher (a much older man); she experienced difficult relationships with a sister-like character, and a mother-character. Within her writing of her story, Rose worked through separation issues and her conflict about growing up. She quickly let go of her symptoms, did well in school, had good friendships, and went off to overnight camp.

Rose communicated her feelings of hopelessness through a total regression into infancy where she needed to be fed, dressed, and carried by her parents. Within her regression was hope.

Lizzie

Lizzie became severely constipated when only six weeks old and was encopretic by the time she was two and a half. There were multiple occasions when her stomach would become distended and she experienced terrible pain. She began to withhold bowel movements for up to two weeks and eventually was admitted to the hospital where she underwent three days of intrusive medical procedures. Once home again, her parents were instructed to insert a rectal tube at night to allow drainage. This took place over a three-month period. The family was referred for outpatient cognitive-behavioral therapy that Lizzie attended for just under a year.

I first met Lizzie when she was three and a half years old, when her parents became frustrated with her current treatment and sought out a child psychoanalyst. At home, Lizzie fell into terrible tantrums at the slightest frustration; she refused to even attempt to use the toilet, and was terrified of bodily harm. If she fell and scraped her knee, she decompensated and could not be comforted for a prolonged period of time. After meeting with her highly intelligent, warm, and caring parents several times, it became apparent that they were terrified and paralyzed by Lizzie's rage, which in turn, caused Lizzie to be petrified of her own aggression.

When I met with Lizzie she appeared babyish, well behind where she needed to be in her psychological and physical development. In her first three sessions she spoke very little, did not seem interested in exploring my playroom or in me, and seemed shut down and depressed. In her fourth session, the following took place:

Lizzie showed an interest in my sandbox. I uncovered it and got her a stepstool so she could reach the sand. She played silently for several minutes, absentmindedly pouring sand from one hand to the other. Then her eye caught a small plastic container. She picked it up and shook it, discovering that there was a tiny something trapped inside of the container.

L: There is something in here.
A: Umm, is it stuck?
L: Yes I can't get it out and it is stinky.
A: Oh my there is something very stinky in there and you can't seem to get it out.
[She became animated and excited]
L: Yes! Yes! It won't come out, I can't get it out, and it is getting stinkier and stinkier!!
A: This is a problem. What are we going to do about this very stinky thing in this container?
L: Do you have paper towels?
[I pointed to the top of my toy shelf to show her my large roll of paper towels]
L: If this thing stays in here the whole weekend, it is going to make a very big mess!! You can never have enough paper towels for this mess! You better go to the store and buy a hundred million paper towels for this big stinky mess!

At this point Lizzie was so excited her body was shaking. She dumped out the tiny stinky thing and flushed it down my dollhouse toilet. However, this was not a big enough toilet for her huge mess and she insisted that we leave my office and go down the hall to the bathroom to flush it down a real toilet. She asked me to help her and together we flushed it down the toilet. When she went back to my playroom, she was ravenous and pretended to eat up all the food in the world and then said: "We got rid of Mr. Stinky!!!" Six weeks later, with parent education, Lizzie was toilet trained.

Lizzie terminated her analysis shortly before entering second grade. She had worked through her fear of bodily intrusion, was coping with separating and growing up, and was able to take risks. She had many friends, tried new foods, learned to ride her bike, perform in her ballet recital and all the other activities appropriate for seven-year-old children. When I first met Lizzie, she had been successful in remaining an angry baby by staying in diapers and demanding that her parents care for her as such or else!! There was painful anguish in this and she seemed hopeless, but like Rose, there was great hope in her hopelessness.

Anita

Anita was five years old when her parents sought my help. She was years ahead of her fellow kindergartners, reading on a fifth grade level. She was also very beautiful with olive skin, piercing green eyes, and hair that could not be tamed. Anita's parents were concerned because she seemed to have absolutely no respect for her teachers or her parents and often ignored them when they spoke to her and was defiant. Anita's teachers reported that she was often mean to the other children and extremely bossy, thus she had no friends. Anita was obsessed about "the meaning of life," concerning herself with existential thoughts about death and dying. She often scared the other children by announcing that their mother was going to die or some other worrisome fact about life and death. Anita's parents wanted me to teach her "life skills." Although disappointed that this was something I did not do, they decided to give psychoanalytic psychotherapy a try. Anita began twice-weekly sessions and I saw the parents monthly.

Anita took command of her sessions immediately, demonstrating her narcissistic defenses against worries about being loved. In her elaborate dramas, Anita was the most beautiful, most intelligent girl in all the land, but nobody loved her and she was always alone, or she was the poor orphan girl who was adopted by an evil queen because her father died in battle and her mother gave her away. In this drama, Anita had special powers where she overpowered the queen and won the king for herself.

After one year, right before summer vacation, Anita's parents informed me that while they respected my work and actually liked me very much, they wanted Anita to see a therapist who would give her concrete skills on how to cope with other children, at home with her family, and with her teachers, as all of her symptoms that brought her in to treatment remained. Anita and I had a final session where she told me how distressed she was that she would no longer be able to see me.

One year later, I received a call from the parents asking to meet with me to discuss returning to treatment. They explained that Anita had done very well with her cognitive-behavioral therapist and had learned several skills that helped her to contain her impulsive behaviors, yet the therapist told them that Anita refused to speak about her feelings or her worries and she could no longer be of help. We agreed to resume treatment.

The following declaration took place in her first session back:

Now seven-year-old Anita ran breathless into my office and threw herself dramatically onto my couch and announced:

> You have no idea how hard I had to work to get back here! The other therapist was very nice, but you are the only one who really understands. Nobody gets it. Nobody understands what we do in here and I can't tell them or they would take me away again! They want me to talk to you. I mean I do talk to you but you know how it works in here!!

Anita got right back to work as if we had never been separated. Toward the end of the school year, as summer vacation loomed near and I was about to have a parent session, Anita became extremely distraught and begged me not to tell her parents that we "played." She was sure that if they knew, she would once again lose me. I imagine that during our yearlong separation Anita experienced a sense of powerlessness and hopelessness, but in her refusal to speak with or share her worries with her new therapist there was hope that she would find her way back and she did.

Sara

I met Sara early in my career when I was working in a transitional housing facility for homeless mothers and their children. Sara spent her first four years of life in homelessness. Her mother (Esther) spent the first two years of motherhood pushing Sara in a stroller by day in search of a warm, safe place to sleep at night. Esther's own history is one of severe poverty, physical abuse, domestic violence, neglect, and ultimately abandonment. Her mother was neglectful of her as a child, and then was murdered when Esther was a young teenager. In Esther's narrative, she is called "stupid" and "retarded" for as far back as she can remember. Esther tells of physical abuse at the hands of her father and was literally thrown out of her father's house by his girlfriend when Sara was one month old. As Esther sat in my office telling me "facts" about her past, without visible emotion, she experienced a vivid memory. She became agitated and recalled: "It was January, I remember. It was January and cold [she shivers]. She put me and the baby out. I was standing on the porch with no place to go. It was night too and really cold." Esther looked at me (one of the few moments where she was able to maintain eye contact) in disbelief.

It was easy to imagine Esther taking off down the city streets with Sara in tow, walking quickly and with purpose. I imagine she was trying her best simultaneously to walk away from her abusive past and painful memories and walk toward a better, safer place. For two years, Esther and Sara lived on the street. There was a kindly old grandfather, who offered his couch many a night, but he died; then there was nobody. When Sara was two, Esther had another baby girl. Esther was no longer able to survive on the streets with two babies. Only then did this young family enter the shelter system. I first met them all when Sara was twenty-seven months old, as they had come to live at our shelter.

Sara was recommended for individual therapy because the daycare and clinical staff were concerned that the mother/child relationship was poor. Staff members observed that Esther seemed not to "see" her daughter and was unaware of the child's emotional needs. During our first session, I was struck by Sara's profound sadness. Though painfully shy, she left her daycare room with me easily. It is important to note that I was a complete stranger to Sara, and she left her daycare with me without any visible anxiety or emotion. When children have not been able to develop a secure attachment in infancy, they often feel little or no distress or anxiety when separation or loss of love is threatened (A. Freud, 1965).

Sara presented developmentally as a twelve- to eighteen-month-old baby. Her vocabulary consisted of fewer than twenty words. She seemed unaware of her own body in space; her movements were stiff and awkward. She did not notice obstacles and would trip over small toys. She stiffened when touched, and it was reported by daycare staff that she would not allow other children to touch her. She cried and fought staff when they changed her diaper. For the most part, her affect was flat and she did not make eye contact.

I slowly began to connect with her through body movements, facial gestures, and responses and shared posture. For example, Sara discovered the sink in my office and began to pour the water in and out of a baby bottle. As she did this she made noises and I joined her, using similar inflections in my voice, as I mirrored her facial expressions. This was the first time she made eye contact with me.

In another early session Sara found the baby lotion on my shelf and gestured for me to help pour some on her hands. She took the lotion and gingerly rubbed it into my cheek while maintaining deep eye contact. I asked her if I could put some lotion on her and began to rub some on her arm. Her affect changed from serious exploration to deep sadness and she became immobilized. I said to her in a very sad voice: "You are feeling so sad." She nodded her head "yes" and two tears rolled down her cheek. Through this interaction, I was able to validate Sara's feelings and at the same time allow her to view herself. Winnicott (1941) relates a vignette about a little girl who sat on his knee, bit his knuckles, cried, and played a game of throwing spatulas. He explained that while playing a game of throwing spatulas from his lap, she was able to express hostile aggression and great sadness. Just as Winnicott's little patient was able to express her sadness through play with spatulas, Sara was able to express her sadness while playing with the baby lotion. Our play with the baby lotion touched a very deep place in Sara. Her longing to be touched was immeasurable. Her lack of physical and emotional proximity with her mother was overwhelming, causing her to feel profound sadness.

Sara's play was mechanical and joyless and possessed an emptiness, which kept others at a distance. However, she included me in her play, and it was through her play that I was able to engage Sara on an affective level. In these early sessions, she would feed a baby doll a bottle, empty out the dollhouse handing me all of the objects, or hold on to one end of a slinky and place the other end in my hand. She played in silence and I provided the narrative. "You are feeding your baby milk in her bottle," or "You want me to hold all of the people in this dollhouse," or "You want me to play slinky with you."

Over the next several weeks she began to mimic me, verbally stringing together three to five words together in sentences. Her sense of her own body seemed to improve. She no longer lost her balance as easily and was better able to navigate her surroundings. She began to laugh and sustain short periods of eye contact without experiencing overwhelming anxiety. Perhaps most important, but painful, Sara began to feel deeply. She now was capable of expressing both hostile aggression and great sadness. In her play with dollhouse figures, she began to act out aggressively toward the mother doll, hitting her on the head with the little girl doll, and finally stomping on the mother doll's head. She played a similar game with a stuffed squirrel family, always attacking the mother figure.

In one particular session I elicited a game of "peek-a-boo" that fascinated Sara and captivated her attention as she maintained deep eye contact, but this game also caused her to feel intensely sad. At first, I found it extremely difficult to maintain the engagement when the therapy elicited these affects. For example, if Sara became profoundly sad in a session, I felt the need to make it all better for her, to make the bad feelings go away. I needed to be able to "hold" Sara in whatever she was feeling in the moment. It was my job to validate her feelings and show her that both she and I could survive them.

The following vignette took place after a weekend absence, when Sara felt abandoned and rejected by me. She seemed to experience hopelessness.

When I went to daycare to retrieve Sara for our session, I found her in a dissociated state. Daycare staff reported that she had been in this condition when her mother brought her in. She was mute, unable to walk, and did not respond when spoken to. When I picked her up to carry her to my office her body was stiff, but she offered no resistance. Once in my office she made an attempt to play by feeding a bottle to the baby doll but was unable to do this as the bottle fell from her hand. I felt at a loss and did not know what to do. I instinctively picked her up and began to pace and sing to her as if she were an infant. Slowly her body began to relax and she molded to my body and fell asleep. I sat down in my chair and, as she slept, I wondered what had happened to this little girl and how I possibly could help her. We sat still for thirty minutes. I hoped she had a high fever, for that would explain the behavior, but I knew that she was not physically ill. However, my need to make her well was very powerful, so I covered her with my coat and headed back outside, across the street, and back to daycare to take her temperature. Her teacher inserted the thermometer under her arm as she slept in my arms, and of course it registered normal. As I spoke with her teachers, trying to discern if there had been some abuse of some sort, she awoke. I did not realize she was awake because she remained motionless; her teachers informed me that her eyes were open. We decided that perhaps she would want to lie on her cot, so her teacher got out her cot and I sat on the floor with Sara still motionless in my arms. She was unable to move from me. I began to talk to her very slowly and quietly, telling her how sad she was and how hard it is to feel so sad. I held her in my arms and we rocked together as I sang a lullaby. At this point the teacher came over and asked Sara if she would like to join her class in a project. Her barely audible "No" let me know she was beginning to feel safe enough to come back. I asked her if she would like to return to my office and she nodded her head "yes."

Once back in my office I continued to sing and speak softly to her. She lay in my arms like an infant at the breast and began to explore my face. She gazed into my eyes as her fingers explored my lips. I responded to her as if she were an infant. As I continued to verbalize her sadness, she slowly became able to move from me physically and began to communicate with me through her play. She handed me the toy phone. When I asked with whom I should speak, her answer was unintelligible, so I asked her if she wanted me to call her. She nodded her head "yes." I began: "Hello Sara, you were so sad this morning that you couldn't even talk, and you couldn't even walk. But now you are beginning to feel better and we are having a safe time together."

She returned to her continuing drama using the squirrel family. This time the mommy squirrel held the baby and did not hold the big sister. The sister became very angry and began to hit the mommy on the head. She gathered up the whole family; the mommy, baby, and sister, and threw them into my lap. I responded: "You are throwing them all at me and now I have the whole family and I can hold them in my arms." Sara had communicated how rejected she felt by my weekend absence, and her sibling rivalry. After this conversation, she came very close to me where I was sitting on the floor and she took my hair and covered my face. I said: "Where did I go? I have disappeared!" I could see her face through my hair and she became very frightened. I moved my hair away from my face and exclaimed that I was back, but that I could see how sad she had become when she thought I had gone away.

She was then able to repeat this several times—both covering me up and bringing me back. As she did this, she maintained eye contact. This interaction was not a happy, funny peek-a-boo game, but rather a very serious use of play.

This session lasted just under three hours. Just as we were leaving my office, Sara deliberately plucked a handful of tissues from a box near my desk. As we walked back to daycare, she was able to talk with me and notice her environment. She opened her daycare door and looked back over her shoulder at me as if to give me one last look before I left her again. I watched her from the window as she rejoined her class, seated around a table to paste and paint Thanksgiving turkeys. She clutched the tissues tightly in her hand as she sat among the other children, struggling not to dissociate once again. I was shaken. I had never experienced such profound sadness and hopelessness in another human being.

That afternoon, I met with Esther in an effort to discover some hidden abuse or mysterious illness that would cause Sara to dissociate. When I began my session with Esther, I was aware of my anger toward her for not protecting her child from such intolerable pain. These feelings quickly vanished as I felt that Esther, too, was like a small child crying out for connection and love. It was obvious that Esther did not abuse her daughter; she was even unaware that Sara was in this state. Sara seemed invisible to her. After two years of intensive treatment, Esther and her children moved out of the shelter into their own home. Esther encountered many difficulties, but she continued to bring Sara back to the shelter for her sessions for well over a year.

Helen

Sixteen-year-old Helen came into treatment in an unconventional way. She had recently been released by the hospital after a forty-eight-hour stay. She had gone to the ER on her own as an attempt to demand that her parents take notice of her distress. Helen had become despondent because of a perceived rejection by her uncle for whom she had formed an attachment. Helen was extremely demanding of his attention, sometimes calling over 100 times in an evening, leaving frantic messages for him to return her calls. He explained to her that his own family and children took precedence over her, therefore he could only speak with her occasionally. Helen construed this interaction to mean that he did not care for her and she experienced it as devastating rejection. In the hospital, she was prescribed anti-psychotic medication, told she was probably bipolar, and released with instructions to see a psychiatrist.

Helen had a plan; her uncle had described his own personal analytic treatment to her. She became intrigued and was determined to pursue an analysis for herself. Helen read a little about Freud and searched the internet until she located me through our institute's referral service. She required an analyst who was located within walking distance from her high school. In our initial phone conversation, she explained her financial situation and her need for a low fee. She was determined to pay for it herself, afraid that neither of her parents would help her. Helen was emphatic that she could not rely on them to financially or emotionally support her treatment.

In her first several sessions, Helen appeared disturbed with her head turned down and away from me, looking only at the floor. She was unable to risk sneaking even the tiniest glance at me. She wore an oversized sweatshirt over torn, dirty black pants that were her uniform for many months to come. Her hair was a stringy mess, and her movements were extremely awkward. I was not at all sure that I wanted to treat her or if I could help her, but Helen *demanded* an analysis. She was determined to find a way out from her pain, a way to alleviate her tormented life. I was struck by her resiliency and her astounding tenacity in spite of remarkable ineptness and difficulties being in the world. With apprehension, I agreed to begin an intensive analytic treatment, uncertain as to where our turbulent journey together would take us.

Helen was the second of three children. She was born when her older sister was three. Her mother became pregnant with her brother when she was two months old. Her mother was not college educated and from Helen's description and memories, she was depressed and overwhelmed. She spent long afternoons locked in her bedroom while the three children ate candy and watched television. Helen's father was a professional who worked long hours and was unavailable to his family. Helen's childhood memories are of verbal and physical fighting, harsh punishment, isolation, and being told she was "retarded" and "crazy." She was unable to read until fourth grade and was assigned to a special education classroom. She remembered feeling enraged all the time. In school, she would act-out by jumping from desktop to desktop, screaming all the while. At home, she would fight with her siblings and parents and hurt neighborhood children. For example, she would ride her bike very fast through a group of small children with the intention of harming them.

Her father told Helen that her mother was depressed after her birth and too tired and weak to care for both a new baby and a three year old. In addition, she became pregnant with her little brother when Helen was only two months old. Her father would often find Helen crying in her crib in a soiled diaper at the end of the day, obviously left alone for several hours unattended. Helen's mother would be asleep, while her sister ate junk food and watched television, also unattended. When Helen was nine years old her mother became romantically involved with a man she had met on the internet. When Helen was twelve, her parents divorced and her mother moved to another state with her lover. Her mother had no friends. Two years later, her mother gave birth to another daughter and a year later was diagnosed with Stage IV breast cancer. She died when Helen was nineteen years old.

Helen wrote the following after three years of psychoanalysis:

> I was born with Autism, and I know no other way of being. Imagine living your life in a skewed reality. You walk into a room and try your hardest to make sense of what is going on and what others are thinking. You have to consciously think about what expression you are wearing on your face and what you **should** be feeling. Everything is confusing. When people talk, you need to figure out how to interpret what they mean, but it is impossible because your brain just won't let you. You see this happening every time someone says something and you just can't figure it out. You can't read their facial expressions or social cues and are trying to think of what to say. And when you try to talk, your words come out confusing and unclear, and may not have much to do with what they just said.
>
> Every single day is a struggle. There is no escape. There is a longing that I feel to bond with others and I die on the inside when I realize that it just is not working. Invisible tears fill me up inside. Right now it is hard to imagine my life being able to connect well with others. I have improved in the last three years. I can connect a little bit, but it makes me so uncomfortable I cannot stop laughing. I get scared. Others can see that I am afraid. It is a very painful reality. I get rejected over and over. I keep trying. I must overcome my condition. One day, I will have a friend. That is my dream.

Helen has been in her analysis for almost seven years. She continues to struggle in relationships and has not yet found that one special friend, but she continues to hope.

Conclusion

Georgie, Rose, Lizzie, Anita, Sara, and Helen all shared their infantile hopes and feelings of hopelessness with me. In the analytic space, old hopes were altered, and within the therapeutic relationship, new hopes took form. Before treatment, all of the children were stuck. They could only express their intrapsychic pain through pathological symptoms. I worked with each child differently, led by the individual child's needs. Georgie told me his story through inanimate objects that came apart easily and needed to be handled with care. As we played and pretended together, new meanings developed and new possibilities opened up. Rose used the written word to communicate her conflicts. Through her narrative of feeling different, alone, and unloved, she was able to give up her infantile demands and hopes of finding the perfect mother who would care for all of her needs and desires. She shared her story with me and together we created a new story that allowed Rose to continue on her journey of growing up. Lizzie's body expressed her rage and aggression in painful ways. Together we put new language to what her body was communicating. Lizzie was terrified to grow up, as she angrily demanded to be cared for like an infant. Lizzie too was able to allow her infantile hopes to evolve into hopes for a future. For Sara, language was a barrier. In our work together, I gave her new words to describe her feelings, but it was feeling understood on a primitive nonverbal level that promoted new growth and development.

Georgie, Rose, Lizzie, and Sara had experienced infantile regressions which could be understood to be defensive and pathological, but these painful regressive states could also be viewed as positive, hopeful communications. Mitchell (1993) reminds us that: "Infantile hopes represent a self-healing return to the point at which psychological growth was suspended. Infantile hopes and longings do not need to be renounced but rather reanimated and brought to life, so they can grow and develop into more mature hopes through natural, organic maturational process" (p. 207).

For Georgie, life was fragile, his body was fragile, his sense of self was almost nonexistent, as he did not feel human. Rose, Lizzie, Sara,

Anita, and Helen also had to come to terms with the fragility of life. Growing up means acknowledging that the people you love the most, your parents, will eventually disappoint and let you down, and ultimately abandon you through death. "To love in a committed fashion, over time, is to hope; and to hope is to impart value in an inevitably uncertain future" (Mitchell, 1993, p. 212).

CHAPTER THREE

Adolescent hope and hopelessness

Rose A. Vasta

A capacity to sustain continuous shifts between the opposing forces of hope and hopelessness is crucial for ongoing psychological development and growth of the mind during adolescence. The changing balance between these states is related to and underscores the ambivalent relationship toward time of the adolescent. The ability to tolerate hope and accept that gratification may possibly occur in the future demands a tolerance for frustration that is not always feasible for the adolescent. When hope dominates the adolescent personality, the future takes on greater importance; however, when frustration is too great due to failures in the environment or other factors, hopelessness ensues. The adolescent overcome by hopelessness feels powerless, unattached, and alienated. This state is marked by a terrifying sense of emptiness that requires faith to believe it can be survived. When hopelessness is overwhelming, desire emerges and the adolescent will seek satisfaction from what is available in the here and now. The fluctuating balance between hope and hopelessness determines, among other things, the adolescent's capacity for ego growth and intellectual curiosity. In this chapter, I will use the theories of Bion, Boris, Klein, Winnicott, and others to examine the concepts of hope and hopelessness in adolescence and address some treatment considerations in the analysis of young people with various antisocial and acting out problems.

Hope and hopelessness and their importance during adolescence

The core of the analytic process with patients of any age is to identify the dynamic sources of the patient's hopes and the inability to find satisfaction for them (Rizzuto, 2004). It is the job of the psychoanalyst to bring those hopes to life through the transference and assist the patient to transform those unachievable hopes that caused suffering and stagnation into hopes that are at least partially attainable and lead to further development. Psychoanalysts who make a special study of development tell us that hope appears as an important factor both in early childhood and again in adolescence.

Erikson (1964) described hope as "the enduring belief in the attainability of fervent wishes, in spite of the dark urges and rages which mark the beginning of existence" (p. 115). Hope, he said, becomes the fundamental condition of all growth (1970). He found that hope was the first and most basic quality of the human infant (1962), noting that in adolescence the capacity to be loyal to a vision of the future and have faith that meaning is possible shows itself as a focused hope that is tuned to an ideologically coherent universe. When life events and the pressure of rapid physical development interfere with the capacity to maintain that focused hope, we can expect to see specific types of problems.

Blos (1967) describes adolescence as the second individuation process, the first having been completed toward the end of the third year of life. He observed that in both periods, there is an extreme vulnerability of the personality organization. In early childhood and again in adolescence, there is an urgent requirement for rapid change to psychic structures to keep up with the substantial physical and psychological development. He concurs with Erikson's notion that if there is a problem during either of the individuation processes, it will be followed by a specific form of deviant development or psychopathology that will in turn reflect the failures of that period of development.

If, during adolescent individuation, the frustration of hope is too severe or comes too quickly, hopelessness develops along with a sense of fear, panic, and urgency. Without relief, a prolonged sense of hopelessness can lead to a premature curtailment of the curiosity, dreams, and aspirations that marked the latency period of childhood. For example, the adolescent who is without hope of having the emotional support to transition from a high school student to a self-sufficient adult can become hopeless and lost without a future plan. This is a state of mind that cannot be tolerated for more than a short time before the adolescent seeks relief in what is available. That young person can seek an immediate sense of achievement and status in a social group through participation in gangs and illegal activities. The young woman who struggles but cannot experience herself as separate from an engulfing mother, may express her need for separateness through self-destructive behavior. The adolescent does not suffer the disappointment and pain of waiting to seek satisfaction of the frustrated hope as the desire has been filled on an immediate basis. This phenomenon, considered as the interaction between hope and hopelessness, will be examined more carefully.

Examination of the vicissitudes of hope and hopelessness

It is tempting to take a black and white approach to the concepts of hope and hopelessness and their role in development. The continuous maintenance of hope, however, is not preferable or possible for the adolescent. The presence of hopelessness is actually a necessary precondition for the development of hope. Hopelessness is characterized by a void and a sense that the youth does not know anything. It is out of this void that the selected fact arises, giving coherence to what previously had been only anxiety and fear (Bion, 1962). While this state of mind is necessary for the development of truthful thinking and hope, there are occasions when surviving the sensation of hopelessness is more than the adolescent can bear. In this situation, the satisfaction of desire in the moment allows the fragile adolescent a much needed sense of achievement and a fantasized halt to the progression of time. This can be seen as a "time out" taken to alleviate the overwhelming pressures coming from both physical and social change. The acting out behavior of a hopeless teen can be the temporary gratifications associated with adolescence such as the failure to attend school regularly, sexual acting out, rebellion against authority, or the use of drugs. The adolescent who "drops out" may do so to prolong the period of adolescence, unconsciously allowing more time to find someone who will provide sufficient emotional structure to permit him (or her) to bear the frustration of the previous hopes and retain a sense of psychological integrity through the periods of time when he must experience hopelessness. If the adolescent remains in the place of hopelessness for too long or finds sufficient pleasure in the short term gratification of desire, there is danger of remaining there, in a closed off mental space that will not be open to further growth. The adolescent will have succeeded in stopping the progression of mental development. A closer look at how hope and hopelessness function as elements in the intrapsychic world makes this more understandable.

The person experiences hope as an enticement toward something that is, as yet, unnamed and unattained. Hope, with its arrow of time pushing always forward, functions as what Bion (1963) first introduced as a preconception. Bion defined the preconception as an element designed to "receive a restricted range of phenomenon" (p. 23). As he described it, the preconception is a type of unspoken question that awaits its realization, the answer. When the answer is finally found and linked to the question, the preconception and its realization together form a concept. This represents an act of true creativity. Of course, the new concept, itself, never fully satisfies the question. There is always a gap in satisfaction that becomes evident. So every new concept functions as another preconception, that is, another question, with the hope that makes the person wait expectantly for the realization that will make it make sense. For the neonate, there is a preconception of something that fits inside something else and gives satisfaction. The nipple is the realization of this preconception and together with the open mouth forms the concept of the feeding breast. If the baby is made to wait too long for the breast, he may fall into a state of hopelessness characterized by fear of the void. If the mother comes quickly enough and is able to soothe him this becomes an opportunity to learn about frustration tolerance. If the baby is unable to wait, he may satisfy his desire by sucking his thumb or whatever is in the environment and close enough to his mouth. Once the baby has formed the concept of the feeding breast other questions arise such as "Where is the breast when it is absent?" The hunger pain in the stomach of the baby may seem to answer that question forming within the concept of the attacking and withholding mother. Later, the warm encircling of the mother's arms around a hungry, cold child fulfills another preconception of the infant to do with something painful that is contained. The container holds him and makes him better.

In normal growth, this exercise of seeking and finding and seeking again, reaching increasing levels of complexity, is repeated over and over from infancy through old age. It is an endless carrot on a stick pattern that entices the mind to advance itself toward the new idea and shed its comfortable place of knowing for one of uncertainty and the possibility of new knowledge. The mind can only approach the truth but can never know it completely. Implicit in all of this is the persistent idea that, with time, the realization will be found. There is also an implied tolerance for frustration as the actual capture of the entire truth continually advances into the future.

This cycle repeats itself innumerable times as the infant and then the child explore the world around them. We can speculate (Boris, 1976) that during the latency phase of development, a period of tremendous intellectual and social growth, this cycle is mediated by an unusually high level of hope. This rapid period of growth meets with difficulty when the developing child reaches puberty. It is during the period of adolescence that the physical and mental changes of this phase begin to interfere more dramatically with frustration tolerance and the capacity to wait for the realization. The sense of hopelessness that ensues is profound and threatens to overwhelm the psyche. At this time, the element of desire, always present and functioning as part of the counterbalance to hope, begins to exert its influence in a distinct and sometimes troublesome manner.

Desire and its special relationship to hopelessness

Desire, related to Sigmund Freud's (1920g) pleasure principle, is sensual, requires gratification and requires it immediately. Desire arises from the sensual concerns of the body. The adolescent experiencing desire has only a limited capacity to tolerate the reality principle's time constraints necessary for hope to flourish. Desire, as described by Boris (1976) "wants a real object and real fulfillment" (p. 141). Desire requires the final complete answer, something that hope can never provide. Desire demands that the object remain static in time. It takes the path of least resistance and, when blocked or thwarted, the object of desire is replaced with something that can be attainable, usually the most recent success. Freud recognized this process as regression.

When hope is lost then hopelessness composed of desire and the hatred of time ensues. This hatred of time induces the adolescent to change what would have been movement through time to "a series of stills" (Boris, 1976, p. 142) which can be used to deny the passage of time. This can be seen in certain behaviors of troubled adolescents such as cutting, eating disorders, and drug abuse, all attempts to stop time. The ultimate behavior with its aim to deny the forward motion of time is suicide. The adolescent personality, under the sway of hopelessness, is aware only of the void and of what he or she does not know. When hopelessness is too much to bear, the adolescent is taken over by desire and is bent on pleasure in defiance of time. The adolescent who is mainly influenced by hope and has a fairly good frustration tolerance lives for the future and longs to realize his or her preconception. Such adolescents possess the concept before discovering once again that there is yet another question with which to reckon.

Hope derives from the preconception of how things might or should be. As long as the realization of this preconception matches fairly closely what was expected, the two forces of hope and desire can coexist. In fact, in the best of circumstances, they function as counterbalances. Bion in a brief note in *Cogitations* (1992) mentioned that hope and desire are related as though knotted together. He advised that whatever the personality used to substitute for the truth was transformed into a poison for the mind. The adolescent under the sway of desire will substitute a type of a "lie" for the truth. Bion thought that this sort of a mechanism could be identified by the patient's assumption of an omnipotent stance to counter the sense of experienced helplessness.

The presence of hope prevents the adolescent from falling into hopelessness and taking the course of least resistance which is desire (Boris, 1976). Hope also prevents the adolescent from becoming mired in a place of desire in which time stands still by continuing to present a greater possibility for the future. When there is too great a difference between what is hoped for and what is realized, hope and desire come into conflict with each other. The adolescent who repeatedly experiences frustrated hopes may substitute a different and attainable goal for the previously hoped-for next step in mental development. This attainable goal will meet the short-term need for satisfaction but may not be in the best interests of the development of the adolescent. In other words, when frustration tolerance is poor or when the environment is too frustrating or dangerous, the mind can substitute a concocted belief system or a lie (Bion, 1970) for the sought-after truth necessary for the growth of the mind. Occasionally, this substitution is useful as it buys time for the adolescent to garner further resources and hope again later. There are also periods when the substituted object of desire provides such a powerful level of pleasure or avoidance of pain that the cycle of preconception seeking realization is severely interrupted. An example of this might be an eating disorder that provides the adolescent girl with an identity and a way of shutting out excessive outside stimuli. When the substituted object of desire works too well, the adolescent can exhibit major problems with learning, social skills, and self regulation that may continue into adulthood. The idea of a retreat from frustration is a topic considered by some psychoanalysts in the treatment of seriously ill adult and adolescent patients.

Steiner (1993) writes extensively about a type of emotional withdrawal he has called a "psychic retreat" that provides a temporary escape from frustration at the cost of mental impairment. He views this withdrawal as both a manifestation of destructiveness and a defence against it. The formation of a psychic retreat, as Steiner sees it, provides a protected mental space at the price of impaired contact with reality and minimal opportunity for development. His belief is that this maneuver is necessary to protect the hoped-for object from the overwhelming destructiveness caused by frustration and envy. This leads to behaviors designed to modulate that frustration and envy and provide a sensation of satiated desire in the present without the necessity for development. The implications of this avoidance of reality are profound for adolescents and represent some of the biggest challenges in their treatment.

Clinical implications of hopelessness and desire

Conditions including cognitive disturbances, physical symptoms, and/or self destructive behaviors are frequently seen in practices that include adolescents. While these behaviors are not viewed as a normal or typical part of adolescent development, they do predictably occur when there is an environmental or constitutional failure preventing the successful working through of the adolescent's internal conflicts and anxieties. The rapid changes to the adolescent's body and mind are such that the previous capacity to sustain hope for the future and tolerate frustration can fail, allowing hopelessness to dominate. In that state, frustrated desire leads to behaviors designed to provide immediate relief of frustration and prevent the formation and mentalization of thoughts that are difficult to accept and work through. When the frustration is severe and prolonged, the adolescent can become mired in the regressive or ego-dystonic behavior, forgoing normal development. These are usually the adolescents who come into treatment. The following clinical vignettes may serve as an illustration of this process.

When sixteen-year-old Jennifer entered treatment, she had been cutting herself for over two years. With her sleeves rolled up hundreds of fine pearly scars were visible, creating a lace-like pattern over both arms from wrist to biceps. Jennifer's self-mutilating behavior began during a period of time when she was frequently embarrassed in the presence of her school friends by her mother's obviously severe mental illness. This was complicated by her mother's long-standing emotionally abusive behavior towards her. Jennifer's mother was fond of telling her that they were like twins and that because of the superior intelligence they shared Jennifer did not need to study and struggle with learning as other people did. She withdrew her love abruptly each time Jennifer asserted her independence and individuality. Her mother presented a notion to Jennifer that it was possible to "know" without the frustration of not knowing first. The chaos and confusion these ideas created in Jennifer's mind resulted in the need to dissociate, thus cutting herself off from her own thoughts and experiences. The belief that she should already know interfered actively with her natural curiosity. As a result a sense of arrogance and hopelessness permeated her personality.

Bion described a disturbance of the impulse of curiosity on which all learning depends, and the denial of the mechanism by which it seeks expression. He noted that this sort of disturbance makes normal development impossible. Under such circumstances, Bion advised that the question "Why?" cannot be formulated. "The patient appears to have no appreciation of causation and will complain of painful states of mind while persisting in courses of action calculated to produce them" (Bion, 1959, p. 108). Jennifer continued to cut for two years, sometimes so severely that she required emergency room care with stitches. Her school work suffered and she began skipping classes to walk endlessly around her neighborhood.

Two years into her analysis, Jennifer recalled that at the time she began cutting, she imagined that her mother could be killed by the street people she often invited into their home. Jennifer was horrified to find herself wishing this would happen. This thought was so unacceptable to the fourteen-year-old Jennifer that she put it out of her mind for several years, continuing to idealize her mother and their relationship. The cutting provided a way in which Jennifer could satisfy her desire by both symbolically reducing the loss of distinction between herself and her mother that occurred when she dissociated and by containing her violent impulses toward her mother—acting them out on her skin rather than holding them in her mind as thoughts that could be manipulated creatively. The use of cutting was effective in keeping her from thinking about her violent wishes; however, that state of mind with its prohibition against curiosity also prevented her from being able to concentrate on school and other activities. A once straight-A-student, she began failing at school. Creativity was globally decreased as the act of cutting became her chief focus in life. With the insight Jennifer gained in analysis regarding her healthy need to separate from her mother and an understanding as well as acceptance of her ambivalent feelings toward her mentally ill and emotionally abusive mother, Jennifer no longer felt the need to cut and was eventually able to return to school and the normal activities of late adolescence. She was able to recover from a more than four year break in the expectable trajectory of the growth and development of an adolescent girl and could once more tolerate the frustration of questioning and thinking about the reality of the circumstances of her life. By the end of treatment, Jennifer was able to verbalize her pride in how hard she worked to achieve at school and, freed from her mother's and her own arrogance, no longer felt ashamed that she had to work to gain new knowledge.

Winnicott (1971) found that hopelessness in a child is often due to a break in the continuity of their life line and the normal developmental sequence that occurs as they grow up. The break is often due to an inevitable massive reaction in the child to an environmental failure. The young person in such a frustrating situation is hopeless but does not know why. Winnicott thought about various behaviors such as stealing or delinquency as attempts to reach back over the gap to recover the lost object and, in that way, keeping the possibility of hope alive. This attempt to reach back over the gap from a place of hopelessness is illustrated by the account of an adolescent who entered treatment because of a profound sleep disturbance, cutting behavior, a sudden onset of a learning disability, and cannabis abuse.

April was seventeen years old when she began analytic treatment. Severe cutting behavior had alerted the mental health system to her potential for suicide and a nearly mute and vacant-eyed young woman was escorted from the hospital on pass for her first session. With her hair tied in two ponytails and dressed in a dirty pink track suit, April gave the appearance of a girl of no more than thirteen or fourteen and did not at all look her age. It was as though she had truly succeeded in holding time still. In that first visit, April revealed to the analyst that she had been sexually abused by a female family friend from age six through twelve. April had not told her parents about this abuse because of feelings of shame and fear of reprisal from the perpetrator. April's mother was exceedingly anxious and April was concerned that if she found out about the abuse that might cause her to have a "nervous breakdown." April began cutting at age fourteen when she entered high school shortly after she witnessed the overt sexual behavior of two of her friends. As time went on the cutting increased and it became the only way April could calm herself down at night. Formerly an excellent student, April had begun failing at school in the last year and smoking a lot of cannabis to get through the night when her suicidal ideation and desire to cut to stop the intrusive and frightening violent thoughts were at their worst. Almost immediately after entering treatment, April's cutting ended. It appeared that finally having someone to talk to about her earlier traumas was enough to help her stop this activity.

Winnicott (1971) wrote about the hope that is often evident in the first session with adolescents. He described how the once hopeless patient suddenly begins to develop hope because of something good happening in the environment such as the presence of the psychoanalyst. At the point when hope reappears, the child or adolescent comes alive and returns to the place where he or she was before the environmental failure. Winnicott gives an example of a child whose stealing at least initially functioned as reaching back over a gap with the hope of rediscovering the lost object, the lost maternal connection or family structure. With the establishment of the attachment to her analyst, April was able to begin to speak of her hope that she could find her way to a normal adolescence, which for her would include being able to sleep at night and stay awake during the day, socialize with her peers, attend school regularly, and enjoy intellectual and sports activities.

Two years into treatment April's problems of sleeping, extensive use of cannabis, truancy, and inability to comprehend the words she read in school continued to be limiting. Winnicott (1965) noted that the more disruptive behaviors of the adolescent are often the last to disappear. The adolescent knows that it is hope that is locked up in the rebellious behavior and that despair is linked with compliance and the lie of socializing on someone else's terms. As long as the antisocial behaviors continue, there is hope that someone may notice and be able to help. Compliance insures that help will never come and contributes to the development of what Winnicott (1965) called the "false self."

During the night, when everyone in her family was in bed, April suffered from extreme anxiety and was able to sleep only when her parents were up and moving around in the morning. As she described her nightly torment, it became clear that frightening and violent sexual fantasies were a part of the landscape of her fantasies and dream life. April felt she could not talk to her mother about sex. Yet her fantasies about both the sexual abuse and her mother's and father's bodies united in sex in the next room were troublesome. This contributed to the violent images that kept April awake at night and tormented her in her dreams when she finally did fall asleep.

Melanie Klein (1975) explained how the child's horror of knowing anything about the dreadful destruction she had caused to mother's body and subsequent retribution the child might have to encounter could be so great as to set up a major disturbance of the child's yearning for knowledge as a whole. The child's original strong and unsatisfied craving to know what goes on inside the mother becomes, instead, a deadened version of itself, taking the form of compulsivity such as counting, measuring, adding things up, cutting and eating disorders to name but a few forms of the obsessional neuroses (Quinodoz, 2008). During this period, April compulsively played computer games and kept meticulous records of her dreams in her journal. Even her use of cannabis had an obsessive quality. April was smoking cannabis heavily every night in an attempt to control her anxiety.

Drugs can be used by adolescents to make time itself seem more forgiving and elastic. As mentioned earlier, the adolescent who abuses substances such as cannabis or heroin can be seen as attempting to alter the sensation of the inevitable passage of time. The Symingtons (1996) cite an example of a patient who was abusing drugs. When this person became aware of emotional contact with the analyst in his sessions, he experienced a feeling of loneliness which he found unbearable, shortly followed by taking drugs. As soon as contact with the analyst became evident, the patient was aware of painful and hopeful feelings. These feelings were intolerable; destructiveness took over, obviating the tentative step forward and destroying progress in treatment. The cycle they outline is akin to what has been described in this chapter. For the adolescent in analysis, there is hope of finding connection through analysis, which is the preconception awaiting its realization. At the same time, the adolescent can experience an inability to tolerate the time it takes to fulfill this longing. The time between sessions, the limitations of the frame, and the abstinence of the analyst frustrate the patient's desire for immediate and total gratification. Hopelessness and desire then become dominant and action is required to cease the passage of time. The need has to be filled with something that has worked in the past even if it is not the thing originally sought. This is the dilemma in which April found herself. The cannabis helped to erase the sensation of the passage of time but it also clouded her mind all the next day making it impossible for her to read and learn. The thing she had chosen to help control her anxiety, cannabis, impeded her return to the normal path of development once she found the emotional support for which she had been waiting.

After recognizing the meaning of her cannabis abuse and the fact that it was helping to keep her mind clouded, April voluntarily tried cutting back how much she smoked. When her reading comprehension improved slightly, she was able to risk cutting back even further until she was no longer using it to try to stay calm at night. It was not until the analyst interpreted her need to stay awake all night until her parents were up and about as the need to protect them from being murdered by her in her sleep that she was able to begin to sleep through the night again. Only when the nightmares in which she found her parents murdered in their beds were understood as her own attacks on their creative coupling could she rest at night. April was finally able to integrate the rage and destructiveness she felt toward her parents with her tender loving feelings toward them.

Realistic hope can be formed and maintained only when one has been able to integrate the oppositional forces of hope and desire. The rage, grief, and disappointment when the object of hope fails to meet expectations have to be worked through. Klein (1975) noted that in her analyses of both adults and children the feelings of hope could only emerge after a full experience of the depression that occurred when the patient struggled to grieve the loss of the ideal parent. She thought that it was this hope that could help to overcome the depressive position. When hope is experienced once more the adolescent can focus on the possibilities of the future and tolerate the frustrations of the past.

What then is the experience of the analyst who deals with the hopeless adolescent and what are the special considerations that the analyst should keep in mind?

Countertransference implications

Bion (1970) admonished clinicians to put aside memory and desire while doing the work of psychoanalysis and the reader may rightfully reflect on how this advice relates to what has been said about desire in the adolescent patient and its relationship to hope and hopelessness. We know that the more the analyst concerns herself (for which read either gender) with memories of the past and desire for satisfaction in the present, the farther away she is from being able to discover the selected fact that rises from the place of hopelessness. If the mind of the analyst is filled with what is or is not said, or with what the analyst does or does not hope, she will not be able to allow the experience of being in the room with the patient to predominate, particularly the part of the experience that is not simply the sound of the patient's voice or his body language. However, the analyst is just as prone to fall into desire as the patient when the pain of not knowing and the void of hopelessness is profound. Winnicott (1965) reported a patient who said the only time he was able to feel hope was when his analyst told him he saw no hope and nevertheless continued carrying on with the analysis. It is vital that the adolescent experience the analyst as able to bear the feelings of hopelessness while remaining curious and expectant against great odds.

It appears that a parallel process occurs in the mind of the analyst and the mind of her adolescent patient. In this situation, it is imperative that the analyst be able to tolerate the experience of hopelessness projected by the young person. If the analyst gives into frustration and desire, moving too quickly to interpretation without the shared experience of tolerating the hopelessness, the adolescent will receive confirmation that his pain is indeed too much to bear.

Concluding remarks

The ability to tolerate hope with gratification at some point in the future demands a tolerance for frustration that is not always feasible for the adolescent. When hope dominates the adolescent personality, the focus is on the future with behaviors in line with that view; however, when frustration is too great due to failures in the environment or other factors hopelessness appears. If hopelessness is too prolonged or if the adolescent personality does not have the capacity to tolerate it, the by-product of hopelessness, desire, dominates. In such a situation, the adolescent seeks satisfaction from what is immediately available. This type of behavior allows the young person to experience the sensation of holding back time and allows him the opportunity to continue to wait until the environment provides a mediator that will permit a return to a hopeful stance. In the worst of circumstances, the adolescent may become entrenched in behaviors springing from desire and lose his focus on hope and growth of the mind in favor of a more immediate psychic escape. The fluctuating balance between these two states, hope and hopelessness, determines, among other things, the adolescent's capacity for mental growth and intellectual curiosity.

CHAPTER FOUR

Hopelessness and midlife

Jon P. Ellman

Among the important contributors to the literature on midlife development and crisis, two names stand out: Erik Erikson (1950) provided conceptual clarity by defining the developmental tasks to be accomplished at different stages of life, including midlife, while Elliot Jaques, in the landmark article in which he coined the term "midlife crisis" (1965), elucidated the central fantasy underlying midlife tasks. Thus, when Erikson posits generativity—passing something of value of oneself on to the next generation—as necessary to achieve a sense of integrity vs. a sense of stagnation, Jaques would attribute such a need to the realization of one's own limited lifespan.

Adjusting to this realization is the central task of the midlife transition. When this challenge creates unbearable conflict, symptoms, or provokes impulsive destructive decisions and behavior, one speaks of a "midlife crisis." However, the term is often used to simply denote the midlife phase of development. Coping strategies and defenses used to deal with the tasks of this period, such as denial in fantasy or action, with its driven pursuit of youth or immortality, will be well known to readers of this volume. In essence, the midlife literature suggests that a middle-aged person is confronted by three distinct but interrelated dynamic issues:

- A confrontation with the loss of youth and the youthful body.
- A confrontation with the personalization of death: It will happen to me. My time on this earth is limited.
- A confrontation with the loss of a mental representation of parental figures as even potentially available as a source of security and guidance in the future—the so-called third separation-individuation process: I am the adult now.

This last task is particularly difficult for those who experienced inadequate parenting. They may not be able to relinquish an idealized future hope of finally getting all that was missed out on or of getting an apology or revenge. Or, if such hopes are relinquished, despair may ensue. This dynamic, in addition to oedipal guilt over replacing parents, can impair the full acceptance of the adult role and the normal role reversal that occurs at midlife.

A few caveats

Articles on midlife written after the heyday of interest in the 1970s and 1980s seem to reflect a need to stress the usefulness of midlife theory. Helpful as their contributions are in this regard, might these authors also be sensing that colleagues do not give it sufficient importance in their day-to-day work (Lowenstein, 1990)? If true, several questions arising from midlife theory may be in play. For one thing, according to which author is consulted, midlife is a developmental phase that spans anywhere between thirty-five (Jaques, 1965) and sixty-five (Colarusso, 2007) years of age. Even making allowance for changes in longevity and lifestyles—like having children into the late thirties or beyond—positing a specific phase of development that can occur over that many years stretches credulity. Taking this a bit further, I have been struck by how many patients in their twenties and also beyond the age of sixty-five appear to be confronting the tasks of midlife. I find myself thinking they must be going through a premature or delayed midlife crisis. For example, young adults in their early twenties can be just as distraught over limited time as middle-aged adults in their forties. They express their disappointment in themselves and what they have done with their lives so far as if they had no future. As one college student put it, in all seriousness and with accompanying despair: "I'm twenty-two and what have I accomplished?" Moreover, a young adult in analysis may discover how difficult it is to mourn the loss of his or her "youth and youthful body," which in such a case refers to the loss of childhood.

In the same vein, I analyzed a highly successful female captain of industry, who was so happily and energetically busy with a family and then building her financial empire, into her seventies, that it was only in the face of a life-threatening illness, which she survived, that she developed all the concerns one usually associates with midlife—in particular a felt race against time. Therefore, I have come to think in terms of "midlife crisis phenomena" whenever I hear these themes from an adult analysand of any age.

Another possible obstacle to picking up themes that are supposed to emerge only at midlife may be that they do not strike the therapist as new at all but as new editions of earlier conflicts and challenges about survival, abandonment, loss, dependence, forbidden wishes—whatever names one's analytic school may attach to the developmental phases during which these themes predominate. Modell (1989) cautions that "human time is cyclical ... conflicts recur endlessly and may be worked through at increasingly high levels of mastery" (p. 19). Colarusso (2006) addressed this issue by concluding that it is a question of both old and new. The analyst must try to discern how prior conflict is woven into the current task, that is, "acceptance of transience in midlife" (Colarusso, 2007, p. 337).[1]

In addition, the central tenet of midlife theory has to do with the passage of time. But time in analysis is not always in the foreground of the work, available for interpretation. It may continue to operate in the background, even in midlife, until some triggering circumstance, like termination or an illness, propels it onto center stage.

Finally, what exactly is one supposed to do or say analytically once the issues of midlife, even if previously unconscious, are recognized? Aging and death happen to be inevitable and as Mitchell (1993) had the courage to suggest, understanding has its limits in mitigating suffering over real loss. On the other hand, in a highly creative contribution to the subject, Perry (1989) illustrated the value of simply being a silent witness as the new realities (in the case he wrote about these concern the changing body) are assimilated by the midlife analysand.

Dilemmas of midlife

Notwithstanding these cautionary notes about midlife theory, certain truths about middle age do seem self-evident. Signs of the passage of time become so numerous and manifest at some point in all our lives that they cannot but evoke, at the very least, a new balance in what comes to occupy one's fantasy life. Fantasies emerge related to taking stock about where one is in one's life relative to earlier hopes and aspirations regarding relationships and career. They may involve the pull of the past such as an old boyfriend or girlfriend, the music or literature of adolescence, a need to take care of unfinished business, or to pursue goals or interests long postponed. A preoccupation with one's body in terms of health and longevity makes its appearance as well. Fantasies may arise concerning the assumption of the adult/parent/leader/mentor role at home and at work or of being supplanted in or not needed in these roles at some point. Eventually, fantasies about what enduring effect one's life will have on future generations occur in some form. The fantasies themselves may give rise to defenses or to creative solutions. Many of these themes, which have occupied the professional and lay literature alike for the past forty years, are, it seems to me, entirely predictable from simply imagining the unpleasant thought that you have just been sentenced to death on a date to be determined at a future time. After the initial shock, passing one's life in review, stocktaking, and many of the other preoccupations attributed to midlife would likely be set in motion. As Samuel Johnson famously argued: "If a man knows he will be hanged in a fortnight, it concentrates the mind wonderfully" (Boswell, 1791).

Clinically, interest is focused on how patients deal with these issues. This, necessarily, has much to do with preexisting experience and character. In that regard, a cartoon comes to mind in which a young girl is seated at a lunch counter ordering a meal. She is saying, "I'd like an order of curds with a side of whey." Below, the caption reads, "Little Miss Muffet Does Lunch." One does midlife as one does life. Elliot Jaques (1965) uses a framework that applies the Kleinian template of infant development to midlife development. To me, this basic Kleinian model seems eminently suited to the task of conceptualizing how character impacts one's reaction to the realization of limited time due to the personalization of the idea of death.

Thus, there are those who, in their mental representation of self and other, tend to split good and bad qualities and feelings and then alternately project them in their pure form onto their image of others or introject them, again in their pure form, onto their image of themselves. Self and other are experienced as either all bad and hated or all good and idealized. When the hate is so great that further development is largely thwarted, this state of affairs persists and its relevance to the midlife encounter with death will be explored presently. In contrast, those in whom loving feelings dominate the mental landscape are able to go on to develop a capacity to see themselves and others as a mixture of good and bad; shades of grey replace a black and white view of experience and self. This capacity is considered a momentous step forward in development. It was originally brought about in early childhood by some form of realization in the young child's mind that the good and bad breast/mother are one and the same with accompanying feelings of concern, mourning for the imagined harm done by hate, and an impulse to make reparations. A healthy ambivalence in one's inner world—the depressive position—is attained when there is an integration of positive and negative mental representations of self and other with an overall predominance of the positive.

As I understand him, Jaques (1965) is asserting that the idea of one's own death is hard enough for anyone to contemplate as the cessation of consciousness. But it is far more difficult for those whose idea of death is unduly persecutory; that is, those who have not achieved the depressive position. (Those who have, must rework it at midlife.) To the degree that splitting continues to dominate mental functioning, it will extend to the middle-aged adult's notion of life itself—all good or bad. The purified bad side of life is death; and therefore onto the idea of death is projected all the unmitigated horrors the mind can conjure. Jaques provides a vignette with a highly graphic example of such horrors.

When aging and death, split and imbued with persecutory hate, are felt to be unbearable, denial in fantasy and action results. This denial can lead to what Erikson called "stagnation" (1950, p. 266) and Jaques called "character deterioration" (1965, p. 511). Clinically, what manifests is everything from destructive life changes or destructiveness toward others to suicide (Cath, 1980). However, even when splitting is not dominant prior to midlife, everyone is assumed to use denial to some extent with respect to his or her own death. For those at midlife in whom denial can be largely overcome through mourning, a more positive outcome is possible. Mourning in this connection is the process whereby the loss is acknowledged and accepted with pain and not denied.[2]

An image of the whole object with its good and bad qualities can now appear—originally that of mother, now of life, that is, death as a part of life. Mourning is only possible when the level of aggression in the personality is not so great that the resulting hate would threaten to obliterate all goodness in the object or self were the split images of good and bad to be brought together.

A new version of this mourning process is thought to occur with respect to the midlife individual's image of life. Until somewhere in midlife, it had been idealized, relatively devoid of the notion of one's own death. Again, through mourning what has been and is to be lost as one gets older, the idea of death, previously split off from the idea of life, with all the bad that was projected onto it, is now in contact with and mitigated by the good that was and still exists in life. This coming together enables the idea of death to be tolerated as part of life and "carried in thinking" (Jaques, 1965, p. 512) without its persecutory sting. Jaques uses the term "constructive resignation" (p. 513) to capture the essence of a favorable outcome to the midlife crisis.

Strenger (2009) cautions that "mortality acceptance is on a continuum between manic denial and the ability for calm contemplation" (p. 249). For him, a positive outcome to a midlife crisis would still fall somewhere along that continuum, as a total absence of any denial of death is not possible. Comforting ideas about the influence of what one has created on those who survive and even future generations would represent a healthy compromise formation that lies somewhere along this continuum. Strenger also puts his finger on a distinctly positive feature of midlife. Realizing time is limited can serve as an impetus to chip away at what is unessential in one's life, focusing down on what one really wants, is good at, and interested in.

This brings us to Jaques's concept of "sculptured creativity," a term that refers to the effect on one's existence of the new equilibrium: an inner state in which the idea of death is assimilated into and modulated by the good in life. As mentioned above, this new ideational and affective attitude is an alloy, composed of the idea of the positive in life melded with the recognition of one's eventual death. And this new amalgam of good and bad, each informing and diluting the intensity of the other, shows itself in many ways at midlife and beyond: As a more philosophic tolerant attitude toward oneself and others in general (wisdom), as a need to care for and mentor or create something lasting, and in the value one attaches to relationships and experience. In the case of highly creative people, it manifests in their artistic creations themselves. Jaques reminds us that at midlife, Shakespeare, for example, turned from writing historical and comedic plays to tragedies, thereby literally incorporating a sense of the tragic into his work.

Hopelessness in midlife

Hopelessness refers to the feelings and thoughts that arise in the absence of hope. Its feeling tone is best captured in its synonym, despair. In the Romance languages despair is the word for hopeless. Thus in French: espoir = hope, and désespoir = without hope = hopeless. If hope connotes an elaborate fantasy of a desired outcome that is simultaneously believed in yet felt to be uncertain and projected into the future, then hopelessness would convey the opposite: The feeling that accompanies the loss of all belief in that outcome occurring at any time in the future. The contributions on the subject contained in this book attest to the complexity of the concept and address a relative lacuna in the psychoanalytic canon.

For me, hope embodies more of a scenario with a more complex goal than a simple wish. In addition, unlike hope, wishes and desires need not comprise doubt or be as definitively oriented in the future. Hopelessness is therefore more than the frustration of a wish. It is the emotion felt in response to a dream that will never come true; to a failed mission or a failure to rescue or be rescued, with no possibility of these goals ever being realized. Hopelessness can form a part of a depressive state or disorder but can also occur independently. It exists along a continuum of intensity and can be about a highly specific outcome in one area of life or a general attitude toward life. Nevertheless, as Fredrickson (2009) points out, it is more often a reaction to what is experienced as dire or catastrophic as well as insoluble and irremediable. Mitchell (1993) makes the point that hope can be viewed as regressive, embodying earlier longings for magical control or for an irreplaceable childhood object, or progressive, as a starting point for resuming development. Hopelessness would then be the negation of either of these forms of hope.

The link between midlife and hopelessness has long been recognized, as in the old psychiatric diagnosis of "involutional melancholia": Hope requires a future in which to play itself out. But to reiterate, Jaques's contribution is precisely that at midlife the perception of the future is foreshortened by the awareness of death as a personal reality. As mentioned, that awareness occurs in reaction to the innumerable and unavoidable signs of the passage of time. From birthdays, hair greying or loss, biological clocks, to children grown, police and doctors looking younger, illness in one's own or the older generation, etc., there is no avoiding the ticking of the clock. It is as if life were now like the twenty-four-hour Cuban news radio station "Radio-Reloj" (clock radio). This station features a continuous ticking-clock sound in the background of all its programs and the exact time is announced every minute!

The relationship between the loss of hope and a shrinking future is well captured in a clinical vignette of Michels (Michels & Auchinloss, 1989) in which his analysand's illusion of future possibilities is shattered by the limitations of time. A related theme is that a sense of limited time spells the end of postponing, which has particular relevance to hope and hopelessness. As Boris (1976) put it, "Hope resides in time and is lost ... to the timelessness of eternity" (p. 140).

In my analytic practice, I have had occasion to treat three patients who were referred to me following near-lethal suicide attempts. As it happens, all three were highly successful middle-aged men with narcissistic personalities whose childhood experiences foreshadowed that particular character organization. Aging and eventual death are narcissistic injuries par excellence. Narcissistic personality disordered patients are clearly at special risk for a crisis at midlife. The inevitable stocktaking that occurs confronts them with failures in having lived up to grandiose ambitions or a lack of fulfillment from what they have achieved; the loss of physical attractiveness or prowess; damage done to loved ones; or previously avoided emptiness. When, in the face of these and other narcissistic injuries, defenses such as omnipotence, projection, devaluation, and denial fail, despair may ensue (Kernberg, 1980). Each of my patients described a period of despair following catastrophic financial setbacks which they felt to be their own fault and believed irreversible. All three spoke of having felt contempt for themselves and humiliated in what they perceived to be the eyes of their wives. The first vignette will be about one of these three men.

Clinical vignette: 1

Mr. G. was a relatively uneducated but highly articulate and personable forty-one-year-old man. He came from a "dirt poor" family. His father was a nasty alcoholic who left the patient and his mother for good on the day of Mr. G.'s sixth birthday. He had promised Mr. G. a bicycle, but when the birthday came, before leaving, his last words to his son were: "You'll get a bike when your dick reaches your asshole." The patient's mother was an invalid, constantly complaining, who was cared for by the patient's kindly but stern and preoccupied grandmother as well as by the patient himself. From ten years old on, he worked at any job he could get, leaving school at sixteen to work full time. He eventually started a small blue-collar service company, which he subsequently expanded to a number of branch offices. He was a millionaire by his late thirties. Under the influence of a feeling of "I'm turning forty, I've worked like a slave since I was ten, now it's my turn," he suddenly divorced his rather dependent wife and married his highly efficient office manager. Unawares, little by little, he left the running of the business to his new wife. This was the first time in his life he ceased being in complete control over every detail of his finances. In retrospect, he described this period as "making up for lost time." However, at a certain point, he learned that his new wife had neglected key aspects of the business, like paying certain tax bills, and discovered just how deeply in debt he was. In the end, he lost the company. He blamed himself exclusively for "taking his eye off the ball" and for having ignored a number of clues about his wife's unreliability. He could envisage no way out, rigged the exhaust pipe into the cabin of his car, locked the garage door and turned on the engine. Had it not been for a neighbor having heard the car's motor behind a closed garage door and calling 911, he would not have been saved.

During our work, material emerged that revealed the link between hopelessness and midlife tasks: He had had two previously unconscious hopes that he had projected into an indefinite and uncertain future. One appeared via my countertransference. I became aware that I often had a pleasurable feeling in his presence. It was like being a student with a kindly and infinitely wise teacher from whom I could learn valuable lessons for life. I noticed that he used "you" instead of "I" when he meant himself, generalizing his own mental life to me and all of mankind. He never lost his calm deliberate lesson-imparting tone and seemed to view his early life, wives, business, and even suicide attempt in a somewhat removed philosophical way. I often felt uplifted after our sessions. Much work and introspection is condensed when I say that it eventually became evident that we were enacting, with roles reversed, an unconscious hope for a relationship with just such a wise gentle father who could be counted on for guidance and support. His reliance on his second wife embodied his other hope: A competent well-functioning mother who would have cared for him, allowing him to have had a normal childhood. He had idealized this woman's abilities in proportion to his need to have her fulfill this preconceived hope for a better mother.

From the type of enterprise he had been running and dreams about vehicles of various kinds, we were able to piece together that his business success represented his ability to do the impossible and give himself the bike. His father's parting remark had other meanings as well. If his dick reached his asshole, he would be "fucking myself up the ass." This had several meanings for him. He could be his own man without any paternal role model while at the same time experience father's harshness as a way of "challenging you into success." Feelings of anger at the humiliating and abandoning father and shame at having been the son of such a loser fueled a wish to defeat him, kill him off. This caused guilt over success. Insofar as his success represented an aggressive oedipal triumph, he had had to lose the bike (fuck himself up), partly accounting for his having "taken his eye off the ball." By wrecking his symbolic bike, he satisfied both poles of his ambivalence toward his father. His failure severed the bond the bike represented while at the same time preserving it by fulfilling father's implied prophecy with its, for him, derogatory homosexual connotation that he'd never amount to anything as a man. This latter dynamic emerged from his associations to the highly condensed symbolic connection between his method of suicide, introducing the exhaust pipe via a hose into the car's back seat, and the phrasing of father's taunt.

Mr. G.'s sudden divorce and remarriage on turning forty had this midlife component: The new unconscious awareness that he could no longer postpone accomplishing a mission to replace his actual parents with long hoped-for better parents. By midlife, success in business and other factors had enabled him to easily enact his hoped-for scenario through a quick divorce and through turning the tables on his childhood mother by having a woman take care of him. Boris (1976) explained how a hope realized ceases to be a hope as it enters the present and coincides with desire—a wish come true. In this man's case, the pressure of limited time propelled him to act precipitously on unconscious hopes with dire consequences. The belief that at his age there would never be time to start anew, a theme of midlife, was a key factor contributing to his suicidal despair.

Consequently, the main point with respect to the topic at hand is that the sense that there was no more postponing had a marked influence on how this man handled success and failure and contributed to feelings of despair that almost cost him his life. Identifying his unconscious hopes enabled us to understand his hopelessness at the time of his suicide attempt. This understanding opened the way for him to begin to tackle the rage and sadness beneath his philosophic calm as they unfolded in the matrix of transference-countertransference. Limited time and financial failure could then be leavened by valuing the mind and determination that had built his successful business and that he still possessed as well as revaluing his wife with whom he went on to have a son. By way of postscript, I subsequently learned that he became a much sought-after life coach, probably in partial fulfillment of his original mission, identification with the analyst, and in line with some natural interpersonal gifts.

The following vignette illustrates a hopelessness that was at once defensive, chronic, and acutely exacerbated by the advent of midlife.

Clinical vignette: 2

Mr. L. was forty-seven when he first consulted with me due to an increasingly anxious feeling following his partner's departure from their business. He was chronically anxious and at the same time "kind of numb." Life for him was "going through the motions" but his present degree of anxiety was unbearable. Mr. L.'s parents were immigrants from a civil war-torn country headed by a truly brutal dictator. His father had heroically fought on the rebel side and was never caught. However, he had witnessed the murder of his parents, wife, and son by government soldiers before joining the rebels. After immigrating, he met and married a woman from the same tribe whose childhood had been spent in hiding. The couple had two children, my patient and his older sister. As a child Mr. L. recalled an aura of unspoken sadness in his home but felt loved and cared-for by his mother and special for his father: "His eyes lit up whenever I entered the room." But his father rarely spoke. In particular, his father never talked about his war experiences and my patient only learned about his courage and leadership from family members and friends who had fought with him. Financially, his father was a modest breadwinner who could not concentrate on his work life and was portrayed by mother as irresponsible. The patient said his father reminded him of the movie character in an old movie he had once rented, *The Pawnbroker*. I had seen it and felt I immediately knew what he was talking about. The patient's mother was described as sociable, talkative, and ambitious for her husband but also as having a "paranoid streak." However, she was a good, loving mother until an abrupt change took place in her behavior toward the family. It occurred about the time the patient was six years old. It coincided with a move into a better neighborhood. His mother suddenly became consumed with envy of wealthier neighbors who were originally from their country of origin and blamed their situation on her irresponsible husband. She lost interest in my patient. From that time on, several nights a week, she made her children watch as she repeatedly hit the father, yelling at him all the while. Father never defended himself or spoke during this scene, which could go on for hours. As a result, Mr. L. was chronically sleep deprived, did poorly in school, thought he was dumb, and was ashamed to have friends over. His parents were unavailable to help him. He said he had never blamed them but only felt sorry for them.

A high school teacher recognized his latent intelligence and encouraged him. He slowly began to realize he was smart, applied himself, and obtained a scholarship to a top university. A remarkably pleasing personality made him very attractive to girls but he had a dread of intimacy with women born of a fear of humiliation at the hands of a woman.

Rarely did he express aggression, "I don't want to be like my mother," but it emerged in other ways: He described family and friends and, subtly, me too, with a good-humored contempt; he had a sexual fantasy of sticking an iron rod into a woman's bum; dreams of being pursued by enemy soldiers; a dream about a subway car running through a couple's bedroom and another in which a guard in a zoo lets a witch out of her cage in spite of my patient's frantic warnings. (We believed I was the guard and analysis would result in his being exposed to what he feared most—humiliation at the hands of a woman.)

Concerning his love life, he had been unable to tell his college girlfriend, whom he loved very much, how much he cared for her and she left him due to his apparent indifference. He eventually married a childhood friend, quite beautiful and non-threatening, but from a troubled family with a cold self-centered mother. Initially, their marriage went well and he was not plagued by fears of being humiliated. This all changed in an eerie replay of his mother's abrupt change when he was six. Several years into the marriage, his wife confronted him with the fact of her cheating. This repetition of the original trauma of a husband's humiliation forcefully revived his identification with his humiliated father. It solidified a sense of hopelessness about women and love to which he now felt resigned. He could enjoy neither vacations nor financial success but blamed his wife's infidelities on some inadequacy in himself. He had not been able to bring happiness to his mother and now to his wife and he doubted that at this time in his life analysis would help. It was too late: "The trauma is too ingrained."

Initially, I saw him face to face. He was never far from tears, especially when talking about his father who had died several years before. As stated, he felt hopeless about ever making a success of his marriage and now of his business, although the latter seemed patently irrational. His role as father to his three children remained his one motivation for living. He was caring, interested in their daily lives, and a helpful, concerned parent unlike his own parents. I soon came to feel that he was a good candidate for analysis and invited him to try the couch. He seemed amenable to the idea but in retrospect his attitude subtly changed from then on and for the next four years. Typically, a session would start with anywhere from ten to twenty minutes of silence. Interpretations of its meaning on both our parts were as numerous as they were lacking in impact. He told me it was simply his way of saying (or not saying) "What's the use?" That is, had he come to see me earlier in life, he might have been helpable but it was too late because of his age.

He never criticized me directly. However, even after a session he had experienced as helpful, by the next session it was back to square one, no continuity, as if he had rid himself of any feeling of the value of what had transpired previously. The notion of "attacks upon linking" (Bion, 1958) came to my mind. He seemed to nullify the good in our work and thereby any hope of feeling better. Theories notwithstanding, I did not feel I really understood what the silences and lack of continuity were about. In my mind, I began to share his pessimism. Was he right that the trauma had occurred from such a young age, had gone on for so many years that it had led to psychic or even neurophysiological changes justifying his phrase "too ingrained"? And was it then reactivated so decisively in his marriage, that he was, in fact, hopeless? Amati-Mehler and Argentieri (1989) well describe the intersubjective dynamics that occur with narcissistically damaged patients who induce feelings of hopelessness in the therapist. They conclude that their patients' protestations of hopelessness paradoxically masked an unconscious unrealistic but persistent hope that "... what is past or lost can still be provided and restored ... the extreme defence against the threat of separation" (p. 299). That is, a hopeless attitude that functions to defend against an even deeper hope about a longed-for but unattainable symbiosis.

In trying to figure it all out, I started with the feeling I had about Mr. L. in general. I liked him. We shared similar views on a number of topics, he had a good sense of humor and an indefinable likeability. Then there was the fact that interspersed among silences and expressions of the futility of our efforts, he was able to associate meaningfully and with affect about his experiences and feelings past and present. And he did keep coming to see me, indicating the presence of some latent hope. Yet his zombie-like feeling state alternating with anxiety persisted. Were my positive feelings toward him and his seeming lack of aggression blinding me to something?

He had reported a number of dreams in which I believed I was being portrayed negatively. At that time, however, he viewed dreams as separate from his real thoughts and feelings and gave them no apparent credence. Several such dreams featured him as a passenger and another man as the driver: A plane he was on crashed in one dream, an elevator with him and an elevator operator in it plunged to the ground in another. In many dreams, he was being pursued by enemy soldiers. Clearly, to me, on one level he could not yet see that he viewed me as dangerously incompetent and, potentially, another humiliator like mother, should he confront me. About a month before the Christmas break of the fifth year of the analysis he recounted two dreams. In one, he was a guinea pig in a medical research institute and in the other, he was going upstairs in the stairwell of his office building when he encountered a colleague going downstairs. As he said hello, he suddenly realized his colleague was deaf and dumb. His associations did not include direct or indirect references to me that I could discern—although mine certainly did.

Nor was he at all responsive to my suggestion to that effect. Mid-December, in the session before what would have been the last session preceding the Christmas break, he announced that he was ending the analysis. He was more convinced than ever that it was too late in his life for anything to change and he was better off feeling anxious or hopeless than chasing rainbows. Now that he was leaving (that it was safe) he would tell me something: When I had "switched" him to the couch, he said, I had acted in an unfeeling and unconcerned way. I had not consulted him sufficiently. For him, the couch had meant isolation. It meant I was only interested in him as a research subject. The word analysis said it all. He had felt unnoticed and dehumanized. I was taken aback. Not at the content of what he was saying, but at the lack of any overt protest or hesitancy on his part then and during the whole four years that had gone by during which he had been aware of how he felt without bringing it up. I restrained an impulse to react defensively or angrily and simply asked if he had ever thought of telling me before? He said he'd think about that. He started the following session without the accustomed silence or lack of continuity by reporting a dream: *There is an infant lying in the middle of the floor while a party of adults is taking place around him. Someone says, 'That baby is dying' but no one notices and the party goes on.*

From the dream I was able to feel the intensity of what he had told me during the last session and I believe he sensed that as we went over it together in connection with the couch. After a pause, he continued by addressing my question. He told me that it was his credo that, in life, when the other person does not realize they have made a mistake or hurt you, and you have to tell them, it's already too late. They are hopeless. Again, I refrained from challenging his belief, even by inviting him to explore it or the dream more. Instead, whatever I might have said in retrospect, what I did say was: That I was sorry I had unknowingly caused him grief; that had he told me what he now had, I would not have insisted, nor would I now insist on the couch; that part of the reason I thought of the couch for him was that I felt it could be more helpful for him, he could go more deeply into things, but that what may be better for some people and at some times might not be for others. I added that I also use the couch because I believe I listen better and that it's more comfortable for me. A long silence followed. It was a different kind of silence from the withholding one at the beginning of sessions. He took up one part of what I had said. He said that it hadn't occurred to him that the couch had been partly for me. His tone conveyed relief at the idea. There was no further talk of leaving treatment. He chose to continue on the couch that he was now used to and the long silences at the beginning grew shorter. He could see the transference distortion that I had not suggested the couch out of a sudden loss of interest in him as a person, like mother.

After the break, a number of sessions were devoted to his new partner who was making foolish decisions while he "still couldn't say anything." I asked him what came to his mind if he imagined confronting the partner. He repeated his mantra about how futile it was to point something out to anyone who had not realized their mistake themselves. I asked what had been the result of finally confronting me? The following session he related that he had had a long talk with his partner, gently getting across all his misgivings. He was surprised when the partner had actually been grateful for his input. He went on to remember with anger how his parents, especially his mother, ignored him. Over time, nothing at home changed. The fights continued. Nothing could restore his mother to her previously caring happy self. "My just being there no longer had the power to make my mother happy. That's what a kid is supposed to be able to do. I realized there were no options."

If his mother, in fact both parents, were going to change, it would have to come from them. He was powerless. It seemed likely to me that it was originally from just that powerless helpless feeling that his hopeless attitude toward life had arisen. For him, hopelessness became a defense against the hope that his earlier mother would reappear and that his parents would come to their senses. "They should have known the impact on a child of violent fights a whole childhood long." His silence with me, his not letting me know his reaction to the couch, his dreams of the dying baby and the incompetent pilot now seemed to make new sense to us as he simultaneously became aware of how angry he had been at me. His hopelessness appeared to morph into a quiet but nonetheless conscious rage at those who should have known.

And yet, he had continued with me for four more years, as he had stayed married to his wife. This "hanging in" betrayed the underlying childhood hope that, with time, parents, wives, partners, analysts, will realize by themselves the harm they have done and right those wrongs. Through his waiting, for as long as it took, he might finally fulfill his mission—to make mother happy and love him and father again. All he could do, now as then, was let time take its course. With midlife's message that time is not infinite, the hope that dwelled beneath the hopeless stance was shattered and true hopelessness with its accompanying dread in the form of his acute anxiety symptoms emerged.

At first, any possible cure that could have resulted from our work together had seemed worse to him than the disease. Eventually, analysis enabled him to tolerate the genuine underlying despair and rage that had been denied, split off, and compartmentalized so successfully that their very inaccessibility gave rise in part to his sense of being incurable.

Analysis for this man took place largely by way of transference/countertransference. For example, although his reaction to lying on the couch had been intensely negative, when he finally learned that the couch was partly for my benefit, he felt relieved, even empowered in that his acquiescence—something he did—had been able to make me/mother happy.

All of the time and work described above appeared to have been a necessary prelude to our subsequent work on the oedipal strivings of a six-year-old boy whose loving mother suddenly loses interest in him and commences nearly nightly tirades, beating and screaming at his seemingly weak irresponsible father, who silently takes it, on a near nightly basis. Following this phase of our work he went on to fall in love.

The analysis lasted fourteen years. An anxiety and a hopeless listless feeling that had been with him since age six had abated. It did recur temporarily in the face of major stressors but he seemed to have undergone real and positive character change. I believe my "hanging in," and all that implies, provided a corrective experience (especially regarding feelings of being powerless to influence others and uninteresting to them) that led to sufficient trust to allow the emergence of the cognitive and emotional understanding of previously unconscious hopes. These hopes had to be worked through and revised to hopes that were consistent with the realities of his phase of life. This involved understanding their relationship to his childhood and then later experience and to their having been dashed by certain setbacks that took place coincident with the midlife realization of the finiteness of time.

Our journey was all the more arduous for his use of hopelessness to defend against becoming aware of his underlying hopeful longings. This dual contradictory attitude toward hope appeared to function for him as a psychic retreat (Steiner, 1993). It was a retreat that had served him relatively well until the confrontation with limited time made failures in his work and marriage seem irreparable, leading to the depressive anxious state that had brought him to consult. Finally, he came to comprehend and mourn as unrealizable the possibility of the now conscious hopes coming true in their original childhood form; but they were not all lost. He was able to revive them in modified form. He came to give himself permission to have, as an important part of a new mission, his own happiness.

The last vignette describes a hopeless feeling at midlife but with a different twist.

Clinical vignette: 3

The patient was a thirty-nine-year-old married woman with four children. Her youngest child was nineteen years old. Ms. T. had always dreamed of becoming a professional writer and teachers had praised her writing efforts throughout school. She had put her writing aspirations on hold in order to care for her family as a stay-at-home mom. However, now that her children had grown, she could permit herself the luxury of devoting herself seriously to her desired craft. She enrolled in an advanced writing course but was mortified, "crushed," when the teacher criticized some phrasing in her first assignment as being "too perfect." The incident plunged her into an amotivational depressed state. She dropped the course and stopped writing. She felt hopeless about ever writing again. It was for this state that she had consulted me.

Ms. T. struck me as extremely nice. She was soft-spoken, expressing herself in a sincere deliberate way. She quietly praised every aspect of my being: my office, my profession, my incredible understanding. I was aware that idealization was at work but could not help looking forward to our sessions. Puzzlingly, she felt that she herself was not a very good person.

Her life story explained that feeling as well as her overreaction to the teacher's comment. She was the elder of two sisters. Her mother was the younger of two sisters. Mother's mother was said to have favored mother's older sister. The patient's sister was born when Ms. T. was three years old. Because she was the baby, mother forced my patient to give her favorite blanket to the new arrival. All mother's attention and affective involvement remained focused on the sister as the two girls grew up. A succession of maids was hired to look after Ms. T. Such approval and encouragement as she got from her mother was for behavior having to do with proper manners, comporting herself like a lady, and looking after household chores. Her father was loving toward her and even-handed with his two daughters but he owned a large company and was away from home most of the time. He was remembered as a warm although distant presence who played a positive but relatively minor role in her upbringing.

As soon as she learned to write, Ms. T. started expressing her feelings in little stories. If ever these were left around the house, she would find them in the garbage the next day. This was not meant to be mean on mother's part, I was told, but mother liked a tidy home and did not have the time to read them. From the patient's description, her mother experienced her first daughter's creativity, curiosity, and lively exuberance as bad traits for a girl. She often told her: "You have a bad soul." It was difficult for me to listen to this material but the patient believed her mother was a good person and parent who had taken fine care of all Ms. T.'s instrumental needs. Mother was simply a product of her times, set in her ways and values.

After high school, where she had achieved top marks, her parents enrolled her in a junior college to learn a trade traditionally associated with women. She recalled, with no particular feeling, having asked to go to a liberal arts university where the education would be more suited to a writing career but her mother overruled her request and father went along. However, by the time her less scholarly sister had graduated from high school, she (the sister) got her way and was sent to an expensive high-status university. Sister's major fit in well with the needs of father's business. In fact, when their father died, everything was left to mother who eventually turned the company with all its assets over to her sister. It only made sense to do so due to the sister's undergraduate degree. Ms. T. did not recount this Cinderella-esque narrative with a hint of resentment. On the contrary, she maintained she had had an ideal family life, even in her solely positive associations to the following dream. The dream occurred early in the analysis. Although confirmed by later associations, the manifest content alone, I felt, well summed up much of her childhood—the before and after the flood of sister's birth: *I'm playing in a stream at our country house. I'm crossing the stream going from rock to rock and I'm very agile and sure-footed. It's a warm sunny day. Suddenly the sky clouds over and there's a storm. The water level keeps rising to the point where I'm not sure I'll make it to the other side. I do, but barely. I follow a narrow path to a house but it's empty.*

About a year into the analysis an enactment took place: Ms. T. had made reference to a book of a technical nature which by chance had been assigned reading in a college course I had taken. I mentioned I had read it. She was impressed. Her being impressed felt good. In retrospect, I had wanted to live up to her idealization of me as all-knowing. Subsequently, she asked if I had read another book, again, rather technical. I said I hadn't. She seemed quite disappointed in me in her tone of voice. And I was too. Her disappointment had tapped into something in me. From one day to the next her whole attitude toward me changed. Now the office was too small, analysis was a much overrated method, etc. And I no longer looked forward to our sessions. She made no link between her changed attitude and the book. I became more silent than usual. Two weeks of sessions like this went by as I was struggling in my own mind to figure out what was happening. I was able to trace the origin of the impasse to the unread book and my reaction in the face of her disappointment in me to its source. It took me back to a relative, a frequent visitor to our home, who was a true intellectual putdown artist. I found an occasion to put my reverie to the test by merely asking her if she had ever felt put down intellectually. The floodgates opened. She answered, with bitter irony: Did I think, with her marks and intelligence and writing ability, that being sent to a trade school, while her flighty sister, who was only interested in looks and a social life and had no interest in books or school, gets an education worth hundreds of thousands of dollars, might possibly qualify as an intellectual putdown? "What does a degree mean anyway?" she continued. "People like you [referring to me, the analyst] haven't read half of what I've read and get all kinds of perks for the rest of their lives that they don't deserve." In this way, there now surfaced from beneath the admiration she had heaped on me, a most intense, if understandable, transference with both sibling and maternal components.

Analysis of her envy revealed that it was all the more intense for never being able to be expressed, as well as for the guilt it induced in her. To have complained about unequal treatment or tried to compete openly with her sister, even now, would have cost her such maternal support as she did get for being well behaved. In addition, to cause her mother any stress would endanger mother's life. That is, in reaction to what sounded to me like normal assertiveness and liveliness in a child, her mother had repeatedly told her "You'll be the death of me." Unfortunately, her mother did have a medical condition whose symptoms, while intermittent, were dramatic and frightening. Therefore, as a child, Ms. T. could actually witness the supposed effect of her supposed bad behaviour on her mother's health. This grounded her guilt and feelings of badness in what for her was reality. Her catastrophic response to her teacher's comment that her phrase was too perfect had to do with the threat it posed to the necessary compliance with mother's image of the kind of person she should be and to the massive reaction formation used to become that person. This work allowed her to resume writing.

A further enactment seven years later proved life changing. By this time Ms. T. had become successfully established in a particular niche in her field. Her romantic life had also taken a happy turn, as avoidance of envy was no longer the main criterion in her choice of love object. We were in the termination phase or so it seemed. Then, at the end of a session she got up off the couch and instead of leaving started to stare at me. I asked what she was looking at. She answered: "I just wanted to see how you look after listening to all the shit that comes out of my mouth for fifty minutes?" I was completely taken aback having assumed that her image of herself as bad had diminished substantially; and yet here was clear evidence it was alive and well and so ego-syntonic!

During the next session, as we continued on the theme of basic badness, I felt myself at pains to find out just how ego-syntonic the feeling still was. I asked if she thought the feeling of being a person who is full of shit or badness was consistent with the reality of what she knew or had come to know about herself. Some might argue that the question itself was out of place because it is her psychic reality that counts and not how congruent with reality to reality. However that may be, my having asked it, her reaction became crucially relevant. She took what I had asked in a way I experienced as surprising: She said that she now understood that deep down I must have always believed she was crazy. For some time, this interpretation of hers of my question had the force of an unshakable conviction; it threatened the analysis and all the work we had accomplished. I tried to make it clear that what I had been referring to as being inconsistent with reality was her feeling of being bad, but she didn't buy it. She had a dream about a bungling workman who left part of her home renovations unfinished and in disarray. It did not take Freud to help her associate the workman to me. In the midst of this therapeutic morass came a holiday break of several weeks.

She returned in a good mood. She told me that over the break she had passed the time considering her life, her accomplishments, her way of handling situations, and her way of thinking in review. She had found nothing to indicate to her that she was anything but a sane rational person as mentally healthy as anyone. I had been wrong. I responded by asking her about the feeling of being full of badness. She said it was gone. Nor did it return.

During the time in which the analysis continued to termination, we came to understand what had been the missing link that caused her to misinterpret the purport of my question, and then go on to lose a feeling of being bad that had always been an integral part of her self-representation. What emerged in the final phase of our work together was that she had needed to use my question in such a way as to disprove her mother's view of her as having a bad soul—being bad in her very essence—without directly contradicting her mother, even to herself. In the maternal transference, I had to be experienced as believing that she was a bad person in order for her to disprove her mother in effigy by demonstrating to herself that I/mother was wrong about her. I stood for her mother because for an analyst, as she saw it, bad equals crazy.

This vignette differs from the other two in that the role played by the midlife confrontation with the prospect of limited time did not create a sense of urgency, pressure, or hopelessness. Rather the advent of midlife was liberating. Now, having rendered unto Caesar in terms of her family in the first half of her adult life, midlife afforded this woman an opportunity to resume a certain important aspect of her development by pursuing a dream from childhood related to a creative gift. Hers was not a hope that had to be mourned or modified. However, what the vignette does illustrate is that when a hoped-for outcome or aspiration is itself laden with conflict, the crisis at midlife may not be mainly the product of dealing with the realization of one's end, but of the emotions evoked by the very opportunities for a new beginning that have been opened up by entering this phase of life.

Each of the patients presented had reacted to significant childhood trauma by forming compensatory fantasies for the future to undo the trauma—in other words, hope. In each case, the full meaning of the hope was unconscious. In each case, their early adult lives went relatively well, I believe in part because of the sustaining nature of their hopes. In each case, by midlife, they were poised to see the fantasy come true. And again, in each case, the midlife encounter with time impacted on certain adverse events in such a way as to render those events synonymous with the dashing of the earlier hope. For Mr. G., the fact that setbacks occurred at a time of life when neither postponing nor new beginnings were felt to be possible meant that he would now never be able to realize hopes that then turned to utter hopelessness. For Mr. L., a pseudo-hopeless attitude had protected him from disappointment until two events occurred in midlife that were so similar to traumatic childhood experiences they obliterated his underlying unconscious hope, doomed as it seemed by destiny and now lacking a long enough future in which to play itself out. A genuine hopelessness and panic ensued. For Ms. T., midlife meant the freedom and the impetus to pursue a realistic hoped-for dream. However, a seemingly minor criticism of her work threatened the entire bulwark of her defenses against the rage, rivalry, and ambition that realizing her hope would have unleashed.

Despite significant childhood trauma, these particular patients were fortunate enough to have had the capacity to use sufficiently positive images of self and other to construct hopeful fantasies that sustained them through the early part of their lives and enabled them to benefit from analysis when the midlife encounter threatened to rob them of those hopes.

Concluding remarks

In my view, the practical application of considering hopelessness in the context of midlife is this: An analyst or dynamic therapist may not be in the habit of hearing unconscious hopes as opposed to desires or wishes. Hopes are more future oriented and complex structures than wishes. As illustrated in the foregoing cases, hopes are often contained in an unconscious mission a person must accomplish, or in a lost or missed out on and longed-for relationship. Because hope exists within a fantasy that is to take place at a future time, to the extent that that future time is felt to be limited, as occurs at midlife, the now never realizable hope may turn into hopelessness. Sensing that one is growing older leads to a realization that one's own life will end. Whether a person greets this revelation by integrating it, through some form of mourning, into ongoing mental life or with renewed, redoubled efforts to split it off, will determine the fate of one's midlife crisis. The word mourning has a depressing connotation but only when its positive outcome is ignored. That outcome enables integration at a higher level. A more genuine, tolerant, wiser individual, with greater depth to his or her being can emerge from it. Poetically put, "A sadder and a wiser man he rose the morrow morn" (Coleridge, 1798, pp. 645–668).

If the mourning inherent in midlife development can lead to a better integration of life's ultimate good and bad, it follows that there will be enhanced integration of the two about all lesser things. Hopes born in childhood and adolescence when unrealized can be mourned and relinquished or modified into something more realistic and attainable by a successful passage through midlife. For some, like the patients in the vignettes, analysis can, one "hopes," bring about conditions that permit them to surmount hopelessness and continue along their developmental paths.

Notes

1. Colarusso (1999) traced the psychological development of the sense of time over the lifespan, progressing from the child's belief that time is limitless and controllable to the mature adult's understanding of it as limited and only partly controllable.
2. In Kleinian thought, due to the child's omnipotence, any loss is partly or wholly believed to result from his own aggression and this connection persists in the unconscious. Therefore, the mourning process must also include an element of guilt and the need to make reparations.

PART II

CULTURAL REALM

CHAPTER FIVE

Literary depictions of hopelessness: a short story, a novel, and a poem

Eve Holwell

The tension between hope and hopelessness is constant. One experience does not exist in the absence of, or opposition to, the other. Both emotional states are often present although to differing degrees and at different levels of consciousness. Childhood experience and temperament—to name just two factors, though there are countless others—can influence whether hope or hopelessness will become predominant in the resulting adult character. Though life's inevitable trials and tribulations can transiently tip the scale in favor of hopelessness, severe and sustained forms of hopelessness constitute clinical phenomena. Hopelessness is a well-recognized manifestation not only in depression but also in most forms of mental illness. Psychiatric literature offers many depictions of hopelessness, ranging from pessimistic character traits through depressive anguish and finally to suicidal despair. To learn more deeply about human emotions, including of course the particular phenomenon of hopelessness, it is always good to look to great literature. Greek and Shakespearean tragedies amply explore despair and its ensuing manifestations. Other works, such as Tolstoy's (1877) *Anna Karenina* and Kafka's (1915) *Metamorphosis* also come to mind as poignant studies in hopelessness. Still other examples can readily be given. However, in attempting to elucidate the nuances of hopelessness, I have chosen works in three different genres. What I lack in scope, I may make up with a wider breadth of genre. With this in mind, and the exploration of hopelessness as a goal, I selected Robert Browning's (1855) poem, *Childe Roland to the Dark Tower Came*, Kate Chopin's (1899) novel, *The Awakening*, and James Baldwin's (1957) short story, *Sonny's Blues*. I will now set to this task.

Three literary genres

A poem: Robert Browning's Childe Roland to the Dark Tower Came

Robert Browning's poem, *Childe Roland to the Dark Tower Came*, depicts Roland's nightmarish journey through a post-apocalyptic wasteland to the dark tower. The dark tower is defeat, and Roland travels there because he has been wandering, hopeless, for many years. The poem opens with the beginning of his journey, when he receives directions to the tower from a "hoary cripple, with a malicious eye" (line 2) who "lied in every word" (line 1). Roland knows the cripple has been set there, to "ensnare the travellers he may find posted there/And ask the road" (lines 9–10). The cripple assumes that in order to get Roland to the dark tower, he must lie, and yet Roland will gladly head to the dark tower of his own accord. He need not be lied to. Despite the depraved nature of his guide, Roland starts out just where the cripple has pointed out the "ominous tract" (line 14) to the dark tower upon which "all agree" (line 14). He submits to his fate without hesitation, "neither pride/nor hope rekindling at the end descried/So much gladness that some end should be" (lines 16–18).

Roland seeks the dark tower after years of fruitless wandering. His failed journeys have made him pessimistic and acclimated to failure. He states:

> What with my search drawn out thro' years, my hope
> Dwindled into a ghost not fit to cope
> With that obstreperous joy success would bring. (lines 20–22)

That Roland calls joy "obstreperous," captures his view of happiness as something unyielding and difficult to obtain. That his hope has "dwindled" over so much time gives the sense that the years of searching have slowly taken his faith away. Having become so used to failure, he now feels himself unable to "cope" with good results. The years of difficulty have left him spiritually distraught, without the ability or inclination for hope and dreams. Hopelessness has become so entrenched that he has set himself on failure, unwilling to exchange his pessimism for a happy ending if one would present itself. He declares: "I hardly tried now to rebuke the spring/My heart made, finding failure in its scope" (lines 23–24). Roland's description of his hopelessness as a spring set to entrap him demonstrates how hopelessness often precedes failure. In Roland's case, such a relationship between despair and failure is clearly outlined. Roland's lack of faith sets him on the path toward the tower, severing any possibility for positive resolution to the years of searching.

In addition to his own failed wanderings, Roland's hopelessness reflects a more pervasive despair that has claimed many people he has known. Roland makes reference to the knights who have come before him and also sought out the dark tower. Hearing of their failure has shaped his view of the future, propelling him toward failure such as the knights have experienced. He explains this pressure, declaring that:

> Thus, I had so long suffered in this quest,
> Heard failure prophesied so oft, been writ
> So many times among "The Band"—to wit,
> The knights who to the Dark Tower's search addressed
> Their steps—that just to fail as they, seemed best,
> And all the doubt was now—should I be fit. (lines 37–42)

Roland's quest has become one toward hopelessness, though it was undoubtedly started with better endings in mind. However, the despair of others has influenced Roland greatly. He not only feels he cannot succeed, he has also begun to view failure as something to be obtained, wondering if he "should be fit" for such an awful ending.

The many ramifications of hopelessness are captured in the hellish, abandoned wasteland through which Roland journeys to the tower. That the path to the tower is deserted reflects the sense of loneliness that accompanies despair. This loneliness is psychic but in the poem it becomes literal as Roland travels alone to the tower. The barren landscape of his journeys further highlights such isolation. Roland, revolted by such lacking, comments:

> I think I never saw
> Such a starved ignoble nature; nothing throve:
> For flowers—as well expect a cedar grove!
> But cockle, spurge, according to their law
> Might propagate their kind, with none to awe,
> You'd think: a burr had been a treasure-trove.
> No! Penury, inertness, and grimace,
> In some strange sort, were the land's portion. (lines 55–62)

The lack of growth highlights yet another feature of hopelessness: stagnation. The ability to grow is often predicated on positive associations for the future and yet Roland is unable to feel that anything good might happen to him. He sees only difficulties and suffering in his surroundings. The suffering Roland experiences as a result of his hopelessness is also evoked. Roland stumbles on a stream and hopes for something nice, yet the water only further reflects his sour temperament. Observing the stream, Roland notices:

> Low scrubby alders kneeled down over it;
> Drenched willows flung them headlong in a fit
> Of mute despair, a suicidal throng:
> The river, which had done them all wrong,
> Whate'er that was, roll'd by, deterr'd no whit. (lines 116–120)

Here the suicidal intentions of the willows powerfully capture Roland's own cravings for the end. Interestingly, Roland interprets the river as doing the willows wrong and then moving on without regret or remorse. This projection demonstrates Roland's own sense of victimization.

Yet another relevant aspect of the environment is the violence Roland interprets as being there. This violence captures his own internal struggles that have ended in hopelessness as well as the stormy world from which he flees. After Roland crosses the river, he hopes for a better landscape on the other side. He realizes that hope is "vain presage!" (line 128). Coming to the other side, he is further horrified by what he finds:

> What war did they wage
> Whose savage trample thus could pad the dank

> Soil to a plash? Toads in a poisoned tank
> Or wild cats in a red-hot iron cage. (lines 129–132)

These fraught images are likely projections of Roland's psychic darkness. That the landscape is not only devoid, but also defiled points to the struggles that often precede hopelessness. Before the defilement, the landscape was something better and nicer. Roland has fleeting thoughts on what has come before the barren and ugly landscape. Coming to a place where there was once a wood, Roland comments:

> Then came a bit of stubbed ground, once a wood,
> Next a marsh, it would seem, and now mere earth
> Desperate and done with; (so a fool finds mirth,
> Makes a thing and then mars it, till his mood
> Changes and off he goes!) within a rood
> Bog, clay and rubble, sand and stark black dearth. (lines 145–150)

Roland's thought to the better past is fleeting. He can only think briefly on it, moving quickly to what it has become. The inability to hold onto good or positive thoughts is also characteristic of Roland's hopelessness. Roland attempts to think of his previous colleagues in order to comfort himself. He first thinks of his friend Cuthbert's "reddening face/Beneath its garniture of curly gold" (lines 91–91) and their loving embraces. Suddenly then, the reverie is broken and he states "alas one night's disgrace!/Out went my heart's new fire and left it cold" (line 95–96). Cuthbert must have committed some transgression; suddenly a once happy memory serves to remind Roland of his despair. Roland tries to recall yet another friend, one who equally at first evokes happiness and good memory. And yet, just as before, Roland's memory quickly sours:

> Giles, then, the soul of honour—there he stands
> Frank as ten years ago when knighted first.
> What honest men should dare (he said) he durst.
> Good—but the scene shifts—faugh! What hangman
> Pin to his breast a parchment? His own hands
> Read it. Poor traitor, spit upon and curst! (lines 97–102)

Again, we understand that Giles has committed some sort of crime or treason. The image of the dishonored comrade captures how Roland flees a shameful and destructive past. This past seems to plague Roland, pushing toward the dark tower because "better this present than a past like that" (line 103).

The poem closes with Roland's arrival at the dark tower. Before entering, he surveys his past once more. He thinks of:

> ... Names in my ears
> Of all the lost adventurers, my peers—
> How such a one was strong, and such was bold,
> And such was fortunate, yet each of old
> Lost, lost! one moment knelled the woe of years. (lines 194–198)

These last thoughts are powerful expressions of his hopelessness. They capture a previous sense of good that is now gone. It feels irrevocably lost, and as such, Roland thinks once more on those who were once "fortunate" and "strong" and "bold." He hands himself over, recalling all that has been "Lost, lost!" and heads to the tower.

A novel: Kate Chopin's The Awakening

Kate Chopin's 1899 novel, *The Awakening*, was widely seen as a landmark work of feminism. Edna Pontellier, the protagonist of Chopin's novel, attempts to break from the limiting roles of women in nineteenth-century America. The novel depicts both Edna's struggle and her eventual hopelessness as she cannot free herself. In this sense, Chopin's novel covers broader experience than Browning's poem, where Roland is already full of hopelessness when the poem begins. While Edna eventually descends into hopelessness, we also come to understand the difficulty of her struggle and the strength and nobility with which she fights against the limitations of her life.

When the novel begins, Edna and her family are summering in the Gulf of Mexico. Edna is still complicit to the expectations of women in her society and yet, there are signs that she is unfulfilled and unhappy. One night, after having been gambling, her husband returns home. On the way to his bedroom, Mr. Pontellier stops to kiss their children goodnight and decides one of them has a fever. Instead of tending to the child himself, he wakes Edna, asking her to go check on the child. Edna has put the child to bed and feels certain the boy does not have one. She doesn't think she needs to check on the boy and when she tells her husband this, he chides her. Shamed, Edna does as her husband wishes and checks on the child. She finds the child is fine and returns to the bedroom, only to find Mr. Pontellier fast asleep. Agitated and upset, Edna herself can no longer sleep. She leaves their bedroom and cries in the other room though she "could not have told why she was crying" (p. 49). We learn that "Such experiences as the foregoing were not uncommon in her married life," though "[T]hey seemed never before to have weighed much against the abundance of her husband's kindness and a uniform devotion which had come to be tacit and self-understood" (p. 49).

Edna soon befriends Robert LeBrun, a young man who summers with his mother at Grand Isle. He is a few years her junior, with a reputation for falling in love with young, pretty married women. He takes to Edna and their ensuing friendship awakens her desire for autonomy and freedom. Their time together charts her first experiences of empowerment and enjoyment. He takes it upon himself to teach her to swim though "... she had received instructions from both the men and women; in some instances from the children" (p. 73). It is explained that Edna has trouble learning to swim because "... a certain ungovernable dread hung about her when in the water, unless there was a hand near by that might reach out and reassure her" (p. 73). This fear mirrors her fear of independence, which she has never experienced as a woman. And yet Robert does not give up on his lessons and finally one night, in a foreshadowing of the independence she will seek in the future, she learns to swim. The experience is empowering and liberating for her:

> A feeling of exultation overtook her, as if some power of significant import had been given her to control the working of her body and her soul. She grew daring and reckless, overestimating her strength. She wanted to swim far out, where no woman had swum before. (p. 73)

These lines capture how Edna is overcome with her new power. Learning to swim has given her confidence in her ability and she enjoys this long-awaited liberation. That night marks a change in her: She starts to think for herself. She comes home that night and finds she wants to spend the night on the porch, which her husband thinks is ludicrous. He calls her to come in, plainly showing his irritation that she will not and yet she does not.

> Another time she would have gone in at his request. She would, through habit, have yielded to his desire; not with any sense of submission or obedience to his compelling wishes, but unthinkingly, as we walk, move, sit, stand, go through the daily treadmill of life which has been portioned to us. (p. 77)

This passage shows how Edna is beginning to reflect on what she wants. She begins to see that she has made choices based on what her husband wants and yet, she has desires as well. She is starting to become conscious of them.

As Edna begins to make her own choices, she spends more time with Robert. The day after she learns to swim, she fetches Robert to sail with her to a small island nearby, though she had "never sent for him before" (p. 80). That this is the first time she has called on him signifies an end to her passivity. During the sail, Edna experiences a spiritual release from her previous bondage.

> Edna felt as if she were being borne away from some anchorage which had held her fast, whose chains had been loosening—had snapped the night before when the mystic spirit was abroad, leaving her free to drift whithersoever she chose to set her sails. (p. 81)

After the sailing trip with Robert, Edna realizes that change has come to her. She understands "that she herself—her present self—was in some way different from the other self" (p. 88). Robert, frightened by his feelings for Edna, departs the next week for Mexico. While Robert's departure saddens and shocks Edna, she does not retreat from her newly discovered freedom. Instead, Edna begins "to do as she liked and to feel as she liked" (p. 107). When Mr. Pontellier became "rude, Edna grew insolent. She had resolved never to take another step backward" (p. 109).

Naturally Edna's husband becomes angry with her. When he has an extended business trip to New York, he leaves her behind. A doctor tells him to let her do as she likes for a while, and so he takes their children to stay with his mother. During this period, Edna takes to painting and spending time with an older, independently minded female musician. She decides to leave her large family house and move into a small four room house around the corner because "she had resolved never again to belong to another than herself" (p. 135). As Edna comes into her own, she also experiences her sexuality more fully. She attracts the attention of a young and handsome womanizer, Aclee Arobin, who kisses her one night, awakening her sense of physical desire in ways her husband never could.

When Robert suddenly returns from Mexico, Edna finds herself with the physical and emotional space to be upfront with him about her love. Edna has also largely been liberated from following the societal norms and she suggests to Robert that they run away together. She tells him, "I am no longer one of Mr. Pontellier's possessions to dispose of or not. I give myself where I choose" (p. 167). And yet, in the end, Robert refuses because he doesn't want Edna to bear the social repercussions of leaving her husband. He knows that if she did, she would have to break with her children and become a social outcast. Devastated by Robert's decision, Edna finds herself alone, without hope for a future. She loved Robert and also saw him as the vehicle for her escape. Now, with those hopes dashed, she sees no future apart from one where she continues on as wife to a man she doesn't love and mother to their children.

The night Robert leaves, Edna experiences something that amplifies her hopelessness. She is called upon to be present while her friend gives birth. The birth is gruesome. Her friend is in extreme pain, exhausted physically and emotionally by the process of bringing a child into the world. As Edna watches, she becomes horrified. She understands how much nature has made it so that women must sacrifice themselves for the continuation of the world. Her friend urges her, when she is about to leave, to remember the children. And yet Edna remembers that she has decided "she would never sacrifice herself for her children" (p. 175). This sacrifice would surely mean, in terms of her life, staying with her husband. Edna refuses to do this and with Robert's rejections, she feels without the strength to set up her own life.

In the final scene of the book, she returns to Grand Isle, where she had begun to find her freedom the previous summer. She decides to take a swim, swimming out far and thinking back on her life. She thinks of children "like antagonists who had overcome her; who had overpowered and sought to drag her into the soul's slavery for the rest of her days. But she knew a way to elude them ..." (p. 175). The way she eludes them is by drowning herself. She swims out far, just as she had the previous summer, after Robert had taught her how to swim. Death becomes her only way to achieve freedom from the hopeless limitations of her life. The irony of this bind makes the ending of *The Awakening* quite tragic. We have hoped that Edna could find freedom in her life but without this possibility, she claims freedom through taking her life. There is undoubtedly a glimmer of triumph in her final act. Edna has, after all, eluded societal limitations. Her suicide, however, is clearly a manifestation of the hopelessness she felt in life.

A short story: James Baldwin's Sonny's Blues

James Baldwin's *Sonny's Blues* is, at a glance, about the impact of the tragic legacy of slavery and racism on African-American communities in the twentieth century. It takes place in Harlem, New York, and tells of two brothers—the elder who narrates the story, and his troubled younger brother, Sonny. The narrator has more or less come to terms with the limitations of his life as an African-American male in America. He has remained in Harlem and become a math teacher. He has married and started a family. Sonny, on the other hand, has struggled to escape from Harlem and the prejudice and oppression present there. He has dreams of becoming a jazz pianist but he falls prey to drug addiction, ending up in jail. It seems that Sonny is unlikely to overcome his addiction or become a jazz pianist. The hopelessness of Sonny's situation mirrors the general lack of hope in the African-American community, which Baldwin makes painfully clear through the story.

The story begins when the narrator, on his way to work, learns that Sonny has been sent to jail for selling heroin. The narrator reads the news in the paper, and at work that day he thinks of Sonny. The two are estranged because of Sonny's addiction and the older brother realizes that Sonny probably starting using drugs when he wasn't much older than the students he teaches in class. The narrator looks at the class and thinks that "Every one of them for all I knew, [may] be popping needles every time they went to the head. Maybe it did more for them than algebra ever could" (p. 108). The narrator knows the limited options his students face because he has faced them himself. Even though he has become a teacher, he still lives in a housing project in Harlem. Though the housing project was new when he moved his family in, it's "already rundown and the people who live in it do their best to make it a parody" (p. 113). The nearby playground is "most popular with the children who don't play at jacks, or skip rope, or roller skate, or swing, and they can be found in it after dark" (p. 113). These are scenes from a poverty-stricken neighborhood, where crime and poverty is rampant and

LITERARY DEPICTIONS OF HOPELESSNESS   95

opportunities are slim. The narrator hopes to shield his own children from what he and Sonny experienced but knows that, "The same things will happen, they'll have the same things to remember" (p. 113).

After the narrator's little girl dies, he reaches out to Sonny in jail. They correspond for a while and once Sonny is out of jail, he comes to live with the brother and his family. The narrator worries that Sonny will return to drugs and from the first moments with Sonny, he is

> ... trying to remember everything I'd heard about dope addiction and I couldn't help watching Sonny for signs. I wasn't doing it out of malice. I was trying to find out something about my brother. I was dying to hear him tell me he was safe. (p. 113)

And yet, we all know Sonny isn't safe. Before Sonny returns, the narrator presses another drug addict as to what will happen to Sonny when he is released from jail. The junkie is at first evasive but when the narrator presses him, he says "They'll let him out and then it'll just start all over again" (p. 108). These words are bold and simple and they clearly convey the hopeless nature of Sonny's addiction.

A powerful scene unfolds toward the end of the story when Sonny opens up about his addiction. The scene begins with the older brother at home, alone, "trying to work up the courage to search Sonny's room" (p. 128), when he sees a revival meeting taking place outside the window. He listens to the threesome holding the meeting sing about the ship of Zion that has "rescued many a thousand" (p. 129), and thinks how everyone in their neighborhood has heard the song before and that "not one of them had been rescued. Nor had they seen much in the way of rescue work being done around them" (p. 129). The narrator then sees Sonny walking down the street. Sonny returns to the apartment soon after, where he tells the narrator that the revival song

> ... reminded me for a minute of what heroin feels like sometimes—when it's in your veins. It makes you feel sort of warm and cool at the time. And distant. And—and sure ... It makes you feel—in control. Sometimes you have to have that feeling. (p. 131)

The narrator wonders if Sonny needs heroin to play music. Sonny says, "It's not so much to play. It's to stand, to be able to make it all. On any level ... In order to keep from shaking to pieces" (p. 131). We understand here that Sonny needs drugs because they help him live. At the root of his disclosure is his desire to escape from his life. And yet, drugs don't help him escape at all. They do the exact opposite, and even eventually landed him in jail. Herein lies the hopelessness of his addiction.

Sonny continues to talk about his addiction and how, even though he needed drugs, they also destroyed him. He says, "I was all by myself at the bottom of something, stinking and sweating and crying and shaking, and I smelled it, you know? *My* stink, and I thought I'd die if I couldn't get away from it and yet, all the same, I knew that everything I was doing was just locking me in with it" (p. 134). The narrator, of course, wants Sonny to never use again but Sonny knows he can't promise that: "'It can come again,' he said, almost as though speaking to himself. Then he turned to me. 'It can come again,' he repeated. 'I just want you to know that.'" (p. 135). The narrator doesn't fight what Sonny says. He accepts the truth of it, understanding how powerless Sonny feels in the face of heroin.

In the next and final scene of the story, the narrator accompanies Sonny to a jazz club downtown. Sonny knows most people there and everyone greets him like an old friend. He is called onstage to play as the narrator watches on. It takes Sonny a little. The narrator thinks how, "Sonny hadn't been near a piano in over a year. And he wasn't on much better terms with his life, not the life that stretched before him now" (p. 138). Sonny continues to fumble and then finally he "began to play" (p. 139). The band stays with Sonny for a while, excited that he is back and playing well, and then the lead singer

> ... stepped back, very slowly, filling the air with the immense suggestion that Sonny speak for himself ... then they all gathered around Sonny and Sonny played. Every now and again one of them seemed to say, amen. Sonny's fingers filled the air with life, his life. But that life contained so many others. (p. 140)

The narrator thinks the song is "very beautiful" and he seemed "to hear with what burning he [Sonny] had made it his, with what burning we had yet to make it ours, how we could cease lamenting. Freedom lurked around us and I understood, at last, that he could help us to be free if we would listen, that he would never be free until we did" (p. 140).

In this final scene, the narrator comes to understand why Sonny plays music. He feels how Sonny, himself more or less trapped by his addiction and his past, can nonetheless find freedom in music. He knows the hope that playing gives Sonny against the backdrop of poverty and addiction and oppression. When Sonny stops, there is applause and the scene and the story ends. There is no conclusion offered on Sonny. Nothing has changed in the world. There is still racism and oppression and inequality. Sonny may in the end prove hopeless in the face of his addiction, but we do know that he has hope and we know too that the narrator finally understands his brother. There is grace, if not resolution, in such an ending.

Some common themes

Relying upon the principles of metapsychology (Freud, 1915e; Rapaport, 1960), contemplation of the three protagonists discussed above needs to be addressed from the genetic, topographic, economic, dynamic, and adaptive perspectives. The genetic perspective can best be taken vis-à-vis Edna who lost her mother at a young age; her trepidations toward motherhood can be traced to these beginnings. In tracing the impact of her childhood maternal loss upon her adult sense of hopelessness, we encounter Balsam's (2000) work. Balsam has examined how a woman experiences her own mother's influence most fully when she herself becomes a mother. A comment from her is particularly relevant to Edna's experience:

> It is inevitable that a woman will internally encounter as "remembered present" (to borrow a term from cognitive science) the intimate actions and attitudes of her primary caretakers as they have imprinted themselves within her ... In such major events as pregnancy, childbirth, and certain aspects of child care—each of which a woman's mother once did to and for her—these life-identical passages most heavily bear the imprint of the mother. (p. 9)

Given that Edna lost her mother at a young age, she might have associated illness and death with becoming a mother. Moreover, her mother's death probably left her without a mothering-image to refer to once she had her own children.

The topographic view toward Sonny's hopelessness is particularly relevant. As African-Americans, the narrator and Sonny are members of a minority with a long and continued history of oppression and racism in this country. Akhtar (2014b) elucidates the nature of the difficulties minorities face:

> Belonging to a minority, therefore, acts like a cumulative trauma whereby breaches in the protective and holding functions of the society-at-large accrue over time and put a silent but palpable strain on the ego, both at the individual and collective level. (p. 3)

Baldwin's story captures, many times over, breaches in the protective functions of society for African-Americans in the United States. A particularly powerful example from the story comes to mind. Once Sonny is back from jail, the narrator reflects on a conversation he had with his mother. His mother meant to urge him to look out for his younger brother and with this idea in mind, she tells him something she and his father kept from both him and Sonny. She tells him how his father's brother was hit and killed one night by a truck full of drunken white men. His father witnessed his brother's death but of course, there was no police investigation into what happened. There was no way to seek justice for his brother's death because the men who killed him were white. The mother tells the narrator this story to warn him that "The world ain't changed" (p. 118) and that "You may not be able to stop nothing from happening. But you got to let him (Sonny) know you's there" (p. 119). Akhtar (2014b) talks about how these traumas accrue over time and put a strain upon the individual and collective ego. In this scenario, one can understand how the uncle's death must have shaped the narrator's father. One can understand how the uncle's death is just one in a long line of past injustices committed against African-Americans in this country, from the time of slavery through to the present. Sonny, as a member of this minority, has inherited this hopelessness.

The economic perspective toward Sonny's hopelessness is also important. The poverty of Harlem, ever-present in the story, is a constant source of both over- and understimulation for a growing child. A greater than ordinary exposure to adults, due to overcrowding, leads to early disillusionment. This, in turn, has ego-weakening effects. The lack of privacy and potential exposure to the primal scene also becomes a source of ego strain. Neighborhoods are run down and the people who live there are always coming face-to-face with the manifestation of their marginalization. Furthermore, there is no sense that one can move past the poverty. Even the narrator, who is a teacher, lives in a housing project in a neighborhood rife with crime. A thought from Symonds (1968) on poverty and hopelessness is relevant in this context.

> What became increasingly apparent to me was that those children who were disadvantaged and defeated by poverty, and who behaved in antisocial and self-destructive ways, grew up in the climate of defeated parents ... This climate of defeat is not unique to poor people, but poverty is the most fertile soil for hopelessness to grow in. (p. 1)

As far as the dynamic and adaptive perspectives on hopelessness go, breaking the three works down into their central components is helpful: 1) the desire to break free from one's situation, 2) the inability to do so, and 3) an ensuing sense of powerlessness. In Browning's poem, we know anecdotally that Roland has tried and failed to escape. He refers to his past and the "whole world-wide wandering" (line 19) and a "search drawn out through years" (line 20). By the time he starts toward the tower, there is a resignation in his manner. He is happy only that "some end might be" (line 18). In *The Awakening*, we witness as Edna first attempts to free herself from her limited role as a mother and wife. She doesn't want to simply take care of her children and make sure her husband is happy. She isn't interested in housekeeping matters. In one instance, the Pontelliers' cook makes bad food and Mr. Pontellier scolds Edna that the kitchen "needs looking after" (p. 102). But Edna has no interest in such endeavors. In the past, however, she would have gone "to her room and studied the cookbook during an entire evening, finally writing out a menu for the week, which left her harassed with a feeling that, after all, she had accomplished no good that was worth the name" (p. 102). Indeed, Edna would rather spend her time sketching and painting than keeping house and mothering, and as the novel unfolds, she begins to abandon her previous role and to act as she pleases.

In *Sonny's Blues*, Sonny wants to escape many things: Harlem, poverty, his drug addiction, and, underlying all this, his own inner helplessness and despair. In a flashback, the narrator remembers trying to convince Sonny to stay in school when all the younger brother wanted to do was be a musician. Sonny gets furious and cries, "And I'm sick of the stink of these garbage cans!" (p. 123). For Sonny, the stink of the garbage symbolizes the rotten state of life in Harlem. Sonny's desire to escape from Harlem manifests as his dream of becoming a musician; this also creates hope and permits freedom from his inner anguish. When the narrator leaves Sonny with his wife's family after their mother dies, his wife writes that all Sonny does is play the piano. No one tries to stop him because they all figured, as the narrator did, "that Sonny was at that piano playing for his life" (p. 125). This line captures how Sonny views music as his vehicle of escape. Sonny needs to play for his life because the racism and injustice and poverty that pervades the African-American experience in Harlem is damaging.

Failure to escape their current situations happens in varying degrees to all three characters. Schmale (1964) offers the view that hopelessness follows an inability to gratify oneself. He states, "Hopelessness ... is a loss of autonomy with a feeling of despair coming from the individual's awareness of his own inability to provide himself with gratification" (p. 1). The gratification that each character seeks is often liberation from his current struggles. One is reminded here of Reich's (1949) emphasis upon the role of conflict between the inner desires and the external realities of an individual upon his or her character. Reich declared that:

> The psychic process reveals itself as the result of the conflict between instinctual demand and the external frustrations of this demand. Only secondarily does an inner conflict between desire and self-denial result from this opposition. (p. 289)

Given this perspective, one can discern the centrality of reality-oriented conflicts in the lives of the protagonists under consideration here.

In Browning's poem, Roland attempts to leave the treachery and failure that pervades his past. He has tried for a while without success and heads to the dark tower with "gladness that some end might be" (line 18). He speaks, too, of his hope "dwindled throughout the years" (line 20). We have found him at the end of his struggles, once he has reconciled himself to their lack of use and failure.

In *The Awakening*, Edna heroically tries to free herself from the limitations of her role as a wife and mother. For a period, she seems as if she might succeed. When her husband is in New York on business and her kids are with her mother-in-law, she takes her own house. She tries to run away with Robert when he returns from Mexico. Then, over the course of one night, two events happen that make her feel she cannot be free. First, Robert refuses to run away with her because, according to him, "I love you" (p. 172). Robert's decision throws Edna into despair. Edna links her initial movement toward freedom with her feelings for Robert. When that love is dashed, she feels she doesn't have the sustenance to continue on her own. The other event which causes Edna to give up is that she witnesses her friend give birth. It is a difficult and bloody birth that demonstrates all the sacrifices women must make in the world. The birth is described as a "scene of torture" and Edna watches "with an inward agony, with a flaming, outspoken revolt against the ways of Nature" (p. 170). Just as she is set to leave, her friend, the new mother, ominously reminds her "to think of the children" (p. 170), and it is this refrain that Edna remembers, on her way home, to find Robert gone. In fact, Edna knows then "that she meant to think of them; that determination had driven into her soul like a death-wound" (p. 172). Edna feels she cannot simply run away. She feels this would ruin her children, and without Robert for support, she feels she can no longer choose the life she would want.

In Baldwin's story, the inability to escape pertains to both drugs and racism. When Sonny is released from jail, he returns to New York. The narrator picks him up and they travel uptown together. The narrator looks out his taxi window and sees young boys just like they once were who "had found themselves smothering in these houses, came down into the streets for light and air and found themselves encircled by disaster. Some escaped the trap, most didn't" (p. 112). The narrator thinks that

> Those who got out always left something of themselves behind, as some animals amputate a leg and leave it in the trap. It might be said, perhaps that I had escaped, after all, I was a school teacher; or that Sonny had, he hadn't lived in Harlem for years. Yet as the cab moved uptown through streets which seemed, with a rush, to darken with dark people, and as I covertly studied Sonny's face, it came to me that what we both were seeking through our separate cab windows was that part of ourselves which had been left behind. (p. 112)

The narrator conveys how their childhood of marginalization and poverty has shaped both Sonny and him. He knows, too, how it shapes all its residents, often entrapping them with a lack of options, apathy, and despair. This inability is reflected in the rampant crime and drug use of the neighborhood, and of course, in the story in Sonny's drug addiction. Even though Sonny isn't using when he returns, his addiction looms above the story as something potent and inescapable.

In all three works, the inability to escape creates a powerlessness that leads to hopelessness. In Browning's poem, Roland heads to the dark tower because he feels he has failed for so many years. After many years of searching for something better, he has become defeated and tired. He feels he can't escape and so he chooses the dark tower simply because it promises an end to his current situation. In *The Awakening*, the powerlessness Edna experiences is derived from her identity as a woman in a patriarchal society. She has tried to break free from societal constraints without success and it is the final sense of powerlessness that seems to seal her fate as feeling hopeless instead of hopeful. She has attempted steps toward hope; she has tried her hand at changing her constrained situation. But in the final scenes of the novel, she is reminded, when watching her friend give birth, of how greatly nature has chained her to the self-sacrifice of mothering. She watches in horror, but also heeds the warning that she should "remember the children" (p. 172). Her remembrance of the children sends her out to swim to her death. She has found a way to elude them without hurting them. Her suicide certainly could be interpreted as an "accident." She had learned to swim the previous summer and it would not be unlikely that she tired easily. The ambiguity about her end will probably work in her family's favor. They may be able to convince themselves that she didn't commit suicide. The reader is not meant to have such luxury. We know that Edna kills herself. Suicide is the ultimate act of hopelessness in life. Interestingly too, there is a degree of power in the act nonetheless. The person who dies has reclaimed some agency in the act of executing one's own death.

In *Sonny's Blues*, Sonny is powerless over his addiction. He can try to stay clean but there is the reality that drugs will always have a pull over him. He has come to rely on them to deal with life and this reliance also enslaves him. He explains this sensation to the narrator saying, "I thought I'd die if I couldn't get away from it and yet, all the same, I knew that everything I was doing was just locking me in with it" (p. 135). This inability to break free fosters hopelessness. The powerlessness, and ensuing hopelessness in the story is also derived from years of racism and marginalization on the African-American community in Harlem. Baldwin brings both these aspects to vivid life in *Sonny's Blues*. But he also offers the hope that Sonny discovers. Sonny finds hope through his music and as the final scene makes clear, it is his music that will offer him redemption and will combat the hopelessness that he experiences.

Concluding remarks

In this contribution, I have analyzed three literary works with the intention of understanding the human experience of hopelessness. Psychological and psychoanalytic understandings have illuminated many features of this hopelessness. I have meant to add onto these conceptions as well as highlight the ways they accurately portray the causes of, and manifestations, of such a state. I keep the goal in mind that understanding hopelessness will bring the ability to mitigate this very common and debilitating human experience.

With these goals in mind, I feel that this discussion would not be complete without a glance toward the experience of hope. Of the three works, *Sonny's Blues* offers a glimpse into how this force is a compelling antidote to the experience of hopelessness. When hopelessness arises, hope must be found to combat such a state and Sonny finds his hope through music. In Browning's poem, little of significance is to be found vis-à-vis the nature of hope. Chopin's novel, in contrast, offers up the transient nature of hope and how fleeting optimism can be. Edna temporarily experiences both hope and optimism but quickly finds herself unable to sustain these moods after Robert's rejection and her friend's gruesome childbirth. In sharp contrast to these two works is the poem *To Hope* by the great John Keats (1795–1821).

To Hope

When by my solitary hearth I sit,
And hateful thoughts enwrap my soul in gloom;
When no fair dreams before my "mind's eye" flit,
And the bare heath of life presents no bloom;
Sweet Hope, ethereal balm upon me shed,
And wave thy silver pinions o'er my head.

Whene'er I wander, at the fall of night,
Where woven boughs shut out the moon's bright ray,
Should sad Despondency my musings fright,
And frown, to drive fair Cheerfulness away,
Peep with the moon-beams through the leafy roof,
And keep that fiend Despondence far aloof.

Should Disappointment, parent of Despair,
Strive for her son to seize my careless heart;
When, like a cloud, he sits upon the air,
Preparing on his spell-bound prey to dart:
Chase him away, sweet Hope, with visage bright,
And fright him as the morning frightens night!

Whene'er the fate of those I hold most dear
Tells to my fearful breast a tale of sorrow,
O bright-eyed Hope, my morbid fancy cheer;
Let me awhile thy sweetest comforts borrow:
Thy heaven-born radiance around me shed,
And wave thy silver pinions o'er my head!

Should e'er unhappy love my bosom pain,
From cruel parents, or relentless fair;
O let me think it is not quite in vain
To sigh out sonnets to the midnight air!
Sweet Hope, ethereal balm upon me shed,
And wave thy silver pinions o'er my head!

In the long vista of the years to roll,
Let me not see our country's honor fade:
O let me see our land retain her soul,
Her pride, her freedom: and not freedom's shade.
From thy bright eyes unusual brightness shed—
Beneath thy pinions canopy my head!

Let me not see the patriot's high bequest,
Great Liberty! How great in plain attire!
With the base purple of a court oppressed,
Bowing her head, and ready to expire:
But let me see thee stoop from heaven on wings
That fill the skies with silver glitterings!

And as, in sparkling majesty, a star
Gilds the bright summit of some gloomy cloud;
Brightening the half-veiled face of heaven afar:
So, when dark thoughts my boding spirit shroud,
Sweet Hope, celestial influence round me shed,
Waving thy silver pinions o'er my head.

Every stanza of Keats's poem opens with a situation that brings despair and trouble to the human heart. The first stanza starts with the experience of hopelessness "When by my solitary hearth I sit/When no fair dreams before my 'mind's eye' flit/And the bare heath of life presents no bloom" (lines 1–3). The following stanzas offer further examples of times when lack of hope prevails, such as when "sad Despondency my musings fright" (line 9) or "Whene'er the fate of those I hold most dear/Tells to my fearful breast a tale of sorrow" (lines 19–20). Each stanza, thus begun, ends with a call for "bright-eyed Hope" (line 21). Hope is called upon to heal emotional pain and to "my morbid fancy cheer;/Let me awhile thy sweetest comforts borrow" (lines 21–22). Hope is variously described as something mystical and uplifting with "heaven-born radiance" (line 23) and "silver pinions" (line 24). It is also—importantly—something outside or other than oneself that needs to be called upon when despair descends. I think such a depiction grasps a keen psychological truth, namely that hope doesn't always feel inherent to an experience. It can, however, be called upon. When it arrives, it feels luminous and a much-needed salve for the wearied soul. To the psychoanalytic ear, Keats's metaphors of "bright-eyed Hope" (line 21) as the "sweetest comforts" (line 22) and "ethereal balm" (line 5) with "silver pinions" (line 6) and wings that "stoop from heaven" (line 41) are all reminders of the mother's reassuring gaze, picking the baby up from the crib, offering her breast for nourishment and love.

The experience of hopelessness, often encountered during difficulties of life, comes to all. And yet, as Keats's poem reminds us, hope is something people must strive for. Sometimes it remains elusive. No doubt, this is a common enough experience. Pervasive hopelessness is seen in countless contemporary situations. The works I have chosen have depicted situations in which such hopelessness is experienced. It is ultimately defeating in *Childe Roland to the Dark Tower Came* and *The Awakening*, while in *Sonny's Blues* the victory of hopelessness over hope is not by any means assured. Sonny calls upon his love of music and the potent human factor of communication to lift him up. This ability reminds us, as does Keats's poem, that hope can be called upon. In the poem, as in life, hope does not change the situation. Yet as Keats aptly puts it, its "ethereal balm" (line 5) and ability to keep "that fiend Despondence far aloof" (line 12) should not be underestimated. It can keep us afloat when hopelessness calls for us to fold and as such is an important force in human experience.

CHAPTER SIX

The illusion of a future: hopelessness in contemporary cinema

Sylvia Chong

Hollywood has often been called a "dream factory," manufacturing fantasies of wish fulfillment and escapism for mass consumption and enjoyment. But what do we do, then, with films that, far from delivering such simple pleasures, actually seem to antagonize and even traumatize their viewers? I refer here not just to horror films that deliver visceral thrills and frights like a roller coaster, which for many viewers are their own form of enjoyment, but rather to films that deny visceral pleasures as well as narrative satisfaction. Why would a spectator spend not only money but precious time, and willingly submit to a film that delivers only quiet, slow, depressing hopelessness? Why would these films recreate this vicious world of suffering and anxiety that we expend so much energy escaping from, whether through religion or leisure? Psychoanalysis would have no trouble placing such films within the framework of dreams, working with the pathways of an individual's unconscious desires and anxieties. Freud (1927c) remarks of such negative illusions: "The sleeper may be seized with a presentiment of death, which threatens to place him in the grave. But the dream-work knows how to select a condition that will turn even that dreaded event into a wish-fulfilment: the dreamer sees himself in an ancient Etruscan grave which he has climbed down into, happy to find his archaeological interests satisfied" (p. 17). At the same time, films of hopelessness do seem to call into question common assumptions about the role of cinema as popular entertainment, in particular psychoanalytic theories of film spectatorship that focus on pleasure and mastery. If the dream-work helps the individual shield himself from the dark desires in his unconscious, what kind of work do films on hopelessness perform for society at large?

I want to use the occasion of this present volume on hopelessness not only to reflect upon a few select films centering on this theme, but also to consider the more general question of how such films function in a modern culture industry—specifically the one we know as "Hollywood."[1] The present moment is ripe for such an investigation, as it seems that dystopic or post-apocalyptic (although not necessarily hopeless) films dominate the marketplace, and personal as well as historical trauma seem de rigueur for the dramatic genre. (As I write, at my local theater, three films are gloriously forecasting the end of the world—*Oblivion* (2013), *World War Z* (2013), *Elysium* (2013)— while another, *Fruitvale Station* (2013), restages the killing of a young black man, shot by a white police officer, that took place in Oakland, California, in 2009, and even the comic-book film, *The Wolverine* (2013), features a tortured, suffering hero.) But not all suffering is unpleasurable, and filmic fear and chaos do not always lead toward hopelessness. Furthermore, true hopelessness is hard to maintain in filmic form; all films, like dreams, do eventually end, thus giving way to the muted hope of everyday life and its mundane bustle of activities. But like dreams, films bleed into our daily lives in both directions, drawing on the detritus of our experiences for their materials, and also infecting our consciousness with the residue of their desires and anxieties. Thus, this investigation into hopelessness on film will perhaps shed light on the hopelessness that enters our lives off-screen.

How did I pick the films for this investigation? As befitting an examination of a mass genre, I went to the masses: I posted a request for recommendations on Facebook and let the suggestions flood in. If we can call hopelessness a film genre, then based on these suggestions (which I list in my Appendix), there are many distinct sub-genres, including historical atrocities (films about the Holocaust or Hiroshima), the alienation from or loss of love, the depiction of poverty or social crisis (often focused on those "other" parts of the world we don't live in, such as Africa), and even the degradation of the culture industry itself (for some viewers, this is exemplified by Adam Sandler's oeuvre). The largest two sub-genres, from which I chose three films for my analysis, are what we might call "end of the world" and "'end of *my* world": in each, we experience the destruction of a world, but the horizon of that world may differ, from the shared environment of a planet (*Melancholia*, 2011), or a social order (*The Road*, 2009), to the horizon of an individual's life, shortened by death (*Never Let Me Go*, 2010). What makes these films seem hopeless, in contrast to other films with similarly dark themes, is how they prey on their audience's expectations of redemption, toying with hope through familiar gestures of sentimentality or aestheticism only to abandon them in deeper despair. If anything, the hopelessness film seems sadistic toward its audience, manufacturing nightmares out of the stuff of people's desires and dreams.

Thus, my title, "The Illusion of a Future," refers to the way such films about hopelessness present images of extinguishing worlds that lack any potential to increase, rebirth, or even continue to exist. Here, I allude to Sigmund Freud's (1927c) short book, *The Future of an Illusion*, where he discusses the role of religion in alleviating some forms of hopelessness born of helplessness in the face of a hostile environment or violent social world. The individual is beset with hostilities from her fellow humans, as well as a menacing natural world that cares not for her well-being. For Freud, religion is a powerful illusion that not only makes such helplessness tolerable but is "built up from the material of memories of the helplessness of his own childhood and the childhood of the human race" (p. 23).

The experiences of hopelessness are inverted into the hopefulness of religious belief, allowing for psychological if not actual mastery over these circumstances. In reversing Freud's title phrase, I mean to show how these films of hopelessness also play upon such beliefs and expectations, but with the result of denying the possibility of a future— whether afterlife or sequel—to redeem the films' (and the spectators') sufferings. With the loss of the future, though, comes the loss of a major frame of reference to give meaning to present experience. How does one confront the disappearance of the future in these films without making both the past and present meaningless? The difficulty of this endeavor becomes clear as we examine the way film critics, marketing departments, and even fans deal with the hopeless themes in these works by reasserting forms of hope, but in ways that in fact dilute the power and meaning of these films.

I am also alluding to another book of the same title, Constance Penley's (1989) *The Future of an Illusion: Film, Feminism, and Psychoanalysis*. For many film theorists, psychoanalysis was a major framework for the understanding of not just individual films but the cinematic industry and apparatus at large. But the influence of psychoanalysis has waned in film studies, in large part due to its gloomy vision of passive spectators devoid not only of individuality but also of agency, as they are acted upon by cinema in ways they could not control. Instead, film studies has turned to more cheerful avenues of exploration, detailing the history of filmmaking, the activities of fans, and the ways new media have multiplied ways for people to both make and consume films and connect with one another. Penley's work harkens back to an era when psychoanalysis was not only dominant but seemingly necessary not only for cinephiles but also for political activists in academe. For Penley, the "illusion" that psychoanalysis helps us interrogate is not religion but sexual difference, and how cinema both shores up and undermines this illusion through various narrative and visual techniques. As she frames her synthesis of the unlikely couple of psychoanalysis and feminism:

> To rewrite Gramsci, perhaps what feminist theory needs to consider is the pessimism of the unconscious at the same time as it touts the optimism of the (feminist) will. What would we stand to lose, in theory and practice, by doing otherwise? Feminism would have to give up the possibility of understanding that there is a part of each of us that does not always do what we (think we) want it to do. So too, we would have to ignore the mechanisms of denial, wish-fulfillment, resistance, and complicity that suffuse all our personal and political life. (p. xvi)

Like psychoanalysis and the "pessimism of the unconscious," hopelessness is often thought of as apolitical, and many popular writers have criticized these films precisely because they indulge in feelings that seem antithetical to political agency. In choosing a psychoanalytic framework through which to view these films on hopelessness, I am trying to return to the concerns of earlier psychoanalytic film theorists such as Penley, and to ask what kind of politics *can* come from hopelessness in film. Although a cinema of hopelessness might seem to subvert the tendencies toward narcissism, action, and mastery found in the mainstream film industry, the difficulty in confronting hopelessness lies in avoiding a reversion to these forms of mastery and action, and thus shoring up the ego's fantasy of power. In short, how do we, as filmic spectators, dwell with cinematic hopelessness in a way that does not simply negate the film (and its hopelessness) and re-center on a fantasy of ourselves as hopeful agents? While I will try to address some of the concerns of the "new" film studies and focus on how actual fans, critics, and filmmakers talk about these films, I will return to psychoanalytic film theory to negotiate this binary between activity and passivity, between mastery and subjection. Hopefully (!), this can point to the value of films of hopelessness as more than a pathological cultural symptom to be cured.

The end of the world as we know it

As a larger category, the "end of the world" genre is not necessarily devoid of hope. It has affinities with dystopian science fiction as well as the disaster film. Although both genres have the potential for social critique, they are also associated with spectacular visual effects, violent action sequences, visceral pleasures of exhilaration: What Susan Sontag (1966) has called the "aesthetics of destruction ... the peculiar beauties to be found in wreaking havoc, making a mess" (p. 144). Danish director Lars von Trier has made what he has called his "anti-disaster film," *Melancholia* (2011), a literalization of medieval beliefs about this dark mood's link with celestial bodies in the sky, as a way of playing with these generic conventions. While maintaining some of the "peculiar beauties" of mass destruction, von Trier also subverts the narrative pleasures of crises averted, removing the potential for heroic salvation through individual effort. As a film about hopelessness, *Melancholia* comments simultaneously on two different scales of the world: The intimate, intrapersonal suffering of the depressed person, and the large-scale, global disaster of a soon-to-be-demolished earth. If hope for the individual might lie in an elusive cure (like in the 2012 film, *Silver Linings Playbook*), the usual forms of hope for planetary disaster—heroic scientific effort, the chance of a missed collision, escape to another planet—are equally missing in this film. Instead, we witness the film narrowing the possibilities of action available to its characters until both melancholia (the mood) and Melancholia (the planet) are inescapable conclusions.

Thwarting the drive toward narrative development, *Melancholia* opens with a montage that essentially gives away its plot, including the eventual swallowing up of the earth by the rogue planet Melancholia. Having dispensed with its climax in the first eight minutes, the film focuses instead on the intimate disasters that accompany the beginning of the end: Its first half portrays the dissolution of the marriage of its protagonist, Justine (Kirsten Dunst), only a few hours after it has begun, while its second half shows Justine awaiting the imminent end with her sister, Claire (Charlotte Gainsbourg), and her family. *Melancholia* unfolds at a lugubrious pace, especially in comparison to most disaster films' frenetic action. The first half seems to last as long as Justine's short marriage (an interesting condensation between narrative time and filmic time), lingering on scenes of inaction and delay. Justine and her new husband, Michael (Alexander Skarsgard), find themselves stuck in a limousine on a sharply curved road, making them hours late to their own reception. Justine and Michael giggle and kiss, behaving as you might expect of two young newlyweds, and eventually abandon the limo to stroll up to the reception. But once before this audience of family and guests, Justine's seemingly carefree attitude devolves quickly into melancholic paralysis, as she disappears from the reception for increasingly long intervals to gaze at the sky, to put her nephew to sleep, to take a bath, to have meaningless sex with a stranger. All the while, her sister, Claire, attempts to nudge her back into the social rituals of the wedding, reminding her to return for the dances, the bouquet toss, the late-night food service, the lighting of paper lanterns on the lawn. But Justine is dragged deeper and deeper into the lethargy of her depression, which has no apparent cause in any of the events or people presented before us, but rather lies in the unspoken prehistory of the film.

Oblivious to her impassivity, the people around Justine try various tactics to rouse her from her depression. Claire bustles about Justine more like a mother figure than a sister, needling Justine to activity in infantilizing ways. "We agreed that you weren't going to make any scenes tonight ... Look at me when I'm talking to you," Claire scolds Justine early in the evening. In a different manner, Claire's husband, John (Kiefer Sutherland), uses the language of economics to solicit Justine's compliance. John, who apparently owns the palatial mansion hosting this reception at their own estate for the bride and groom, complains (and brags) to Justine about how much this evening is costing him—"for most people, an arm and a leg"—but then brushes off Justine's concern by asking her to "make a deal" with him: He will consider the money well-spent so long as she promises to be "happy." What may seem as material generosity comes off as psychic coercion, since Justine has no ability to make good on her bargain to John, deepening her sense of failure and indebtedness. Even her husband, Michael, applies pressure on Justine through his seemingly selfless declarations of love. Late in the evening, as Justine's disconnection with the wedding has become apparent, he pulls her aside to reveal a special gift, a photograph of an apple orchard he has purchased for the two of them. "In ten years' time," he explains, "when the trees have grown, you can sit in the shade in a chair, and if you still have days when you're feeling a little sad, I think that will make you happy again." Michael's romantic gesture betrays his blindness to the depths of her depression, as well as his naïve hope that his love alone can somehow salvage her psyche. When Justine wanders from the room after Michael's gift, she absentmindedly leaves the photograph of the orchard behind, already too deep into her funk to hear his attempt to reach her. All of Justine's loved ones are impotent to heal her melancholia, just as they prove to be impotent in the face of the planet Melancholia's impending collision with earth in the film's second half.

Von Trier has elaborated in an interview with Nicholas Rapold (2011) that *Melancholia* was drawn from his own experience of deep depression, but even with this personal backstory, the depression portrayed by the character Justine seems starkly impersonal, in the sense that it exists without any narrative background or psychological causality in Justine's individuality. Justine's melancholia is merely a given, just as the destruction of the earth is a given—neither has a cause, and thus, a cure. At one point, resisting from being roused from a nap, Justine whispers haltingly to Claire, "I'm trudging through this grey, wooly yarn. It's pulling into my legs. It's really heavy to drag along." This description, we realize, had been visualized in slow-motion in the opening montage, although at that point we had no idea whether these yarns were literal or figurative. While this metaphor may dramatize how depression feels to Justine, it obscures any sense of the losses that might underlie her depression. Are these strings growing from the earth itself like a mutant plant, or are they woven by unseen hands? Is Justine's depression a natural fact, or of human origins? A hint lies in the musical soundtrack: the opening bars of Richard Wagner's prelude to the opera, *Tristan und Isolde*, had previously served as a leitmotif for the appearance of the planet Melancholia in the sky, but we hear this music for the first time indoors when Justine describes her wooly restraints, as if the leitmotif now refers to Justine alone. Although many reviews have read the planet as an externalization of Justine's internal state, the analogy could just as easily work in the other direction, as Justine personifying the planet's impersonal approach towards the earth. The passionate love-death of this film, à la *Tristan und Isolde*, will not be between humans, but between planets. At the end of the reception, just as Michael is saying farewell to Justine for good, he murmurs to her, "This could have been a lot different," to which Justine replies, "Yes, Michael, they could have been. But Michael, what did you expect?" It's as if Michael's hope of intervening in Justine's depression is as absurd as expecting rocks to roll uphill or the sun to rise in the west. Michael nods, and in doing so acknowledges that Justine's vision of her melancholia has overridden his narrative of romantic salvation. It also foreshadows the planet Melancholia's own unalterable course in the second half of the film.

Of course, this vision of melancholia as inevitable and unmovable is not necessarily true, but it matches the melancholic's narcissism, as Justine asserts her psychic reality as reality for everyone around her. In the second half, Melancholia's collision with earth becomes the manifestation of Justine's suicidal death drive. Justine and John switch places as figures of authority, while Claire's maternal instincts and social skills devolve into hysteria. At first, Justine arrives back at Claire and John's estate even more disabled by depression than at her wedding, and unable to even bathe or eat without Claire's physical assistance. John, an amateur astronomer, has been gleefully tracking the planet's approach, convinced that it will simply fly by the earth harmlessly, even as he hedges his bets by stocking up on provisions like a survivalist. Meanwhile, Claire becomes increasingly nervous, convinced of a horrible outcome but infuriated by her inability to do anything about it, and her only practical response is to buy a bottle of pills with which to commit suicide before the planet can kill her and her family. Justine, however, seems to grow stronger and more calm as disaster looms. Soon after stockpiling her suicide pills, Claire finds Justine drinking tea and picking through a box of chocolates. Claire reports that John, who "studies things," is apparently calm about the planet and convinced that "it will pass us by tonight." Justine responds flatly, "The earth is evil. We don't need to grieve for it." For Justine, having abandoned (and been abandoned) by the world in her depression, it is easy to welcome its destruction, as it has already disappeared for her.

Ironically, it is this deathly certainty that helps Justine endure the end, whereas John quickly abandons them all upon learning of Melancholia's certain approach by stealing Claire's pills and committing suicide alone. John's worldliness fails dramatically in the face of this super-worldly disaster, and even his death is a shameful one, witnessed off-camera only by the horses of the estate.[2] Claire, denied her own suicidal escape, tries to take control of her death by trying to stage it in a civilized manner: "I want us to be together when it happens. Maybe outside, on the terrace. Help me, Justine. I want to do this the right way ... A glass of wine, together, maybe." Justine promptly declares this plan to be a "piece of shit," mocking Claire's attempt to glamorize the end of the world with a meaningless social ritual, recalling the empty rituals of the failed wedding in the first half of the film that filled Justine with such dread. The only concession Justine makes is to her nephew, Leo, as she helps him to build a "magic cave" in which they will face the end. Although the cave seems as much an escapist fantasy as Claire's glass of wine on the terrace, the solemn tone of the final scenes suggest that the characters, and perhaps even Leo, know very well that the cave they are building is little more than a grave. The cave resembles the empty frame of a teepee, barely the pretense of a shelter, under whose fragile lines they sit and hold hands until a giant Melancholia rises on the horizon and obliterates them and the world in a brilliant burst of light. Just as Freud (1917e) imagined the melancholic subject incorporating the whole of its lost object into its ego, the planet Melancholia swallows the earth whole, both destroying it and preserving it forever.

Despite the dark mood of the film, von Trier invokes a visual tone of lush romanticism that seems to contradict its narrative of hopelessness. In contrast to the sparse visual vocabulary he employed in earlier films (and also advocated in his minimalist "Dogme 95" movement), here he evokes rich colors and textures that seem to elevate the theme of melancholia to sublime heights. In the first half, the wedding reception is depicted with such extravagance, suffused with golden tones and luxurious surroundings, that what seems like a critique of petty bourgeois customs through Justine's eyes also comes off as a celebration of Old World wealth. The sole use of Wagner's *Tristan* prelude as musical soundtrack also perpetuates the "Gilded Age" atmosphere, weighting down the science fiction elements of the plot with an operatic, costume-drama feel. As *New York Times* reviewer, A. O. Scott (2011), puzzled: "'Melancholia' is emphatically not what anyone would call a feel-good movie, and yet it nonetheless leaves behind a glow of aesthetic satisfaction," and the *Los Angeles Times* critic Betsy Sharkey (2011) proclaimed the film to be "hopeful" as a result of its "amazingly romantic—lush, ripe, rich, delicious" tone. While one way to read von Trier's aestheticization of melancholia is to view it as elevating, compensating for its narrative bleakness, another interpretation might follow from his enigmatic and controversial comments at the Cannes Film Festival in 2011, where he ramblingly claimed at a press conference, "I understand Hitler … I am a Nazi," leading the festival to ban him from its premises.[3] Von Trier later tried to explain his comments, coming from his own struggle upon learning that his Jewish father was not his real father, but that instead he was born from his mother's affair with a conservative German businessman; he clarified that what he meant to have said was, "We are all a little bit Nazi, we are all a little bit Jewish."[4] The reference to Nazism in the context of *Melancholia* was not simply a nod to his references to German Romanticism—as one reviewer joked, "Von Trier may not be a Nazi, but he sure embraces Wagner like one"—but also perhaps a warning not to be lured in by the aesthetics of destruction, even as he crafts his film as a visual seduction. The *Tristan* chord of longing and desire pulls the spectator into the planet Melancholia's orbit, making us view Justine's fatalism and bluntness as even heroic. But this celebration of sublime hopelessness makes us accept the violence of *Melancholia* more easily than we may have embraced the sadistic, brutal endings of von Trier's other films: Bjork's hanging in *Dancer in the Dark* (2000), Nicole Kidman's massacre of her rapists in *Dogville* (2003), Charlotte Gainsbourg's self-clitoridectomy in *Antichrist* (2009). To use von Trier's crude analogy: If we are a little bit Jewish—victims of violence, we are also a little bit Nazi—conscripted to violence by the compensation of aesthetic pleasure.

Survival of the hopeless

In the post-apocalyptic dystopia, we pick up where the disaster film ended. The present world has ended, and we watch as another, often more horrific one takes its place. Some critics like Fredric Jameson (1982) have accused the genre for "dramatizing" our inability to imagine the future, a lack of utopian imagination that leaves us trapped in the constraints of the present. For Jameson, these dystopic futures are symptoms of our incapacity for political change, their totalitarian or anarchic contours revealing a lack of conceivable or viable alternatives for organizing our present societies. Yet, even the most terrifying dystopias have potential value, as Constance Penley (1989) points out. These "critical dystopias" can suggest causes rather than merely reveal symptoms of our present political predicaments, thus helping us to analyze our current situation, even if they cannot conceive the kind of collective political strategies necessary to change or ensure that future. The apocalypse may even be a source of optimism, helping to wipe our political slate clean through a narrative *deus ex machina* that does not require the messy work of revolution. Commenting on the current vogue of the zombie apocalypse genre, cultural critic Paul Cantor (2013) finds the expression of a certain exhaustion with governmental, financial, and social institutions in the early twenty-first century, sparked by financial crises and a global recession. But his conclusion finds a certain libertarian silver lining in these visions of the end of the world: "We can see how the American nightmare can turn into the American dream when rampaging aliens or zombies descend upon a quiet American suburb. The dream of material prosperity and security is shattered, but a different ideal comes back to life—the all-American ideal of rugged individualism, the spirit of freedom, independence, and self-reliance" (p. 33). These imagined survivors of the apocalypse are able to shed the corrupt institutions of modern life and emerge with more authentic, idealized social relations with their fellow men and women. They face their zombie or alien enemies not as existential threats, but as tests of their personal strength, over which they inevitably triumph. Like a secular eschatology, the end of the world simply hastens the birth of a glorious new world order.

This is far from the vision of *The Road*, a 2009 film directed by John Hillcoat and based on a celebrated novel by Cormac McCarthy that won the 2007 Pulitzer Prize for fiction. In many ways, it is like the sequel to *Melancholia*: What happens if you survive the end of the world? Reviewer Ann Hornaday (2009) called the film "one long dirge, a keening lamentation marking the death of hope and the leeching of all that is bright and good from the world," Yet Hillcoat (cited in DiGiacomo, 2009) described his film adaptation as essentially hopeful, since "... hope is all the more special when it's surrounded by hopelessness." In order to bring this thin strand of hope into relief, *The Road* razes nearly everything else in sight, literally leaving nothing but a scorched earth behind. Hewing quite closely to the novel's plot, the film depicts an unnamed father (Viggo Mortensen) and son (Kodi Smit-McPhee) in a post-apocalyptic landscape as they travel southward, toward the coastline, all the while fighting and dodging the perils of roving gangs, thieves, weather, hunger, cold, and despair. There is little explanation of what caused the end of the previous world, but the landscape that the father and son pass through is not only devoid of social institutions—government, businesses, communities—but is also barren of flora and fauna: no wild animals, no greenery, not even sunshine. The state of nature is so far from a prelapsarian paradise that these two only find sustenance or shelter in the detritus of human civilization, rather than in the natural world: abandoned buildings, empty cars, discarded cans of food. Neither is there any rebuilding of human relations after the apocalypse; nearly all other humans the pair encounter are cannibals, killers, thieves, or victims of these previous aggressors. Despite its title, *The Road* is not really about a journey toward any kind of destination. With the landscape emptied of place names and landmarks, everything merges into a muddled grey blur, including the coast they eventually reach, and events experienced along the way take on the feel of a traumatic repetition compulsion: look for food, sleep, hide from others, and keep walking. At the film's end, the road they have been following simply disappears into the ocean, as grey as the landscape behind them. Thus preoccupied with the bare necessities for survival, the father and boy have little time or energy left to create or even imagine a new world.

The Road draws from the conventions of two popular genres: the zombie apocalypse, alluded to through the threat of cannibalism practiced by many starving survivors, and the Western, a genre in which both McCarthy and Hillcoat had worked previously, with its invocation of lonely bands of people at the frontier of civilization. But unlike the zombie film, *The Road* does not draw many distinctions between the human and the monstrous. Although the father and son try to convince themselves repeatedly that, as the "good guys," they don't eat other people, the "bad guys" we witness appear as normal human beings who have been driven to difficult choices: eat others, be eaten, or starve to death. In one scene, the father is wounded in the leg by an arrow fired from a nearby building, and he instinctively shoots a flare gun at his attacker. Running into the building to confront his attackers, he finds an older woman weeping over the burning corpse of her husband. "Why are you following us?" the father yells at her. She responds, "You're the one who's following us!" Although we are otherwise aligned with the father's point of view, this brief exchange reveals how our "good guys" are easily reversed into the "bad guys." Also, in contrast with the Western, *The Road* reveals that the frontier has disappeared, so has the civilized world that is usually contrasted with the Wild West. Even in nihilistic Westerns like *Unforgiven* (1992) or *The Wild Bunch* (1969), the violence of the genre is a proving ground for the assertion of individual will in the absence of institutionalized morality. In one flashback, the father tries to convince his wife that he would do "whatever it takes" to make sure they survive, but the wife's reply exposes the emptiness of his boast: "Like what?" Indeed, what individual action would be sufficient to fend off all of the hardship present in *The Road*? There is no climactic gunfight or confrontation to purge the world of its threats, not even a noble but futile "last stand" to celebrate. The ultimate force that threatens human life in the world of *The Road* is not other humans, or the awesome power of natural disaster, but simply the slow slog of depravation that is only momentarily held at bay by the cannibalism so sensationalized in the film.

Given that both the zombie apocalypse film and the Western privilege masculinity and violent agency, *The Road* disappointed many spectators with its defenseless, helpless protagonists. On the review pages of the Internet Movie Database (IMDB), some viewers complained about the main characters being "whiny wimp[s] with apparently no survival instinct at all" and "simply pathetic," faulting them for not trying to create their own weapons and fighting back more effectively.[5] These expectations reveal how invested many viewers are in the fantasy of survival in the wake of destruction. Like the narcissistic paranoid who believes he is somehow chosen by his visions, the survivalist believes he is immune to the dangers that face his fellow man, and hence feels betrayed by *The Road*'s ordinary, vulnerable figures. In particular, the son is an overdetermined figure for vulnerability and helplessness, one that shifts our emotional cathexis away from other representatives of the human in *The Road*. Marxist critic Mark Fisher (2010) faults *The Road* for taking capitalism's obsession with individualism to an extreme: "The man and the boy exist in a world in which Margaret Thatcher's dictum has come true: Here there really is no such thing as society, only individuals and their families ... As contemporary capitalism tries to do,

The Road forecloses the possibility of collectivity" (p. 15). In the father's flashbacks, we learn how the boy's mother reluctantly gave birth to him during the beginning of the end, hesitant to bring life into a world so unwelcoming. This nuclear family seems to weather the first years of the apocalypse in their home in isolation, surviving on stored food and candlelight, but eventually the harsh winters, loneliness, and lack of hope wear on them. But we never see any attempt to counter these fears by joining with other families or individuals for mutual protection. The mother eventually gives up, opting to walk out into the night and die of exposure rather than devote any more energy to the hard task of living. She opts for death over mere survival, but she leaves the boy with his father, as if to give him something to live for: "I would take him with me if it weren't for you."

It's unclear whether the son's presence is a gift to either the father or the film spectator. On the one hand, the son's presence burdens the father with someone to protect, someone to care for, and ultimately, someone to fail. When the son complains about being scared after watching his father strip a thief of his clothing and leave him out to die, the father yells back: "You're scared? I'm scared. You're not the one who has to worry about everything." The son's immaturity is most apparent in scenes where he whimpers in hiding, alarming his father who worries that they will be discovered, or falls asleep while guarding their food supplies, threatening them with starvation again. These childlike traits seem an unnecessary luxury in a world as far gone as that of *The Road*, which has no room for such sentimentality. Likewise, the film spectator's fears are also concentrated on the boy. As Hornaday (2009) wrote of the experience of watching the father and son repeatedly imperiled, "Viewers may be forgiven for wishing for *No Country*'s Anton Chigurh [the villain from another McCarthy film adaptation] to show up with his stun gun and put all of us out of our misery." Another critic, Peter Bradshaw (2010), pointed out that the novel went even further than the film in assaulting the privileged ideal of childhood since Hillcoat's adaptation omitted a chilling scene McCarthy wrote, in which the pair stumbles upon a couple preparing to eat their recently born infant. The emphasis on the son also diverts sympathy from other figures outside the father–son dyad. In one of the film's most wrenching scenes, the father and son break into a house to look for food, but come upon a cellar filled with people being kept like cattle awaiting slaughter. The naked prisoners swarming upon the pair is the closest image *The Road* gives us of zombie-like creatures, but rather than being soulless monsters, they are merely other human beings desperate to seize a chance to escape, and appear to be begging for help. Suddenly, the house's inhabitants return, forcing the man and boy to hide in a bathroom upstairs. The boy cries and clutches his teddy bear, while the man readies himself to shoot his son in the head before they suffer the same fate as the prisoners below, but the pair escapes at the last moment when the cannibals are distracted by their unruly human livestock. In a world where all humans are as vulnerable and helpless as children, it seems arbitrary to focus our attention on the child alone.

On the other hand, the son is an important carrier of ethical regard for others, precisely because his utter vulnerability would seem to absolve him from this responsibility. While the father is mono-maniacally focused on his son's welfare, the son remains open to, and thus emotionally and physically vulnerable to, the suffering of others they encounter. Although he has never known a world other than this post-apocalyptic one, the son has never adopted his father's paranoia toward people outside their dyad. When they encounter an old man on the road, it is the boy who convinces the father to offer the man a can from their precious food stores, even though this generous gesture seems wasted when the man vomits the food immediately after eating it. In another encounter, a thief steals their cart of provisions, the man chases after him and forces the thief at gunpoint to strip naked, enacting a bit of frontier justice: "I'm going to leave you just the way you left us." The boy is aghast, even frightened at his father's cruelty, and when the father explains, "Think of what would've happened if we hadn't caught up to him. You've got to learn," the boy retorts, "I don't want to learn!" As they argue, the boy pleads, "Just help him. He's hungry. He's going to die," and eventually convinces his father to return and leave a pile of clothing and food for the thief, even though there's no guarantee their act of kindness will reach its intended recipient. In each of these instances, the extravagance of the boy's actions contrasts with the stinginess of not only the adult figures but the entirety of the natural world; he refuses to accept the zero-sum moral calculus that seems to rule in *The Road*. These gestures are not sufficient to reconstitute the sense of community lost in the apocalypse, but they suggest a concrete example of "carrying the fire," the phrase the father uses to teach the son to carry the last remnants of civilization through this barren world.

The son represents the last glimmer of hope remaining in *The Road* for the renewal of mankind.

But what does it mean to make this small child carry the burden for symbolizing the future in such a hopeless world? *The Road* concludes ambivalently on this question. Having reached the coast but finding no improvement in the state of the world, the father dies in his sleep on the beach one night, leaving the son to continue his journey alone. Miraculously, another nuclear family—the first to materialize in the film since its start—appears to adopt the boy, reawakening the possibility of his survival. The mother of this new family embraces the son, exclaiming, "I'm so glad to see you. We were following you ... We're so lucky. We were so worried about you, and now we don't have to worry about a thing." This phrase could easily speak for the film spectator's hopes for the boy as well, but the artificiality of this last-minute salvation should make us pause. Like the audience, the woman wants to be able to intervene in the boy's fate rather than simply watch it passively and suffer. However, are the new father's and mother's promises to protect the boy any easier to keep than the original father's promise never to leave him? The dire conditions of the world in *The Road* highlight the impossibility of keeping either of these promises. The son's new family cannot simply escape the cycle of cannibals, thieves, hardship, and hunger that has governed this narrative thus far, and there has been nothing to suggest a turn for the better in the near future. Thus, the woman's worry for the child's safety is not erased by his joining their ranks; it has only begun anew. In a world emptied of meaning and potential, survival seems a worse punishment than death itself.

Not enough time

Whereas both *Melancholia* and *The Road* must manufacture extraordinary catastrophes to erase all sense of hope from their narratives, *Never Let Me Go* (2010) represents a less destructive variation on hopelessness: Rather than it bringing about the end of the world, we witness the agony that accompanies the end of an individual human life, often through illness rather than by another human's hand. The slow, impersonal progression of a chronic disease—cancer, Alzheimer's, substance abuse—refutes dramatic interventions of heroic doctors and miraculous technologies favored by modern medicine. They expose the fragility of the human body as well as the finiteness of human life as universal conditions, and not just anomalies. But not all narratives of illness are filled with hopelessness: Many fall into the genre of sentimentalism or melodrama, and attempt to transform personal suffering into meaningful forms of redemption or virtue. Melodramatic films such as *Terms of Endearment* (1983) and *Steel Magnolia* (1989) use death and illness as an occasion for the renewal of bonds between the surviving characters, or to affirm familial ties through teary-eyed, deathbed reconciliations. Film scholar Linda Williams (1991) has described how the melodrama works through a temporal fantasy of always being "too late"—"The quest for connections [between parent and child, between lovers, between friends] is always tinged with the melancholy of loss" (p. 11). But Williams identifies a value in these forms of melodramatic suffering, to counter the accusation that these emotions are simply a form of masochistic impotence: "The fantasy of the meeting with the other that is always too late can thus be seen as based upon the utopian desire that it not be too late to remerge with the other that was once part of the self" (p. 12). Hence, the passivity of mourning is reversed into the activity of desire, and the sentimental structure of these melodramas helps preserve a sense of hope in the living.

In order to manufacture a different orientation toward death, and perhaps foreclose these elements of sentimentalism, *Never Let Me Go* relies on a peculiar narrative twist: Its main characters are doomed to death not simply because they are ill, but because they have been born into a dystopic world in which they are destined to become organ donors for others in the prime of their lives. The 2010 film, directed by Mark Romanek and adapted from a 2005 novel by British author Kazuo Ishiguro, focuses on the brief life of three young characters, Kathy H. (Carey Mulligan), her friend Ruth (Keira Knightley), and their shared love interest Tommy (Andrew Garfield). We learn that the three main characters have been cloned, and are being raised apart from the rest of society until such time as their organs are needed. The film adopts the novel's euphemisms for the program: the clones are divided into "donors" and "carers" who willingly submit to surgical procedures called "donations" that extract their vital organs; after three or four donations, the donors "complete," or die. But the plot seems uninterested in the details of this social arrangement, and instead the film proceeds as if it were a tragic young love story. In the first part of the film, we encounter the three as children attending the boarding school, Hailsham. Although its ivy-covered halls and stately grounds recall the sheltered, privileged settings of many boarding school *Bildungsroman* tales, Hailsham is in fact a beautiful prison, designed not to nurture these children to adulthood, but rather to hide their existence from the outside world that depends on these children's deaths to sustain their lives. Taking note of their budding romance, the more assertive Ruth intervenes and steals Tommy away from Kathy, who endures this quietly while maintaining her friendship with both. In the second part, the three are young adults who have moved from Hailsham to The Cottages, a commune-like system from which they make their first forays into the outside world. Ruth's and Tommy's relationship has continued, alienating Kathy and leading her to apply to be a "carer," or a donor who is trained to help other donors through the donation process, and thus receives a postponement of her own donation for a few years. In the last part, Kathy reconnects with Ruth after one of Ruth's donations. Ruth has broken off with Tommy some time ago, and tries to make up for her past cruelties to Kathy by reuniting these would-be lovers, giving them a brief window of happiness together before they "complete." At least on a manifest level, *Never Let Me Go* frames the tragedy of the organ donation system as an issue of thwarted romance, as death eventually parts these young lovers. However, beneath this sentimental romance is the banal evil of the system affecting every aspect of their lives, governing not only the timeline of their love affair but their very relationship to temporality and agency in their lives. Here, hopelessness is exposed as the foundation of everyday life, lurking beneath the placid surface of these seemingly normal characters.

One way *Never Let Me Go* normalizes this condition of hopelessness is by evoking a sense of past-ness, rendering the extraordinary brutality of the organ donation system into a historical given. Although the plot seems to draw on something like a science fictional premise, there is nothing remotely futuristic about the film. Ishiguro's novel is set between the years 1978 and 1994, and Romanek pushes the time period even further back by employing a muted color palette, costumes, and settings that recall the faded tones of an old color photograph from the 1960s. The first images of the film also reinforce this sense of historicity, as a series of sentences silently presented on-screen trace a timeline that suggests a sort of teleological inevitability: "The breakthrough in medical science came in 1952. Doctors could now cure the previously incurable. By 1967, life expectancy passed 100 years." Having taken place over forty years ago, the "breakthrough" is by now a fait accompli, implying that any public discussion of the donation system is also of the distant past. The pull of the past extends to the characters' nostalgic orientation as well, in particular that of Kathy, the narrator of the film. In the opening scene, Kathy watches an unidentified person being prepped for surgery, and introduces herself to the spectator:

> My name is Kathy H. I'm twenty-eight years old. I've been a carer for nine years. And I'm good at my job. My patients always do better than expected, and are hardly ever classified as agitated, even if they're about to make a donation. I'm not trying to boast, but I feel a great sense of pride in what we do. Carers and donors have achieved so much. That said, we aren't machines. In the end it wears you down. I suppose that's why I now spend most of my time not looking forwards, but looking back ...

Kathy's backwards-looking orientation carries a sense of resignation that comes with the knowledge that she is already at the end of her life span, which jars with our knowledge of her age and youthful appearance. The remainder of the film is presented as Kathy's flashback, traveling through her past before returning to this same moment at the film's end, when we realize that the person we saw on the gurney is Tommy. Thus, the film is one long deferral of the inevitable death that awaits Tommy, and soon will await Kathy as well. By employing such a familiar looking, almost nostalgic recent past to stage this chilling alternate reality, the film suggests that the present-time of the spectators might itself be *unheimlich*, an uncanny replica of life that is in fact suffused with death.

The hopelessness of this situation is intensified for the audience by the characters' stoic acceptance of their fate. Unlike more overtly political dystopic narratives, *Never Let Me Go* avoids describing either the technological or social processes that led to and sustain this situation. Far from being a source of social unrest, the organ donation program is treated as if it were an uncontroversial fact of life. In Kathy's opening monologue, she frames her role as carer/donor as if it were a professional duty she chooses to take on, and even expresses pride in her "achievements," obscuring the fact that she belongs to an unchangeable social caste that condemns her to an early death. There is also no trace of a sinister police state enforcing compliance with the program; rather, we open with what seems like the happy consent of one of its victims. In many ways, the story's lack of resistance is one of its more realist elements. Writing about Ishiguro's novel, literary critic Bruce Robbins (2007) noted, "The organ-donation gulag, tucked away from public view and yet not kept secret, has its obvious real-world counterpart in what we call class" (p. 292). As such, the film draws more from the mundane disciplinary regimes of modern democracies than the spectacular autocratic police states favored in typical science fiction dystopias. Marxist film critic Mark Fisher (2012), comparing this film unfavorably with *The Hunger Games*, remarked with frustration, "There is no such conversion of fatalism into resistance in Mark Romanek's *Never Let Me Go*. The peculiar horror of the film, in fact, resides in the unrelieved quality of its fatalism" (p. 31). However, the element of coercion is not entirely absent; it emerges as a sinister undercurrent of violence and death, alluded to only obliquely in the film. When a new teacher, Miss Lucy, arrives at Hailsham, she is puzzled about why the children did not go outside the walled boundaries of the schoolyard to fetch an errant ball. The children quickly respond en masse with tales of children who reportedly had transgressed those boundaries, only to end up tied to a tree with their hands cut off, or left to starve at the foot of the gates. Aghast, Miss Lucy questions the children as to how they know these stories are true, and Ruth replies matter-of-factly, "Who'd make up stories as horrible as that?" The donor children have accepted these violent myths as fact, and effectively police themselves through these internalized images of death.

Even when the donor characters express something like resistance, it is either as an inchoate emotion with no effective target, or a misdirected anger that fails to subvert the system. While donors never refuse their duties, they do not always face them with equanimity, becoming "agitated" and requiring carers like Kathy to calm them down. Or sometimes they fail to finish their entire series of donations, like Ruth, who completes only after her third surgery. This "failure" might read as an act of suicide that reclaims their lives as their own—as one nurse explains to Kathy, "When they want to complete they usually do"—but it hardly impacts the system, as it takes place after value has already been extracted from their bodies. One rumor that circulated among the young donors living in The Cottages was that donor couples who could somehow prove "they were really, properly in love" with each other could receive a "deferral" so that they could have "a few years together before they began their donations." Such deferrals are hardly a reprieve from the ruthless demands of donation, but it is a vain hope that the donors cling to, a miniscule recognition of the psychological toll of their limited lives. However, when Kathy and Tommy, reunited at the end of their lives, attempt to seek this very deferral through "Madame," a benefactor of Hailsham, they learn that the deferrals never existed, extinguishing this slender opportunity to extend their time on earth. Tommy's primal scream of anguish after the visit to Madame's house is a frightening display that veers from the usual, restrained comportment of these characters throughout the narrative. Sadly, it finds no witness in the film except for Kathy, who has already repressed her anger as polite disappointment and resolved to carry on with the rest of her short life. Tommy is not only helpless to control his fate; he cannot even find the means to articulate his rage or identify an audience for his complaint.

It is possible to interpret *Never Let Me Go* as a poignant meditation on human mortality in general, reimposing the sentimentalist frame that the film's uncanny social system attempts to avoid. By focusing on the tragic love affair between Kathy and Tommy, and ignoring the premise of organ donation and cloning, this interpretation resignifies the deaths of these donors as that which gives meaning to their emotional bonds. The film adaptation seems to lean more heavily in this direction than the novel itself, as witnessed in the way each stages the ending of the story. Kathy drives to an empty field, where she mourns Tommy's death and lets herself "imagine that this is the spot where everything that I've lost since my childhood has washed up." As Mark Jenkins (2010) complained, the film script "changes Kathy's resigned words to a few sententious lines about collective humanity." In place of the last line of the novel: "I just waited a bit, then turned back to the car, to drive off to wherever it was I was supposed to be," the film ends with this elaborate reflection:

> I remind myself that I was lucky to have had any time with him at all. But what I'm not sure about, is if our lives have been so different from the lives of the people that we save. We all complete. Maybe none of us really understand what we live through, or feel that we've had enough time.

Here, Kathy abstracts her fate to the fate of all mankind, as if promoting the moral of her tale as the importance of seizing the day, living life to the fullest, and so on. Yet, if we recall the cheery tone of her opening monologue, which we know by the film's end to have been spoken on Tommy's deathbed, we should understand Kathy to be an unreliable narrator, lying to the audience as much as to herself in these clichéd justifications of her melancholic fate. Although it is true that "none of us live forever," that does not erase the fundamental gap that the dystopic society of *Never Let Me Go* constructs between the donor clones and their recipients. The human agency behind the organ donation system is obscured behind such naturalizing rhetoric and its bureaucratic, self-perpetuating structure, leaving something that resembles natural human finitude but is actually quite different. While this society may justify its exploitation of its underclass by denying their humanity and similarity to the privileged class, Kathy cannot restore her equality with "the people that we save" simply by sharing some sentiments with them. If anything, this attempt to sentimentalize the film reveals that sentimentalism is part of *Never Let Me Go*'s structure of hopelessness, anesthetizing its characters from a full appreciation of the source of their fate. Like the false promise of "deferral," sentimentalism's utopian fantasy of regaining lost love, lost origins, and lost time is but another version of Pandora's last gift to mankind: The hope which Friedrich Nietzsche (1844–1900) called the most evil of evils because it prolongs man's torment.

Hopelessness and film theory

Of the three films under discussion here—*Melancholia*, *The Road*, and *Never Let Me Go*—each has its own strategy for staging hopelessness and playing with the film spectator's expectations. I have foregrounded each film's relationship with a preexisting genre—the disaster film, dystopian science fiction, and sentimentalism, respectively—in order to characterize its effect of hopelessness as not merely inhering in the psychology of its characters, but also deriving from the system of thwarted desires and expectations coming from these genre relationships. In other words, they are hopeless films only in relation to the kinds of hope*ful* films that dominate these genres, and Hollywood films in general. One common feature of their hopelessness is the unwavering insistence on passivity and impotence in situations that typically call for an active and empowering intervention. Such assertions of agency often compensate for the suspenseful terrors to which these films subject their audiences: Killing the monster after a long chase, surviving the apocalypse with family and values intact, reuniting with the mother on her deathbed.

Without such compensatory pleasures, what do films on hopelessness offer their audiences?

But first, we must understand the peculiar role that passivity has played in psychoanalytic film theory, and in particular the apparatus theory arising out of French post-structuralism in the 1960s and '70s. The term "apparatus" refers to cinema as not merely an industry but also as total institution, in which the industry is an "outer machine" coterminous with what Christian Metz (1977) calls an "inner machine (the spectator's psychology)" (p. 8)—coming together to form a dual libidinal/political economy. Part of what the cinematic apparatus projects is not only the film being viewed, but also the film spectator's subject position as well. Following Freud's (1927c) own rhetorical strategy in *The Future of an Illusion* to compare man's existential state of helplessness with that of the infant, these theorists also conceive of the film spectator's position as infantile with respect to cinematic apparatus. Jean-Louis Baudry (1986a, 1986b) likened the situation of the film spectator to not only the dreamer in psychoanalysis but also that of the prisoners in Plato's allegory of the cave in *The Republic*, chained against a wall and forced to watch shadows that are but a simulacrum of the reality outside the cave. For these theorists, the film spectator is not a preexisting subject who comes to the cinema of her own free will; she is a creation of the cinematic apparatus itself, thrust into a passive viewing experience not entirely of her own choosing.

Despite these glum characterizations, the lure of cinema lies not in the direct experience of such passivity and impotence, but rather in the compensatory pleasures of narcissism, scopophilia, and mastery that come from different forms of identification encouraged by the apparatus. For these theorists, the spectator's primary identification is always with the apparatus itself, in the form of a "transcendental subject whose place is taken by the camera which constitutes and rules the objects in this 'world'" (Baudry, 1986a, p. 295). This scopophilia, somewhat akin to the Lacanian notion of the gaze, positions the spectator as an "all-perceiving" subject who is outside of the world created by the camera, and thus is not vulnerable to any actions taking place in that world, including looking (Metz, 1977). In other words, in this fantasy of visual mastery, the subject can see all, but can never be seen. Another, more secondary form of identification, is with the characters in film narratives. Given the cinema's complicity with patriarchy, Laura Mulvey (1986) has famously pointed out that this form of narcissistic identification often favors male characters, who become filmic proxies for the (male) spectator's desires, over female characters, who are reduced to fetishes whose role is to be desired, to be looked at, or to be acted upon.[6] Both forms of identification allow the spectator to disavow her fundamental passivity before the cinematic apparatus, replacing that captive experience with scopophilic mastery or narcissistic agency.

Typical mainstream narrative cinema satisfies one of these two identificatory pleasures, drawing our attention to main characters bursting with purposeful narrative activity, or aligning us with the camera's voyeuristic gaze at spectacles of technological wizardry or other objects of desire. Although filled with potentially distressing content, the three film genres under discussion nonetheless fulfill these pleasures: The disaster film, by depicting the aesthetics of crisis while escaping catastrophe; the zombie/Western, by staging the conquering of nature/chaos by rugged individuals; and the sentimental melodrama, by separating loved ones so as to enable tearful reunions and reconciliations. But these films on hopelessness put pressure on these pleasures, subverting their ability to disavow our underlying passivity before the apparatus. Even as von Trier indulges in lush imagery and musical accompaniment to depict planetary collision in *Melancholia*, his film lingers on the helplessness of waiting for inevitable disaster, with a snail-like pace replicating the temporality of mundane, everyday life rather than the accelerated tempo of an action film. Hillcoat's *The Road* delivers the tension of endangerment for its extremely vulnerable father–son dyad, but without ever releasing that tension through a glimpse of narrative salvation for these characters, resulting in a cinematic experience of repeated assault. Finally, Romanek buries the dystopic society in *Never Let Me Go* beneath a banal tale of thwarted love, but that dystopia seeps through the film as an atmosphere of oppression and death that dampens the emotional payoff of its melodrama. Obviously, the spectator's secondary identification with film characters is undermined by presenting such passive, helpless victims. But these films also replace the mastery of the camera's transcendental gaze with a masochistic experience, more akin to being *subjected* to a tortuous spectacle rather than being the subject choosing to look on. This passivity of the gaze recalls Jean Laplanche's (1976) description of the primal scene fantasy, in which "… the child, impotent in his crib, is Ulysses tied to the mast or Tantalus, on whom is imposed the spectacle of parental intercourse" (p. 102).

The trend in academic film studies in the last two decades has been to move away from psychoanalytic film theory, and in particular apparatus theory. As Constance Penley (1989) has noted in her study of psychoanalytic feminism, "The picture of human subjectivity that emerges from psychoanalysis is not easily compatible with that espoused by American feminism and other political movements, which presume notions of 'idealism, voluntarism of the will, and a traditional American strain of utopianism'" (p. xiv). One response has been to reject the psychoanalytic vision of passivity in favor of "active" spectators: fans who "talk back" to the film texts by blogging about them, forming fan groups and conventions, dressing up like their favorite characters, or even writing their own sequels and alternative versions of these texts. We have witnessed examples of this type of active spectatorship in the film critics and ordinary fans who have responded to these films on hopelessness by violently rejecting them—criticizing the films in public forums, revising the premises of the films by singling out elements that are unrealistic or unsatisfying, or simply dismissing the films as a waste of time. Riffing on the analogy of the cave employed by Baudry (1986a, 1986b), one might describe such spectators as prisoners who have cast off their chains, turning away from the cinematic shadows on the wall and toward the light of "reality" outside of the cinematic cavern. This form of psychic defense against hopelessness allows the spectator to not only literally walk away from the film about hopelessness, but also to use this separation between film and viewing subject to reject the very notion of hopelessness presented in the film. Mark Fisher, the Marxist critic who unfavorably reviewed both *The Road* and *Never Let Me Go*, went so far as to excoriate both films for their political complacency, symptomatic of the kind of inaction favored by contemporary capitalism. Instead, Fisher celebrates the kind of populist, pulp cinema whose anarchic energies point toward utopian forms of political activity:

> What is missing from *The Road* can also be inferred by contrast with a more recent apocalyptic thriller, *Terminator Salvation* [2009]. What is its pulp existential slogan, "There is no fate but what we make," if not an alternative way of saying that, against all the odds, another world is possible? (2010, p. 16)

And,

> If the bleakness of *Never Let Me Go* arises from its not even broaching the possibility of collective escape or insurrection, then the

margin of hope in *The Hunger Games* and *In Time* consists in the young exploited characters groping toward new kinds of collective action. (2013, p. 33)

If psychoanalytic film theory's emphasis on passivity seems politically conservative, modeling acquiescence of the status quo, films on hopelessness are even more reactionary, depriving the film medium of any revolutionary impulse through their narratives of submission, impotence, and resignation.

However, this superficial rejection of psychoanalytic film theory risks overstating the power and agency of any film spectator, especially in confronting any sort of political situation found outside the film text. Even the gaze, which critics of apparatus theory misunderstand as simply an assertion of mastery over the visual field, functions in Lacan's thought as an enigmatic and impossible object of desire, one that, far from affirming the fantasy of being a transcendental subject, reveals the subject's essential castration in the field of the Symbolic.[7]

While we can stand up and walk out on these unpleasurable films, and we can criticize them so as to show our independence from their worldviews, these actions do not negate our existential passivity that constitutes our embeddedness in a social order not of our making. Slavoj Zizek (1997) has mocked this myth of the "democratic potential" of such forms of media participation, asking sardonically, "Is not the other side of this interactivity, however, interpassivity?" (p. 112). That is, rather than active spectators defined in contrast to the passive film object, interpassivity offers the fantasy of outsourcing one's essential passivity to the object—"*I am passive through the other*," who suffers (or enjoys) on my behalf—thus freeing the spectator to engage in what is essentially "*false activity*: you think you are active, while our true position, as embodied in the fetish [object], is passive" (p. 115). The hopeless film becomes a fetish disavowing the hopelessness of the spectator, as interpassivity assigns such sufferings to the film alone. Active spectatorship allows the spectator to demonstrate his superiority to the film, fantasizing through his resistance an alternate narrative to its hopelessness: I, who know better than the film, would never succumb to this end of the world, these cannibals, this organ-donation gulag, because I would behave differently …

Even those who find ways to embrace these films on hopelessness might fall into the trap of interpassivity and its false activity.

After all, films like *Melancholia*, *The Road*, and *Never Let Me Go* are not run-of-the-mill Hollywood productions; they accrue status from being foreign films or independent productions, or by having auteurist directors or acclaimed literary sources. Their themes of hopelessness and deviations from mainstream genre strictures may elevate these films to the status of "art," thus justifying their challengingly sad narratives and slow pacing. Spectators may think of their consumption of such dark films as a mark of their own cultural capital, distinguishing them from the *hoi polloi* of action film or melodrama audiences. Although the sentimentalist embrace of hopelessness does not try to "solve" the problem of the film like the active spectator, it nonetheless substitutes its own form of false activity to displace the dangerous vulnerability and passivity displayed in these films. In so doing, these spectators tap into a long tradition of sentimentalist literature, a middlebrow art form that, as I discussed earlier, privileges feeling over action as its utopian gesture toward the world. In the words of Harriet Beecher Stowe (1852), author of the classic sentimentalist text, *Uncle Tom's Cabin*, "There is one thing that every individual can do,—they can see to it that *they feel right*" (p. 375, italics in the original).[8] An analogue to such voyeuristic sympathy may be found in one of Zizek's examples of interpassive suffering: "… the Western liberal academic's obsession with the suffering in Bosnia … One can authentically suffer through reports on rapes and mass killings in Bosnia, while calmly pursuing one's academic career" (p. 119). In both cases, one again denies the fundamental passivity that underlies all subject positions and assigns that passivity to the Other (text or person), from whom one distances oneself in the act of sympathizing. Likewise, the middlebrow film spectator congratulates herself on enduring the hopelessness of these films, and then returns to the safety of her own life, secure that such hopelessness has no real bearing on her existence. This form of sympathy expresses the same desire for mastery as the revisionist active spectator: I, who know better than those other film spectators, feel sorry for the subjects in this film because I myself am so unlike them, yet I understand them so well.

How, then, do we avoid the Scylla of false activity or sentiment on the one hand, and the Charybdis of paralyzing passivity on the other? If we are to find some value in the viewing of films on hopelessness without either negating or succumbing to that hopelessness, it is in the difficult task of dwelling with these difficult portraits of mortality, impotence, and vulnerability and acknowledging their presence in our own lives. Academics such as Judith Butler (1990) and Anne Anlin Cheng (2001) have been attempting to recuperate this type of melancholic subject position, not as a pathological entity, but rather as a position that acknowledges the fundamental role that loss and trauma play in constituting ourselves as racialized and gendered subjects in the world. Films on hopelessness offer a glimpse of these losses, which we should not prematurely turn away from by restoring hope through frenetic activity. Their visions of a lost future give the lie to the fantasy that our lives should otherwise take place in a boundless, temporal field, that this is not a dystopic alternate reality, but simply the truth of our being-in-the-world, or what Martin Heidegger (1962) calls "thrownness" (*Geworfenheit*). Film viewing, then, might serve a different function than that envisioned by the metaphor of the escapist dream factory. Rather than taking us away from the world, film viewing might return us more fully to that world in all of its glorious, traumatic, hopeless reality.

Appendix: a few categories of hopelessness in film

Africa

The Constant Gardener (2005)
Darwin's Nightmare (2004)
Hotel Rwanda (2004)

Death and illness

Amour (2012)
Away from Her (2006)
The Dreamlife of Angels (1998)
Never Let Me Go (2010)

The death of the culture industry

Jack and Jill (2011)

Dysfunctional relationships

Breaking the Waves (1996)
Happiness (1998)

Revolutionary Road (2008)
The Wrestler (2008)

The end of the world

Blindness (2008)
Children of Men (2006)
Melancholia (2011)
The Road (2009)

The Holocaust

Life is Beautiful (1997)
The Pianist (2002)

Poverty

Dancer in the Dark (2000)
Ossos (1997)

Substance abuse

Leaving Las Vegas (1995)
Requiem for a Dream (2000)

Notes

1. I realize that the term "Hollywood film" is often meant as a pejorative, even by those within this industry, and that both industry professionals and academic critics make distinctions between the Hollywood studio film and variants such as independent films, art house films, foreign/transnational films, etc. But all of the films discussed for this article, and listed in the appendix, are mainstream in the sense that they are (1) widely distributed in the US, both theatrically and on DVD; (2) widely discussed by film critics in major newspaper and online publications; and (3) designed for commercial consumption, however boutique an audience they might reach. This distinguishes them from more experimental or avant-garde films which mainly reach audiences through special film festivals, museum exhibition, or academic distribution, and whose profits and audience are miniscule by comparison.

2. It is somehow fitting that John was played by the actor Kiefer Sutherland, well-known as the counter-terrorism agent Jack Bauer on the television series *24*. The show races against the clock (twenty-four hours, matching each season's air-time of twenty-four one-hour-long episodes), frantically trying to thwart multiple terrorist plots.
3. "Lars von Trier: 'I Am a Nazi ... I Understand Hitler,'" *Huffington Post: Entertainment*, 18 May 2011.
4. Geoffrey McNab, "Lars von Trier: 'If I Am an Idiot in the Eyes of the World, So Be It,'" *The Independent*, 14 August 2013; also Nick James, "The Confessions of Lars von Trier," *Sight and Sound*, 21.10 (October 2011): 30–32, 34.
5. Comments from "Slim Jack Rabbit from Planet KzOrp" and "Rene from Netherlands," *Reviews and Ratings for The Road*, IMDB.com <http://www.imdb.com/title/tt0898367/reviews?start=20>, accessed 14 August 2013.
6. Although Mulvey's gender binaries have been heavily critiqued, it is notable that even female spectators often identify with masculine characters, and that female characters in films are often masculinized when they are promoted to roles with agency and purposeful activity.
7. For Lacan's explication of the notion of the gaze, see Todd McGowan's (2003) critique of the misunderstanding of Lacanian thought in discussions of film theory.
8. Critiques of Stowe and her version of sentimentalism abound in literary studies, but some useful ones that have informed my reading are Berlant (1988); Greeson (2010); Wexler (2000).

PART III

CLINICAL REALM

CHAPTER SEVEN

From hopelessness to despair

Jeanne Bailey

Hopelessness is a dysphoric state that involves the loss of expectation that adversity will yield and better days will come. It is also accompanied by sad mood, lowered self-esteem, and a pessimistic outlook on life, at least in that particular moment when one is seized by the experience. Hopelessness is painful, but a modicum of it is developmentally necessary (e.g., at renouncing infantile omnipotence, at giving up oedipal aspirations) and growth-promoting. In fact, it is from giving up childish hopes that mature hope is born. Despair, in contrast, involves losing all hope and confidence. In despair, we not only abandon, relinquish, and renounce hope, but also resign, surrender, and yield to the bleakness of our inner worlds. We lose heart for courage, faith, or hope. Evident in rash and reckless behaviors, despair can be expressed in a precipitate and headlong manner which contrasts with the ability to await, depend, look, trust, and expect. Despair is linked with despondency, desperation, and melancholia; cynicism and pessimism may be present, as well as feeling oppressed and weighed down. The despairing individual feels circumvented, foiled, outwitted, and thwarted. Feeling collected, and composure, assuredness, and confidence elude those who are filled with despair.

As analysts, we explore the what, when, and how of despairing states. We track associative flow, transferential expression, counter-responses and countertransferential experiences, as well as reconstruction, to determine, elaborate, and understand contributing factors. Despair appears in shifting associations, distancing withdrawal and apathetic discarding of our attempts to be helpful. Sadomasochistic repetitive reenactments may hide underlying and unexpressed misery. The analyst must manage her own despair of helpless ineffectiveness. We must manage our feelings of impotence, shock, and horror without criticism or retreat as we listen to and experience in the room the traumas of our patients. This may take the form of managing yet another withdrawal, attack, or dismissal in order to understand the predicament of our analysand, which prevents assertion and interdependency with another.

I will share some descriptions of despair from the literature and elaborate in more detail some techniques for working with despair. This seemingly daunting task was rewarded by exploration of the rich literature in our field. Individuals come to us out of hope, but carry skepticism, worry, and dread for repeating past hurts. Bringing light into the dark requires standing at the brink of the abyss without falling in to join our analysand's despair. The recognition of protest submerged beneath various forms of accommodation begins the mourning process of working through loss and disappointment. Goals can be reset in order to participate in life with an integrated and sturdier self. As predicaments are understood, compassion develops for the patients' own contribution to their predicament. A stoic independent self learns to rely on others after accepting shortcomings. A capacity for humility develops in place of humiliation. Bit by bit, increments of internalization occur in the work of sorting out different aspects of the dilemma. As the losses become tolerable, rage diminishes and internalizations occur to create a sustaining psychic structure. When expressions of hate, and victimization, can be understood as identifications, defensive maneuvers, or even expressions of will, more solid self-assertion can occur.

We learn together how autonomy was undermined and submerged beneath adaptive efforts. These attempts at self-reliance and independence deny such individuals the pleasure of interdependent relationships. Accepting vulnerability as well as the imperfections of others is essential for the working through and mourning of past disappointments. A milieu of safety is created by acknowledging all parts of the analysand as well as our own inadvertent errors in listening. Managing our own destructive urges or masochistic passivity facilitates our understanding of the analysand's predicaments. Giving up our need to be helpful lets us explore the experience of despair as well as inviting in the experience of us as the disappointing parental figures of the past.

Developmental substrate

Abraham (1924) noted disappointment in early maternal responsiveness as an etiologic factor in depression. Winnicott (1965) noted the patient's use of the analyst's minor failures but required the analyst to put up with being misunderstood: The patient now hates the analyst as an original environment factor which is out of the patient's omnipotent control. This optimal disillusionment is not an instinctual renunciation as Freud asserted but rather more in the nature of Ferenczi and Winnicott where the needs of the self are negotiated with the needs of the other.

These patients have overly adapted to the parents' will as described by Ferenczi (1931, 1933) and abandon themselves into a passive object love. The inevitable disappointments must be worked through as in Balint's ideas of a new experience. Ornstein (1974) relates Benedek's (1938) description of the gradual development of "confident expectation" to the transmuting internalizations that follow the ordinarily occurring frustrations in the course of an analysis. Ornstein goes on to state that Benedek:

> ... describes the disruptions in infancy related to the mother's minor empathic failures and ordinary delays, such disruptions in the analysis occur because failures in the analyst's empathy reactivate archaic, automatic, defense patterns' as expressed ... by infantile rage directly, but also by the masochistic and depressive or paranoid behavior patterns which had been firmly established in his personality in response to infantile and childhood disappointments and frustrations. (p. 238)

Brenner (1975) notes the calamities of childhood which cause depressive affects when a loss has already occurred. He defines depressive affect as "unpleasure associated with an idea that something bad has happened" (p. 11). A spectrum of intensity or type of loss is elaborated in loneliness in love or shame in falling short. "Despair implies the idea, conscious or unconscious, that the 'something bad' that has happened will never change" (p. 11).

Several other authors find despair to be rooted in the shame of not being true to oneself with subsequent inhibition of action in the world. Tougas (1999) cites Kirkegaard's idea that "despair involves an unconsciousness of Self or an unwillingness to be oneself" (p. 317). Tougas asserts:

> Analysis that does not recognize the Self as an intimate personal presence is neglecting what helps an individual the most ... It does not see as essential the mixed condition of being an individual subject, in which an ego may hate, attack, or try to hide an intention that it cannot separate itself from, that it judges to be bad. In this way such analysis fails to do justice to the fundamental complexity in feeling and living. (p. 319)

Similarly, Goldberg (1989) describes the predicament of being for Shakespeare's Hamlet as the loss of "innocence and the realization of betrayal (which) so overcame his being that he no longer preferred to live. ... he has become humiliatingly aware of the temptations, the sins, and the errors of the flesh." (p. 596). Hamlet finds it "better to [have] not been born than to fail and suffer as a common man" (p. 596). For Goldberg, the humiliation of realized vulnerability is followed by the shame of inaction. Now aware of temptations, we feel despair in realizing we have failed to proceed along an important and perilous avenue of our inner self. Shame tells the sufferer he has inhibited a necessary and legitimate action and is now aware of neglected ego-ideals.

Stekel (1933) describes a vulnerable self who cannot weather moments of preoccupation in the needed other: "Every unfaithfulness leaves them in despair as to their own worth: they are jealous because their self love is wounded" (p. 118). Other writers (e.g., Laing, 1960) describe how the splitting off of protest causes an apathetic going along or a false self that disavows responsibility for action. Bowlby (1960) describes despair as depression and apathy with a mix of angry protest. Horney (1967) regards despair as a state of being unable to feel anything. One feels clogged with inward rage, self-pity, self-contempt, and an overall sense of wretchedness. Zetzel (1965) describes anger which impedes internalization and structure building. We are well familiar with Freud's (1917e) description of a return to a narcissistic state through introjection of the disappointing object. In an attempt to protect the relationship, rage is now directed at the self and seeps into surrounding relationships with its misery. Klein (1935) described hateful and destructive urges which impede achievement of the depressive position due to attempts at protecting the good object. Bibring (1956) describes the problems inherent in disappointments leading to withdrawal. The object is not relinquished and aims are repressed while the goals remain but become unachievable. Modifying the goals aids in relinquishment as the defenses are lessened against the experience of affect.

Also pertinent is Fairbairn's (1943) description of children who put forth their own moral shortcomings as justification for the neglect and abuse of parents. This attempt to maintain a fantasy of control implies that if one were only good the parents would be good and caring. Fairbairn further elucidates such 'moral defense' in the following passage.

> "It is better to be a sinner in a world ruled by God than to live in a world ruled by the Devil. A sinner in a world ruled by God may be bad; but there is always a certain sense of security to be derived from the fact that the world around is good …. in a world ruled by the Devil the individual may avoid being a sinner; but he is bad because the world around him is bad". (pp. 66–67)

In a review of Seinfeld's (1996) book, *Hope Beyond the Void*, Borden (1997) notes the former's criticism of Fairbairn's failure to appreciate "the centrality of the internalization of good, reliable, sustaining experience for the development of a secure, stable sense of self" (p. 223). If those who have suffered such lapses in care and violations of self are to release themselves from their internal persecutors, Seinfeld believes, they must come to internalize their therapist as a good-enough object.

Joseph (1982) describes misery covered by the pleasurable experience of sadism. The perverse sadistic attitude is a regression away from hurt in an attempt to cope with the trauma of absence. The analyst risks getting caught up in a thwarted, masochistic position which may lead to either critical counterattack, or joining the patient in despair of ever resolving the issue.

The clinical realm

The patient's attempts to get the analyst to be critical and harsh end up repeating the experience of going down in misery while retaining the "thrall of the dominator" (Joseph, 1982, p. 452). Steiner (1984) elaborates the use of projective identification to get rid of an unwanted part of the personality and to control or attack the analyst, but it can also be a primitive and effective form of communication (Bion, 1963; Rosenfeld, 1971). Projections of this sort communicate what it is like to be in the patient's shoes; however, when particularly intense, they prevent us from developing such empathy (Joseph, 1983).

The despair and excitement must be noted over and over again in what Joseph describes as a chuntering of murmur, muttering, and finding fault. This living out is the antithesis of thought. Consequently, the hurt and being hurt must be noted. The analyst must manage his or her resentment and not be drawn into agreement with the patient's anguish or to criticize his arrogance which would shatter him and create despair in both.

Alvarez (2001) agrees with Joseph and highlights the retreats which follow an attack. When an analysand dismisses the analyst's transference interpretation, Alvarez asserts: "Actually you do feel I am [the crooked referee], you don't believe I'm here for you" (p. 496). Also, avoiding the tendency to be too pushy or active in response to the apathetic and passive aspects of our analysands can help us to analyze the interaction and facilitate their getting back their lost identity.

Steiner (1984) describes the essential piece of the analyst who is prone to receive the projection of despair. This projection comes out of a need or a fantasy to utilize the analyst's ego due to a fear of separateness. The projection may also be an attempt by patients to rid themselves of intolerable states: leaving behind a cold pseudo-stupidity. When the analyst listens to the action in the room through symbolic meaning and

> ... remain[s] open to acknowledge to himself the effect the patient's actions are having on him; [he can] characterize the mood ... link it to the patient's verbal communications and ... observable or inferable external events ... [as] the total situation of the transference ... (p. 461)

Steiner tells us the mood and utterances interplay by orienting and illuminating each other. If the analyst can contain the action and utilize its meaning, the patient may eventually become able to enhance his own capacity for containment. He also asserts:

> A critical point in the depressive position arises when the task of relinquishing control over the object has to be faced. The earlier trend, which aims at possessing the object and denying reality, has

to be reversed if the depressive position is to be worked through, and the object is to be allowed its independence. In unconscious phantasy this means that the individual has to face his inability to protect the object. His psychic reality includes the realization of the internal disaster created by his sadism and the awareness that his love and reparative wishes are insufficient to preserve his object which must be allowed to die with the consequent desolation, despair, and guilt. These processes involve intense conflict which we associate with the work of mourning and which seem to result in anxiety and mental pain. (1987, p. 70)

He emphasizes the need to work within the moments of transition into the depressive position which is followed by retreats due to fear of experiencing guilt and despair.

Many other authors describe despair evident in miscommunication or pseudo-stupidity. Modell (1984) believes that miscommunication is used to protect a vulnerable self beside angry and critical parents. He views his patient's inability to terminate her analysis as a problem with depending. Her fantasy of bondage to a mad scientist is then seen as an erotized defense against her worry of relying on one who attempts to insert ideas into her. Her miscommunication and pseudo-stupidity become attempts at autonomy which paradoxically prevent her from gaining actual autonomy. The difficulty taking in the analyst's comments expresses the fear of depending, since that might lead to submission to a critical authority. Any depending risks being subsumed by an angry critical presence. Therefore, in making interpretations emphasizing the unempathic, early parental matrix is insufficient. One must also get at the subsequent defensive stance.

This is similar to Jacobson's (1943) account of a woman who goes back and forth between ineffectual parents. She attempts to hide her need for love behind self-sufficient independence. She tries to ward off her destructive impulses by identifying herself with the image of her "good" parents and by being an overly submissive child. Yet, in her ambivalence she aggressively deserts one parent for the other. Similarly, Tolpin (2007) speaks of the teeter-totter between the trailing edge of previously adopted internalizations and the leading edge of growth. Awareness of vulnerably is achieved by the safety of knowing that the analyst can speak to both sides: the badness of identifying with the traumatizing object as well as the recognition of goodness. She notes that emphasizing the goodness may emphasize the constructed false self to please others which leaves despair in recognizing the internal badness. The analyst needs to witness, welcome, and participate with the positive movement. She also notes the difficulty sitting with the "shock" and "horror" of a patient's childhood trauma. The analyst may attempt to back away from this knowing by focusing on the goodness of the patient. Then the charming and entertaining "good self" is split off from the "bad self" which identified with the parent's abuse. Avoiding the disgusting self colludes with the defensive splitting off of this part of herself which is left to putrefy, reappear, and remain unintegrated in a perpetuated false self-promotion. "The theory of a needed alliance with the analyst can act as an iatrogenic insistence that the analyst's views are inevitably correct and can lead to the analyst mistaking tendrils of healthy self-assertion, protest, and even despair as signs of pathology and resistance to cure" (Tolpin, 2009, p. 39).

Tolpin describes the resistance brought in by the analyst's inadvertent negation of her analysand's psychic reality in an identification with her soiled self during activities with her father. She encourages seeing and explaining the origins of her loathsome self, that is, her childhood submission, pain, disgust, and despair. The analyst becomes reachable when she no longer tells her analysand what to think. The analyst must be able to move out of a wish that it wasn't so. This gets expressed in: "You are not disgusting; your father did disgusting things to you," which isn't mutative. Asking "How easy or difficult is it to trust me?" opens the door to interpretations and reconstructions by confirming and mirroring the patient's experience. This "catalyzes a change in the passive and silent resistance of the despairing child" (Tolpin, 2007, p. 54).

Then, they can work through the idea that the bad self is real and the good self is fraudulent. It is when the analyst inadvertently does not recognize her bad self and seemingly joins others in only wanting to see her as the one who is there for the appreciation and enjoyment of others that revives the compliant self. Similarly, exploring a gift of cookies invites an expression of having something to give with pride and pleasure rather than the imagined burden of caring for others. These exchanges allow a reestablishment of disrupted bonds between the pair. The acceptance of and enquiry about the despairing loathing allows for the development of a twinship and she is less alone with her other side.

Benedek (1956) describes the importance of self-state safety in relation to another in order for growth to occur. Addressing empathic failings in the analytic process is what provides the safety for forward movement and the development of an ability to rely on another and risk disappointments. Benedek considers the availability of a "libido reservoir" which supplies "mobile integrative energy" essential to structure building during infancy. Once the infant can sustain shorter and longer waking states, he begins to establish communication on a psychological level. The infant's ability to establish psychological communication and his ability to wait depend on the maintenance of a relatively undisturbed narcissistic equilibrium with his mother:

> If the mother fails to respond, the infant's "integrative field disappears"—his smile turns into crying, and the mother is lost as the needed object for the maintenance of his narcissistic equilibrium. Since it is the mother's response to the infant's smile on which the infant's ability to wait depends, when the mother fails to respond, the libidinous affects become dissociated and "the aggressive affects take over and mobilize the undirected 'storm of excitation'" (p. 400). Whereas such experiences are also internalized and may constitute nuclei of hostile self-perceptions, they are not structure building, for only when the infant is "protected from the sense of frustration by an integrated, libidinous, emotional state, can he learn to wait". (Benedek, 1956, p. 401)

Ornstein (1974) sees this as created by a willingness to be humble in our misunderstandings and respond to mistaken responses which allow our patients to be humble and bring their varied experiences into the room to be explored and understood in a two person matrix. But other writers remind us that the despair runs deep and identifications with the analyst must be linked with interpretation as well as the new experience of responsive sorting out in the dyad. Slochower (2008) writes of the need with some patients to contain their affective discharge without falling into despair, boredom, or judging impatience. She describes the strain on the analyst in doing so of having to manage his or her internal states when the patient is not able to work with interpretations or bear to think about transference implications. Safran (1999) writes of the difficulty in accepting our limits as the helper and a tendency to respond defensively or shrink from pain and despair. She elaborates that longing for a sense of completion through magical transference is present in adults and is not merely a regression to dependency. Accepting this notion helps us to avoid condescending treatment of our analysand's longings. Difficulty accepting the limits of our role as a helper may cause us to shrink from the pain and despair in our patients. The therapist may fall into countertransference distancing through anger and condescension in order to avoid feelings of impotence, futility, and despair when dismissed by the analysand. Safran (1999) writes about the importance of "will," which she differentiates from "willfulness." The latter is desperate and aggressive. She defines will as a feeling of self-assertion that can have an impact upon the world. Ferenczi (1931, 1933) and Rank (1945) discussed "will" as the ability to imagine responsiveness and effectiveness as a part of growth in patients. The patient must also be able to bear the disappointments that occur from asserting oneself. But Safran's point is that these individuals are not able to imagine doing so out of their feelings of hopeless despair and victimization. For her, despair comes in from the missed experience of agency: actions or efforts make no difference. Mitchell (1988) relates the need to enquire about conscious willful commitment to choices. Rank (1945) parallels accepting the counter will of patients in therapy as in counter will against parents. Aron (2000) suggests we rethink resistance as the beginnings of self-assertion on a developmental path. These assertions, criticisms, or withdrawals can then be worked through and analyzed. When we treat this willfulness as resistance we miss the opportunity to note that their reaction implies our stance is not mutative.

When seen as growth, the development of will can be explored for evidence of identifications with split off dissociated aspects of self. Tolerating opposition to ourselves might evoke the fear of being conned; this is especially evident when the analyst becomes unduly reassuring. Picking up a hint of cynicism is the thread to underlying longing and vitality.

Safran remembered her own experiences of despair when a depressed sister described her absence of will. This "reverie opens up the analytic space … one's own history of success and resentment providing less need to 'help' and lessening our resentment of being stuck by unrelenting process" (p. 11). Once the analyst allowed this reverie, she was able to let go of her need to help with less resentment and more curiosity about the analysand's experience. She could learn through inquiry how discerning a need in the analyst might trigger worries about coercion.

She then shared with her analysand a feeling which "might be between you and me, or just me ... that nothing I'll say will be meaningful", which let in a skeptical fantasy about the analyst's motivations. Her patient feared being conned or taken in by the analyst's reassuring comments. These moments of hope were followed by pain.

Safran (1999) highlights Kaiser's idea that we do not ask the patient to take responsibility for changing but to experience responsibility for actions. The recognition of owning one's contribution for problems can be hard to bear for the analyst and the analysand. Realizing compassion for one's self for moment to moment choices is crucial. Safran's self work and inquiry serve as a model of such a transaction which likely shifted the mood in the room.

Zetzel (1965) writes about the capacity to bear depression as an achieved state in development elaborated by Winnicott. She compares this to the capacity to bear anxiety. She notes that some individuals fare better within the connection to the therapist as an object that holds them and without this connection the patient falls into psychotic states of despair colored by paranoia. Difficulty managing rage impairs internalization. Psychoanalytic technique has evolved to describe the necessity of provisions which move stalled developments into new growth. Davies (2005) refers to the "evil demons and wild beasts" rooted in unmourned separations and abandonments which must be worked through in individual object experiences to achieve a sense of others as subjects. These unique internal organizations of self and other can develop into tools for constructing other relationships as patients learn to accept each other's imperfections. Holding Davies's analysand's destructive elements required owning and metabolizing her own destructive urges. This internal awareness and acceptance allowed the analyst to see the complexity of her patient's motives. Her analysand overcame her shame by working through her narcissistic outrage. Exploring the clouding of positive living when resentment and contempt reign allows new resolutions to identifications to occur. This occurs through the procedural relational knowing of enacted moments which are rehearsed and practiced beside the unsatisfying counterpoint within the dyad.

Analysands also must work through notions of being seduced and then abandoned. Recognizing the inevitable end of the therapeutic relationship facilitates "renunciation of illusory love which cannot be consummated or lived out with the analyst (Davies, 2005, pp. 787–788). By working through this disappointment the analysand can move onto real relationships. Loewald (1962) also writes about the lengthy process of termination which involves internalizations through the work of mourning. Accepting each other's imperfections in the elaboration of overstimulation and retraumatization allows the renunciation of illusory love which is not consummated or lived out. Only by accepting and tolerating disappointments does the patient move on from idealized perfect love to one which accepts imperfection. The consequent emergent self-states are resilient to manage disappointments.

Tolpin (2009) describes this through Stern et al.'s (1998) ideas of "moments of meeting" which provide the something more of now moments which welcome the forward edge. The sorting out of the teeter-totter requires welcoming the forward edge which may include evidence of compensatory actions as well as embracing the trailing edge. Tolpin's idea of the patient daring to think she has something to give could be likened to the idea of will proposed by Safran (1999).

Loewald (1962) relates the complexities of managing where we aspire to be which are intertwined with varied experiences with teachers, ancestors, and heroes:

> Inner ideals, expectations, hopes, demands, and equally, inner doubts, fears, guilt despair concerning oneself—all this is reaching toward or feeling defeated by a future. The voice of conscience tells us what we should do or should have done, speaking from a future that we ask ourselves to reach or tell ourselves we are failing to reach—perhaps a future whose image in the course of development becomes imbued with all that is still alive from the hopes, expectations, demands, promises, ideals, aspirations, self doubt, guilt and despair of past ages, ancestors ... and heroes. (p. 500)

Abend (1986) describes how our own compromise formations may limit our capacity to hear and process the material. Busch (1997) notes that our investment in a transferential understanding may prevent us from following the shifts in associations:

> ... the patient's free associations as a unity. They are viewed as the result of one side or another of the ego's attempt to deal with conflict in the here and now of the transference regression. What one responds to at a given time depends on which side of the conflict

is uppermost in the patient's associations, a technique that allows the analyst to stay close to the surface of the patient's thoughts, (p. 420)

Tolpin similarly speaks of the teeter-totter between the trailing edge of previously assumed adaptations beside the leading edge of growth which encompasses an awareness of vulnerabilities achieved by the safety of knowing that the analyst can speak to both sides. The internalizations of these varied parts of identifications are pointed to by Davies who describes the evolving sense of the analyst as a subject rather than an object after working with the varied object representations in the analysand's experience. Safran describes the need to utilize one's own states of despair in managing roles and identifications in order to tolerate the despair in the treatment. Letting go of the need to help and cure helps us sit with tolerance and curiosity beside affect states. This awareness of experience allows the space for wonder and growth. Our work in psychoanalysis and psychotherapy involves a similar journey of getting our patients to explore despair in an atmosphere of safety where all parts of them can be explored, understood, and integrated. This entails a willingness to be humble in our misunderstandings and to respond to mistaken responses which allow our patients to come forward with previously unknown aspects of themselves.

Conclusion

In summary, despair is different from hopelessness as it involves fear of unrelenting pain which the individual feels helpless to manage and hopeless to remedy. By bringing the elements of identification into the room we can work through various object representations. The analysand can begin to integrate prior split off aspects of the self and begin to accept himself and develop the capacity to meaningfully use others and risk disappointments.

Despair enters the treatment in moments of empathic failures or misreadings. It may be fleeting: only represented by shifts in associations or retreats into defensive modes of sadomasochistic enactments, passivity, or withdrawal. Despair may be at the forefront, in momentary whispers or hidden behind armor which needs to be understood, as well as tolerated. Despair may occur at many levels of experience and development; it may also represent a chronic state of depression from abuse, and the chronic strain of unresponsiveness. The analyst must access her own feelings of shock around horrible experiences of her analysands, welcome discovery of her own states of despair past and present, and tolerate misunderstandings in order to offer a mutative experience. Listening for shifts and managing her own reactions are crucial.

CHAPTER EIGHT

On the edge of hopelessness and despair: an uncertain landscape

Judi B. Kobrick

Hopelessness and despair in an oppressive landscape, hope buried somewhere beneath and barely perceptible ... I find myself immobilized in giving life to a chapter I have been asked to write. I frantically search the literature, poetry, and symbolic realm to unlock a way to begin. I discover Salman Akhtar's (2000) article "Mental Pain and the Cultural Ointment of Poetry," replete with psychic helplessness alongside hopelessness and mourning and the capacity to bear pain in the clinical situation. Mental pain is elaborated as a wordless state of self-rupture for which it is difficult to give shape and form. I search for the poetry and words of Salman's ointment to unleash the unbearable. I also find myself searching for Christian, the analysand of this narrative who presented himself as the adopted and unworthy son of his parents and psychoanalysis. My limited investigative capacity leads me to finding others of his namesake that are deceased, incarcerated, political pundits, financiers, professors, and many others. I muse that like Philomena (Sixsmith, 2009), I am searching for the son that I have lost in order to find myself.

The fear and desire for recapturing the compelling hopelessness and despair transported me back in time, evoking the affective storms and tensions of an analytic treatment that has never left the recesses of my mind. There standing before me was the apparition of Christian proclaiming his "hubris" and "misogyny," declaring that he has trapped himself and I am there with him. The landscape we inhabited exuded both hope and hopelessness.

Christian

Christian was twenty-eight years old when he began an analysis that would traverse through the battlefields of his youth in his desperate search for recognition and accomplishment. He was the adopted son of a revolutionary scientist and a mother who was on an odyssey to become a world-renowned anthropologist. He was consumed with having no one to compare himself to, lacking a historical and genetic sense of himself and his origins. "It's sort of like you came out of nowhere." He yearned for a sense of connection whilst experiencing himself as the undeserving son of admired and accomplished parents and an unworthy participant of psychoanalysis. He believed that his biological mother had been a young university student and fantasized that his biological father was a television repair man. At the age of six, he walked between two parked cars, was hit, and landed on his head which left him in a coma for two weeks; his left side was paralyzed for a period of time. His rehabilitation was miraculous and he returned to excel in school beyond the capabilities of his peers. This set the stage for his sense of invulnerability and hubris. Christian viewed his father as honest and dedicated, filling his life with professional pursuits and activities that cloaked feelings of depression and loneliness. He believed that his mother had potential for understanding his struggle but the "ice queen" remained aloof, demanding servitude and admiration. Although Christian disavowed physical and psychic abandonment, he disguised his sense of profound loss, torment, and pain. At the age of seventeen, he moved out of his parents' home consequent to his attending university, his parents' divorce, and as a reaction to "an assembly-line education and plebeian activities." This was in contrast to his stellar academic achievements and admission to a prestigious and competitive upper school that his father had attended, for which he did not feel recognized. He viewed himself as strong and resilient, he referred to his own "hubris," unaware that his life was unraveling and that his construction of his state of affairs had limited his experience, feelings, and relationships. Underneath his protective façade, emotional turmoil was erupting and interfering with his life. He later revealed and reviled himself as an "exotic swamp creature partially submerged." He repeatedly and intensely became involved with and committed to young women whom he openly regarded as needy, immature, and demanding. These "childlike" women challenged his invulnerability, they eventually becoming unfaithful, negating, and abandoning.

The five years prior to his analysis were painfully difficult. He had been living on relatively little resources consisting of part-time employment, an inheritance, and occasionally financial assistance from his father. He experienced difficultly working, sleeping, regulating his eating, and abuse of alcohol, and was avoidant of committed relationships. He had undergone an emotional and physical metamorphosis, gaining sixty pounds, and found himself attired daily in the same sweatpants and T-shirt as his life became unbearable. Alienation from his body became the instrument for the expression of affects in the psychosomatic enactments that foreclosed self-reflection and mentalization (Fonagy, Target, Gergely, & Jurist, 2002). He wondered whether he could reclaim a sense of his resilient self while inhabiting a lost and damaged self. He pondered potential catastrophe, a fear of breakdown that had already occurred à la Winnicott (1974), empathizing with: "… what if in the process wanting to change, I drop dead?" (p. 104).

Ghent (2002) evocatively stated:

> Every day in our practice we pay homage to, and stand back in awe of, the marvels of the human mind caught up in the struggle to heal and transcend itself, while holding back in fear, jousting with itself in dread of walking through the valley of the shadow of death. (p. 803)

Christian presented as a somewhat glib, bright, sensitive, hypervigilant, and articulate man who was fearful of trusting another person who potentially could seduce him and then lead him to destruction. As he entered upon the stage of analysis, he voiced his concern, saying, "I feel like I am a spectator of my life, as if it's not really happening to me." He regarded his "despair, despondency, and depression" as serious, feeling humiliated and crushed by the inimical world that engulfed him. He viewed himself as an obstacle to the future he hoped for—was I to become an obstacle in the position of power he placed me in as his only hope? Christian spanned the chasm between who he was and who he imagined he could be with trepidation and fear that the other will engulf him with expectations, annihilating and depleting his sense of self. If I was meant to be his biographer, how would I edit, interpret, and change his story? As a fairy and selfless goddess, I may have offered a sense of cohesion; as a witch, I might seduce and rob him of his uniqueness, individuality, and potential creativity that was linked to pain and destruction: "the iron first and velvet glove." He referred to the presence of the art work in my office as if I had painted "the cells to keep the prisoners calm." "You are not a god but a demigod, you are human, you make mistakes … this process is not doing what I expected it to do."

The oceanic countertransference was filled with emptiness, loneliness, and hopelessness as I was pulled down by the undertow. Christian revealed that in his private reverie, I was the fantasized listener who was in concert with him and in my presence there was a fear of breakdown and disappointment. The illusive paradox of hope and hopelessness accompanied both of us. Christian, a master of language, set in motion a lengthy discourse, spewing evocative words that disrupted, confused, and fragmented my self-states. The words pierced links to the unknown and unformulated (Stern, 2010) landscape we both inhabited. I was the confused and inept spectator, unable to make sense of the incomprehensible words he loved and embraced. My consultant became *Webster's Dictionary*, which was needed to navigate the subterranean depths and create meaning. I revealed my consultant and uncertainty as I attempted to grasp words and possible meaning to bridge the relational gap. Christian laughed warmly, only to reveal his nocturnal engagement with the same consultant. He had been searching for rare and unknowable words to give life, vitality, and uniqueness to our engagement. We had both traversed the same unconscious landscape searching to find one another. In the presence of his mother, he felt obliged "to part the Red Sea and to turn water into wine" in his desperate struggle for recognition. Gerson (2009) highlights the affective responsiveness of the witnessing other, creates a "live third," between experience and meaning, "whose engaged recognition and concerned responsiveness to the individual's experience creates liveable meaning" (p. 1342).

Christian expressed ambivalence regarding his sexuality, proclaiming himself a "misogynist," opposing his desire for a meaningful, emotionally, and sexuality-charged relationship. He then reconnected with an important love interest of his adolescence, Mary, who he idealized as his "only true and understanding" friend. This woman's image of him that was linked to their relationship as adolescents together was one of "a dashing romantic figure, a poet, an artist never settling down." She brought to mind the sterile and pristine home environment of his youth—"that white apartment, white furniture and white walls." This relationship fueled desires for affection, connectedness, and the reexamining of his frightened defiance of women as potentially ruthless, exploitive, and withholding. All his desires were pitted against the reality that his adolescent love and torchbearer was now a married woman. Christian looked toward Mary as a secure place from which to grow and "emerge from a period of self-destruction and alienation." He entered the consulting room, averted his gaze, and banished me to the place of spectator. Mary enters the present from the past to rescue him from the bowels of despair and to revitalize his sense of self, desire, and potency. He again found himself in a relationship that cannot be reciprocated as she withdraws both sexually and emotionally. He finds himself retraumatized, in a rage, vulnerable, and attempts to contain himself and ward off feelings of disintegration, fragmentation, and abandonment.

I remark this is not an unfamiliar story, that Mary has joined the traumatizing women he has encountered before and it was painful to address the insults of the past in the present. I was also viscerally implicated in the trauma of disappointment and unable to provide the sustenance he craved. He imagined she has abandoned him for someone more important, that he is "damaged goods." He was unable to protect himself in a relationship which now seems unreal as if it never happened—does this foreshadow the fate of his analysis?

New possibilities for experience and the analytic relationship can become trapped in repeated enactments of the familiar, given the fear of venturing into the unknown, both for the patient and the analyst. Mitchell (1988) reminds us that the "adhesive devotion to the relational matrix" (p. 276) and the "deep loyalty to the familiar" is inexorably tied to the terror of losing oneself and the sense of connection with others.

I dreamt of his shoulder brushing up against mine and the following day as if we had met on an unconscious landscape he effused:

> When I come in, I hardly look at you ... a little dance protecting myself and any strong feelings I may have ... a core I do not share with anyone except you ... more important things I do not share

with anyone, it has reduced my ability to function ... I have so far to go ... I often inhibit myself.

Christian later presented me with his "manifesto" of what he expected to unfold in analysis. He trusted all would be revealed in the fullness of time and that his submission and passivity "may indeed be more efficacious than aggression in the face of chaos." The seduction of submission and the yearning and desire for surrender were held between the fear and peril of exploitation. Ghent (1990) left us with the legacy that what may appear to be masochism, self-destructiveness, and aggression was the veil obscuring profound longings to know and be known by the other. There were times when I felt nonexistent, writing my name in the middle of process notes in attempts to reclaim myself lest I be lost among the ruins and destruction. Cooper (2011) reflected on the reciprocal influence and "sheer weight and force of dissociation" (p. 593) within the patient and the analyst attempting to understand states of nonrelatedness. Christian expressed elation that he believed that I was compassionate and "in concert" with him and paradoxically reviled disappointment that I have unleashed his anger and contempt. He arrived at the next session inebriated, for the first time recoiling, calling me "nasty," exploitative, and that women drive him to drink—he could not eat, sleep, had no sex life, craved touch, and felt alienation from his body. He needed more, his relationships were consumed with unspoken anger, and the only anger he has been able to openly express had been with me. He revealed that it was a point of honor that he endure his mother and that his doing damage to himself interfered with her life that was more consumed with intellectual pursuits than common sense.

In the analytic encounter, Christian unleashed profound rage and destructiveness, disavowing and displacing a sense of linkage and dependency, withdrawing and releasing himself from potential exploitation as the presence of the "good" had been tantamount to the presence of the "bad" (Bion, 1959). The attacks on linking, on the analytic process, and on the analyst's understanding challenge the analyst's survival of the patient's dread and psychic pain without withdrawing (Mitchell, 1993). Christian stated that he was unwilling to accept that I was "the high goddess of psychoanalysis" but also willing to be convinced, and predicting that he "probably will not be." He wept in a state of despair and alluded to his masochistic stance of "relieving pain through applying pain" and his reluctance to engage in "ostentatious displays of emotion." The analytic dyad inevitably struggled to rearrange and recreate meanings that embraced the need for recognition and mutual recognition (Benjamin, 2004) in a landscape of fear and potential loss and abandonment. The desire to remain alive and resilient in the wake of deadness and hopelessness could not be ignored.

I had a dream that Christian was intruding upon my "white" apartment, while I was absent; he was in a rage throwing newspapers all around. I opened a door, he grabbed me in a forceful and sexualized manner, he then was reduced in my arms to a crying baby saying, "Mommy, am I going to be all right?" This dream foreshadowed the arrival of his own mother which he had not mentioned. She resided with Christian between her living in Europe and her country retreat. He announced his mother's arrival: "She wants open warfare … to sail along unruffled … she's not much of a fighter, she may be emotionally unstable … she's going to ice me out." Although I believed myself to be a resonant, and affectively immersed, I found myself adrift with the desire to barricade and protect myself from the unbearable and at times unbridgeable gap between Christian and myself. He had put me on a pedestal as his only hope—who was I?—the one who seduced, entrapped, and destroyed or the one who claimed to be protective but inevitably abandoned him. His intense feelings of worthlessness, inferiority, and having failed to live up to others' expectations, losing credibility and approval, crash against the rocks and reverberated within me—for what had I to offer to calm the maelstrom of desperate seas?

C: "You know I can be very irritating. I'm not crazy enough to be in pain all the time—I seemed to have trapped myself."

Christian was silent for twenty-five minutes, his withdrawal profound; he sighed, coughed, his hands and fingers poised together in extreme physical tension—by one measure, the silence was experienced deeply, and on another, there was the feeling of urgency on my part to intervene and I say, "I'm not sure what I'm listening to …"

C: "For some reason I'm plumbing the depths, I'm loathing myself, I haven't done it in a while—I can be pretty good at it."
JK: "Something you do silently …"
C: "It is the first time this has happened so profoundly in a session, and it is the first time with someone else present. It's basically very pleasant—I don't have to do much, I'm a pretty easy

target—reflecting on myself, being pretty tough, being pretty hard on myself—it's pretty simple really—it's been awhile. It happened here—I was trying to think what I was going to say—I thought isn't that a bunch of shit, that's what started it—it's not something I do frequently, I wouldn't get out of bed if I did all the time."

JK: "Censoring what you say, evaluating it as not worthwhile or meaningful."

C: "I evaluate it as stupid."

JK: "It is like you turned the knife on yourself."

C: "And twisted it a few times, maybe I deserve it."

JK: "It's a very painful withdrawal into the self which excludes others, and now you experience it here with me."

C: "I don't experience you, it's purely a personal thing, I wouldn't want to drag other people into it. It's not something I can explain, I know my shortcomings more intimately than anyone else. I don't need to articulate them, something would be lost in the translation. It's not something specific, it's all encompassing—intellectual defects, physical appearance, my standing in life, the clothes I'm wearing.

—We're talking razor blades—in a manner of minutes, I can reduce my life to nothing—not a healthy thing to be doing this. It is important to be self critical. It stops me from becoming complacent. I'm becoming too communicative.

—Take your life, minute to minute. Imagine it's on film, and it's being shown to someone who intensely dislikes you, and who feels superior, who sees every wart, every peculiarity. It's an experience of the self looking at the self. I'm not sympathetic to myself ... like showing every imperfection of your life to someone who didn't like you and who wasn't sympathetic ... it's deeply personal, not something you can share with another person who would not understand. I'm telling you this so you can imagine what it's like to be me."

JK: "To feel ashamed, embarrassed, and vulnerable."

C: On the day of his thirtieth birthday, he presented me with a "gift" and "more objective data" to shore up his credibility and his lived experience. He presented the most recent typed "form" letter received from his mother, who is researching her next book, a handwritten letter from his father, and a newspaper article with the headline "For some, Oxford brings too-great expectations" highlighting disaffected Rhodes scholars. His mother has written at the top of her generic letter that details her hobnobbing with the intellectual elite, "Darling Chrisie" and adds in the postscript "... heaps of love, how about a letter?" His father's letter, in contrast, expresses compassion and love for his son, Christian's brave attempts to move forward, and his own sadness in being unable to stem the tide of his destruction and attune to his needs. The newspaper article reads: "Disaffected Rhodes scholars are rare: they become alcoholics, they have breakdowns, they disappear ... with a brilliant future behind them."

I was deeply moved; he apprehended and experienced my change of tone as compassionate that was far more important to him than my words.

C: "I was very careful to watch my language: I didn't want to upset you. I felt if this was going to work ... it was tied up with my self-image. I wanted you to like me beyond my appearance, which was disgusting; I wanted to be accepted and liked. One of the things I wanted from mommy was a reflection back of myself. I didn't get it from mommy, perhaps I can get a sense of myself through you. I noticed a change in you ... detected a real change. I caught the tone in your voice that was real. It was very encouraging. I got the sense that you like me genuinely, that there was a basic affection or sympathy ... that was very nice. One of the things I read in Freud about idealizing the analyst: if anything I undervalued you."

Christian then telephoned to advise me that he would be late for his appointment and obliquely mentioned that he has been involved in an accident in which he had been thrown off his motorcycle by the impact of a car driven by a woman. When he entered the consultation room, he insisted that the accident is an insignificant detail and was more concerned that I be at my office when he arrived. He was distressed and shaken, displaying his bleeding abrasions and torn pants. He communicated his internal turmoil to what is unmistakeably visible without words but with feelings that previously he was unable to formulate. I was reminded of the car accident when he was six years old, his remarkable recovery and resiliency, a time when he felt cared for and recognized.

Christian ultimately decided to leave the analysis after several years, disillusioned that it had not brought the "monumental" change that he had hoped for. He became frightened by the surge of affective storms in the presence of the other and his need to disavow his attachment to me who in turn left him disappointed, alone, and excluded from the world of important others. He acknowledged his filibustering disaster on the wake of momentum and sabotaging his own efforts. He prepared his biographical history to present for an upcoming psychiatric consultation in his desire to be understood and experienced as "real." He related to me that he will probably feel lost for the first two weeks but then his analytic experience with me would be forgotten. Several months later, I saw him through the window of my office standing beside his motorcycle in the parking lot. I went out to greet him and invited him in. He presented me with a gift, a copy of his autobiography that was "the least I could do for you under the circumstances." It had taken him six weeks, 300 hours and spanned fifty-two typed single-spaced pages without a break, accompanied by a chronology of his life and a handwritten note: *I should mention that without the benefit of our discussions over the past years, it would have been much more difficult to accurately write this autobiography, not to mention coming to a meaningful understanding of many of the events which transpired.*

I read his eloquent and coherent treatise of his life which was no longer presented in fragments—yet I could not help but muse about the life not yet lived. I was depicted as well-intentioned, compassionate, but ultimately unhelpful. I reconnected with him, shared both my hopes and disappointment that together thus far the intersubjective landscape that we shared had not been able to bridge the chasm and tension between who he is and what he hopes to become. I had been unable, as others before me, to adequately provide him with what he needed—I was a "stand-in for an ideal" (which were his words) depicting the "hubris" self of his youth for a life that was in his grasp yet unobtainable. Christian then revealed that the consulting psychiatrist had not the time or inclination to read his story. He appreciated that I had been there for him, offered new threads of thoughts and perspectives to the tapestry of his life, and hoped someday he could make use of our experience together. He no longer felt that he "came out of nowhere" and that he had a story to tell. He believed (and I believed) that our work together had been overshadowed by forces beyond his control—the ghosts of the past could not become ancestors. New possibilities collapsed into repetitive patterns (Mitchell, 1997). Had the analytic relationship reawakened the passion and desire he preferred to disavow averting disaster? Had I been unable to protect him and ultimately become abandoning, a reenactment of the trauma and fear of his past? Had I been able to give him some hope in the face of hopelessness? Christian seemed to disappear into the ether but always remained present within me, yet I was left with a sense of loss. What was related, lived, and imagined seems incomplete.

The analyst and analysand search for ways in which the deadness of hopelessness can be exhumed and transformed. There is a desire to flee from despair and dread and embrace a sense of hope. There is the inevitable collision with the loss and mourning of a life not lived and a life lived. Paradoxically, Christian's decision to leave the analysis eclipsed the abandonments of the past and left us standing on an uncertain landscape.

To Christian:

Hidden Things

*Let them not seek to discover who I was
from all that I have done and said.
An obstacle was there that transformed
the deeds and manner of my life.
An obstacle was there that stopped me
many times when I was about to speak.
Only from my most imperceptible deeds
and my most covert writings—
from these alone will they understand me.
But perhaps it isn't worth exerting
such care and such effort for them to know me.
Later, in the more perfect society,
surely some other person created like me
will appear and act freely.*

—C. P. Cavafy (1886–1904)

CHAPTER NINE

Hope and hopelessness in the couple relationship

Sarah Fels Usher

Couples, married and otherwise, usually come to a psychotherapist as a next-to-last resort, often after many years of unhappiness. They bring their most private selves, in some way urgently needing to expose problems; in another, embarrassed and shamed by what they often perceive as painful personal failure. Even though patients in individual psychotherapy and psychoanalysis often choose to focus on their romantic relationships, or lack thereof, patients in couple therapy have no choice but to expose these issues—with their partner in the room and with a therapist (referee?, judge?, parent?, friend?) observing every detail (Usher, 2008).

Working with couples can be draining or enlivening: Therapists are bombarded with a myriad of dynamics—projections, projective identifications, fluctuating transferences from each partner, fluctuating countertransference to each partner, secrets, resistances from each or both, manipulation by each or both, as well as exposure to a degree of rage and fighting. Yet the therapeutic environment of couple therapy can be a crucible for incredible learning for all three parties, sometimes for healing, and often, perhaps surprisingly, to develop a sense of humor about life. There are several factors that can make a couple's problems seem hopeless, or indeed, hopeful when treated. I will focus here on what I currently understand as the most important two: Developmental issues, particularly unresolved oedipal issues manifested in difficulties in separation and individuation in adult life; and a partner's use of the defense of acting out manifested in an affair which can be a fatal attraction. It is sometimes difficult to separate these two factors. As it happens, the cases portrayed here are well-educated, heterosexual couples. These hurdles also occur, of course, in same sex and transgendered couples and in couples who are not professionally educated.

Developmental issues

The focus in the following examples is on that part of the couple therapy that pertained to developmental issues.

Clinical vignette: 1

Pamela and Tom, professionals in their early forties, came for therapy because Tom had declared he had no sexual feelings for his partner and felt their ten-year relationship was over. When they were first married, Tom's parents, who lived about an hour away, expected the couple to visit often, which they did on weekends. About two years into their relationship, Tom's father died suddenly of a heart attack, and his mother, for whom he had always been the "good son," began to deteriorate rapidly, her condition of diabetes worsening due to her increased smoking and drinking. Pamela and Tom were then expected to visit every second weekend, and now to stay overnight in her chaotic home, in order to take care of her. As she became more and more ill, she did not want to hire help; the couple were then required to do the heavy care, including toileting, themselves. Pamela reported that she had actually been happy to be involved with her mother-in-law, as she never criticized her and seemed to really appreciate her. Tom acknowledged in our sessions that he had known earlier in his life that he would never marry anyone who could not get along with his mother, even though she was a very difficult and demanding person. He was happy that Pamela had a good relationship with her.

As time went on, Tom and Pamela were becoming more like siblings than partners, and their sex life, never very active after their marriage, was more and more infrequent, in a manner that was seemingly agreeable to both. When Tom's mother died, they were in their late thirties. No longer preoccupied with traveling to Tom's mother's house on weekends, this seemed to them to be a good time to think about having a child. They set about—ovulation thermometer in hand—trying to have intercourse at the "right" time. Tom found sex on demand even worse than no sex. They ultimately managed to conceive, and had a baby boy. However, even though they had wanted a child, both felt totally unequipped to care for an infant. Tom's response to his anxiety was to work harder, and he spent many evening hours at his company, leaving Pamela alone with the baby.

Pamela's parents rushed to help. Her mother, delighted with the opportunity to make up for her own negligent parenting, immediately offered to get involved, and took over a great deal of the care of the baby. Pamela's father became responsible for some of the nighttime child duty. With this arrangement, not only did Pamela experience relief from the stresses of child care, but she was also able to please her parents which she still desperately needed to do, by giving them a purpose in life. As well, this much parental involvement ensured that there would be no space for sexual—or any other—intimacy with Tom, who became angrier and angrier, feeling he was only being used for the money he brought home. When discussions of their having another child surfaced later, although both partners had previously thought of having two children, Pamela yielded to the advice of her mother who said that one was enough, especially since Tom was not at home very much, and when he was, he was "useless."

Although developmentally, at least in terms of separation issues, these partners were more or less aligned—that is, neither one had separated from their family of origin—the nature of the couple's pathological fit meant life together as adults was difficult, if not impossible. In the therapy, both were able to acknowledge that they had been relieved, and unconsciously complicit in, their families' impingements on their marriage. When I broached with them the possibility that forming a new, adult relationship can assist people in pulling out of the quicksand of their original families, Pamela chirped, "I jumped right in with them!"

As we explored the details of their sexual histories, Tom described his parents as wandering around the house naked, and using the washroom with the door open, which had aroused in him conscious feelings of disgust. This disgust, probably a defense against sexual excitement, became associated with something we referred to roughly as "sex within a family." In the months after their son was born, when Tom was spending more time at the office, he developed a compelling flirtation with a colleague ("outside the family"), which consumed his sexual fantasies and arousal. For her part, Pamela, whom our therapy revealed had been molested by her father at ages seven to eight, maintained an immature view of sexual interaction, manifested in her wanting to play childish games with Tom if they ever attempted to have sex. However, despite our gaining at least a partial understanding of the roots of their problems, Tom's statement at the beginning of the therapy, that he had no sexual feelings for Pamela, and probably never would, did not change. In an emotional last session, with both of them sobbing (they had really liked each other, after all), they decided to separate.

Karen Horney (1967) was one of the few early analytic writers to discuss the effects of early development, mainly oedipal love experiences, on individuals' later relationships. In her paper, "Problems in Marriage," she writes that the problem for males who "recoil" from the forbidden female is the notion of saintliness of women, which interferes with sexual desires for the wife, and also raises the dread of being unable to satisfy the woman. She goes on to say that divorce is less related to the "annoying qualities of the partner, and much more [to] the unresolved conflicts we bring into the marriage from our own development" (p. 131).

Later, Loewald (1979) refers to Freud's concept of the turning away from the Oedipus complex as "more than a repression," saying that it amounts, when ideally carried out, to a destruction of it. "First: no matter how resolutely the ego turns away from it and what the relative proportions of repression, sublimation, 'destruction' might be, in adolescence the Oedipus complex rears its head again, *and so it does during later periods of life* [italics mine], in normal people as well as in neurotics" (p. 753). It is my contention that the Oedipus complex often rears its head in the marital bed, whether or not we are aware of it.

Loewald introduces the term *parricide* in connection with the destruction of the Oedipus complex, referring to the necessary destruction of the parent by the child, in order for the growing (and grown) person to become a separate individual. Settlage (1994) states that separation-individuation theory is a part of the life span of human development.

In "Divorce: Separation or Separation-Individuation?", Cantor (1982) states that many divorces result from a couple's working through the task of separation only as adults. "In a marriage, through the gratification of sexual desires, each partner introjects the other as a gratifier of needs and becomes a part of the self-system of the other" (p. 308).

In the treatment of couples, often both partners are not at the same developmental level when confronting serious developmental achievements, such as the resolution of oedipal and separation issues. We could surmise that if one partner is motivated, consciously and/or unconsciously, to separate and the other is not, or cannot, there may be more conflict than if they are closely matched. If this is the case, the striving partner may describe the relationship as suffocating; the less separated partner may describe it as insecure, and fear abandonment. But, as we see in the example of Tom and Pamela, above, who were closely matched on their inability to achieve separation, conflict did occur, when issues of sexual intimacy and maturity (the baby) arose.

There are instances, however, where the partner who is able to separate can help the other to achieve this developmental task so that the relationship can become hopeful again.

Clinical vignette: 2

Carol and Nathan, both professionals in their middle forties, were referred for couple therapy by Nathan's individual therapist. In our first session, Nathan stated, "We both have tough mothers." Carol vehemently agreed. He continued, "This is causing so much stress, it may be fatal to our marriage."

From the beginning of our work together, much of every session was spent on Carol's difficulties with what she perceived as an intrusive, demanding, and controlling mother. Throughout their marriage thus far, Nathan had been able to see how unmanageable this relationship was, but he felt helpless to do anything about it—even when his mother-in-law was moving furniture around in their living room! When any command performance, such as Mother's Day, was on the horizon, Carol would collapse into panic. I referred Carol for individual therapy as her problems with her mother were consuming a disproportionate amount of time in our sessions. This helped somewhat—but our work, which included Nathan, was what helped Carol most.

Nathan's family, who lived in the southern United States, was fairly conventional and financially comfortable. His father was the head of a large corporation and his mother did not work outside the home. He had an older brother and a younger sister, both of whom were married, had children, and lived not far from their parents. Nathan was the only one who had moved away.

Carol's family was quite different. She was the only child of professional parents; her father had abandoned the family when Carol was two years of age, after which she had very little contact with him. Unlike Nathan, she had experienced the trauma of parental separation. The mother and daughter had lived together in a sticky symbiotic unit, her mother adopting a "you-and-me-against-the-world" attitude. Yet Carol's mother was often outrageously mean to her and extremely critical of her. Carol was trapped in an insecure attachment to this hyperemotional, probably borderline, mother. Nathan's and Carol's method of dealing with Carol's mother had been to avoid her as much as possible, up to the time when they entered treatment; for example, they lied about when they went on vacation so that her mother would not "surprise" them by joining them, or make them feel guilty for not inviting her along. "Every decision I have ever made has been with my mother in mind. I don't know my own mind," Carol said.

When Nathan's parents came to visit, there were problems for both of them with his mother. Nathan's mother felt that Carol was overprotective of their children, as Carol did not trust them to be alone with the children on these visits. Despite this, Carol was told quite harshly that she was too lenient with the children in terms of discipline. Both Nathan's parents, but particularly his mother, repeatedly reminded them that they did not visit enough. Nathan had been brought up to honor and respect his parents, and to not go against them. Therefore, he felt guilty about having moved away and not having visited his parents as much as they would have liked. Carol's discomfort with them dictated the paucity of visits.

As our work progressed, Nathan, using both his individual therapy and the couple therapy, came to the realization that the "right" thing to do when his parents visited, or when he and

Carol traveled to see them, was to stand up for Carol—not his mother—particularly in terms of their children. This took some time and painful intrapsychic work. As we deconstructed his parents' visits to Canada, Nathan and Carol described going out of their way in preparation—planning time- and energy-consuming events, during which Nathan's mother never seemed happy and often complained of fatigue or physical illness. During our therapy, Nathan gained an understanding of his mother as suffering from a depression for which he was not the catalyst; he could then start to relate his mother's behavior to many events in his childhood. As he became more and more able to see the positive effect his new support had on Carol, he was determined to allow himself to change. Carol, for her part, now feeling supported, made every attempt to make the previously dreaded visits with Nathan's parents a better time for all of them. It is interesting how crowded the office can become in couple therapy.

There are often times when one or the other partner's parents—or, indeed, both—are in the room with us, as each partner's relationship with them is highlighted in a unique way, often quite differently from how we see it in individual work.

The situation with Carol and her mother reached a peak over a long holiday weekend, when Carol and Nathan and their children visited her mother at her country home, and had planned to see their own friends one day for lunch during that weekend. Hearing about this lunch with their friends, Carol's mother became enraged and a horrible fight ensued. When I heard this story in our next session, I advised that Carol take a break from seeing or speaking to her mother; her individual therapist concurred. Her mother's response to Carol's attempt to pull away was, "This is just like a divorce," thereby revealing her unconscious need for Carol as a spouse and life partner.

After this episode, Nathan was very much onside, and was able to understand Carol's tortuous dilemma—a seemingly intractable desire to meet her mother's needs, her unconscious conviction that she needed her mother to survive, and her low self-esteem and lack of confidence that were the result of her mother's constant criticism. Things then moved along more quickly. Nathan, feeling more valued by Carol as she no longer participated in conversations with her mother which excluded him, and as she put their relationship ahead of her mother's demands, could not only be genuinely helpful in supporting Carol's endeavors to free herself from the pathological enmeshment with her mother, but he could also provide Carol with a mature, loving, and healthy alternative.

At this point, Nathan terminated his individual therapy, although Carol remained in hers. Separation for Nathan was achieved more easily, in part because the dynamics in his family were not as pathological as those in Carol's family—his mother, although chronically unhappy was not sadistic, and his father was present. This had imbued him with more ego strength from his younger years. Perhaps being a male and having other siblings made it easier as well. Therefore, he was able to make use of the experiences in the two kinds of therapy more easily.

Mahler, Pine, and Bergman (1975), reporting on the practicing subphase in toddlers, found that girls have greater difficulty in resolving the rapprochement crisis than do boys. In her research, she found that boys were more able to turn away from the struggle with mother and invest their energy in the outside world; girls, on the other hand, were found to become more enmeshed in the struggle.

We are reminded in the above two examples of the importance of Modell's earlier (1965) concept of "the right to a life." He states, "The belief that one does not have the right to a life is a derivative of separation guilt. In those people who are burdened with intense ambivalence, from whatever source, separation is unconsciously perceived as resulting in the death of the object" (p. 328). Couples need to see that they have a right to a life together separate from parents. Of course, it is extremely difficult to separate from a parent who will not let go. However, due to a combination of factors, Nathan managed it even though his mother maintained that she still felt angry and abandoned. Were it not for the three therapies (his, hers, and ours) this relationship might not have survived the impingements of both families. However, in the case of Pamela and Tom, described earlier, not only was the lack of separation from their parents more ego syntonic and therefore less conflictual for both, but Tom had known that he wanted to leave the relationship from the beginning of the therapy; it was just a matter of his acknowledging that to himself and to Pamela. In this example, their mutual pathological involvement with their families of origin, which neither one was ready to relinquish, and which was partly manifested in their sexual difficulties, needed to be worked on intensively in individual treatment before either was ready for an intimate adult relationship.

Acting out: the affair

When I was first invited to contribute to a book entitled "Hopelessness", I thought this was definitely not going to be a best seller. Even hopelessness in treating couples is not something one necessarily wants to read about; and perhaps, especially, hopelessness in treating couples having affairs. However, since the chapter was given the title "Hope and hopelessness," I had some hope that the work involved in the writing could be productive for others in the reading.

Affairs, I have learned, are like dreams, and should be analyzed by the people who created them. Their origins lie in the latent unconscious of the individuals involved. As in other matters of this sort, the therapist cannot know what is right or wrong, and what anyone should or should not do. Partly for this reason, when I treat couples, I always see both partners together. This puts the issues squarely where they belong, between the two people, as much as possible, and not between one or the other of them and me. It also avoids the game of "I've got a secret," which if permitted, paradoxically, leaves the therapist in a position of decreased power, holding and withholding information.

There are many manifest reasons why affairs happen: Dissatisfaction with the relationship, either emotionally or sexually; unavoidable life stressors like a death or the loss of a job; babies and their libido-draining tendencies for the mother along with feelings of exclusion for the father; young children and the resultant decrease in opportunities for intimacy; a sick or incapacitated partner; financial strain; drug or alcohol abuse; and so on. And there are many varied outcomes that can occur as the result of an affair. The two examples that follow describe couples where the affair was, or became known to both partners, and where the issues involved were responsive to longer term, psychoanalytic couple therapy. Again, these examples are necessarily brief and omit significant parts of the therapy.

Clinical vignette: 3

Doug, a thirty-three-year-old designer stated that his family was "chaotic," describing the dinner table thus: "My mother can fly into unpredictable rages and terrify the rest of us; my sister (unemployed), is phobically anxious and often leaves the table in the middle of the meal to retreat to her room; and my father, often reads the newspaper at dinner."

When Maureen was in the latter part of a pregnancy, Doug had an affair with a colleague at work, who was described as very sexual, who dressed in a provocative manner, joked a lot about sex—and who eventually told everyone in the office about the affair. After the baby was born, the affair now (mostly) over, Doug and Maureen came for help with their relationship. I say "mostly" because, of course, it is never over for the partner who did not act.

During our work together, Doug became conscious of how different Maureen was from his mother, at least on the surface—controlled, and emotionally even—and said that these were qualities he had sought out in a partner. What was more difficult for him to acknowledge was how exciting his "crazy" mother had been for him, and how much he resented Maureen for her formerly admired "perfectness."

In these situations, the old adage that we team up with someone who possesses qualities we wish we had seemed true for both Doug and Maureen. Unfortunately when this happens, partners often drift to extreme ends of a shaky spectrum. The result is that they become unable to develop and nourish their other part—that part is allocated to their partner. Here, libidinous freedom, fun, and irresponsibility were the province of Doug; seriousness, rationality, and responsibility had become the province of Maureen—especially after the children were born. Although Maureen missed her former active, adventurous self, still she had felt secretly happy that she was the "good, responsible" one—that is, until the affair.

Since both partners wanted to stay together, we talked about their differences that had not been so noticeable until they had children. We also worked at uncovering Maureen's "wild" side and Doug's responsible side—which turned out not to be very difficult, since both had been vaguely missing these now "unknown" parts of their former selves. Doug, who had moved out of the home when the affair was discovered, was noticeably agitated in the therapy seeing Maureen's exhaustion from trying to care for their young children. After about two months, he moved back home, just to help. Time with his kids became a priority. He was feeling guilty and depressed, often crying in our sessions, and sought out his own individual therapy, although only briefly. As with all people who do "wrong," the remorse factor played a part in the forgiveness.

Even so, Maureen had enormous difficulty dealing with her incredible pain and anger at the betrayal. Their plans for a life together collapsed as her internal representation of Doug was destroyed. The disillusionment was almost palpable: He was not who she thought he was; they were not who she thought they were. She found herself breaking into uncontrollable rage, not at all characteristic of her, every time she thought about what had happened. She felt she would never be able to trust a close relationship with Doug again.

As time went on, and they were able to discuss their complaints about their relationship before the affair, Doug became noticeably calmer and more engaged in the sessions, often adding to the interpretations. Maureen began to feel cautiously optimistic. About eight months into treatment they planned a holiday together—something they had not done since their honeymoon. Doug took responsibility for the children and for ensuring Maureen was enjoying it. Maureen reported that she felt freer than she had for a long time, and Doug said happily that she was fun to be with.

As our work progressed following the holiday, Doug, feeling less defensive, was more willing to work at gaining an understanding of how and why the affair happened, and Maureen became more able to express her rage honestly and without fear of alienating Doug. This helped with her feelings of depression and hopelessness about the relationship. Both our exploration of their relationship before the affair, and their need to keep their family intact, contributed to their halting success.

Clinical vignette: 4

In another example, Janice and Bob, in their late forties, had been having relationship problems for some years when they came for therapy. Their sexual relationship had ended after the birth of their second child; their arguments at home, and in the session, were manifestly around putting out the garbage and buying groceries—for which Bob felt he did the lion's share. Both partners worked in demanding jobs. About three years earlier, Janice's mother, who lived in a nearby city, had become fatally ill. Janice had spent whatever time she could at her mother's side until her death about two months prior to their entering treatment. This illness and Janice's preoccupation with it had been the icing on a very bitter cake. Bob felt relegated to the bottom of Janice's list of priorities (mother, children, job, Bob), and saw himself as the parent of their children. In addition, he had lost his job about one year before and was trying to get his own business started.

About four months into couple treatment, Janice and Bob came to my office and rearranged my furniture. I have two chairs at an angle with a small round table in between. I sit opposite the chairs. Janice moved the round table out of the way, put the two chairs close together, and they held hands. She looked tired and very upset. "Bob has had an affair." Bob was crying, hiding his face in his hands.

Janice had found romantic and highly detailed sexual emails from Bob to another woman. After she discovered the emails, Bob had confessed to the affair, claiming it was now over, even though it had still been ongoing after our therapy had begun. In the intervening week, Janice had developed phobic anxiety—for example, she could no longer ride the subway—and had stopped sleeping. The very recent loss of her mother became conflated with her fear of losing her husband and her children.

Still, Janice was able to take an active role in working through the situation. She contacted the husband of the other woman, whom she had not known before, and they shared emails. They met for coffee and talked about how they felt. The other couple was now heading for separation, but Janice felt that she and Bob had a stronger foundation and she wanted to stay with him. She related to us that she took pleasure in having the upper hand at last in her relationship with Bob, as he was the one who was guilty. As the therapy progressed, Janice talked more about her own difficulties with intimacy, and Bob revealed that losing his job had been so awful for him that he had not been able to confide in her, feeling he should be "cheerful" for her and for the children. He began to understand how this narcissistic injury had been soothed by the excitement and overvaluation of the affair.

In both the above cases, it happened that the women had been distracted for some years before the affairs occurred: Maureen was preoccupied with academic work when not with the children. Janice had tried to be with her dying mother as much as possible. Both men felt they were not important to their partners or appreciated by them. Both men had experiences they had not had in early adulthood: Doug in promoting his business which involved travel, dinners, and parties with his fellow employees; Bob, in dealing with his first "failure"—losing his job. In both of these examples, it could seem that the men had married Madonnas and had affairs with, well, let us just say, women who were seen as sexually freer.

For both partners in a romantic relationship, the shift from the swirling idealization of a new love to the reality of the actual person can be difficult, and sometimes impossible. Dicks (1967) describes this idealization as the main defense mechanism in couple relationships, as it makes love "blind." Can both people keep their partner front and center when life intervenes? Idealization involves the unconscious projection on to the chosen lover of the features of an ideal image, whether or not he or she actually has these qualities. This idealization often becomes strained and continued disappointment may be evident for both. Altman (1977) describes the process of deidealization in this way:

> In latency and adolescence, love acquires more intensely instinctualized altruistic and self-seeking components—components that war with each other. A little later, in the full flush of the springtime of love, love will surmount all obstacles—nothing must stand in its way. It is a compulsion. For the moment, love for someone other than oneself has the upper hand. Then marriage—husband, wife, children—puts love to new tests. No small bitterness crops up at the dashing of expectations. The love object is found to be in default of all those perfections attributed to it by overestimation—that projection of one's own narcissism; now, taking inventory, the stock is found to be short. (p. 40)

The partners' reactions to the inevitable deidealization may be different, and this difference may lead to serious problems in the relationship, and at times, to the acting out of one or both of them, seeking a new love who can be more easily idealized.

The other part is maintaining passion. In the late Stephen Mitchell's book, *Can Love Last?* (2002), he states that love and marriage may go together like a horse and carriage, but it is crucial that the horse of passion be tethered by the rein of reality acceptance. His answer to the question in his title is: Yes; but passion cannot. Mitchell maintains that our needs for safety and passion are conflicting—since deadness is a requirement for security. Perhaps this is part of what affected the couples described above. "Passionlessness in long-term relationships is often a consequence not of the extinguishing of a flame but of collusive efforts to keep the relationship inert in a sodden stasis" (p. 55). What is so dangerous about desiring someone you love, in Mitchell's words, in "full frontal intimacy," is that you can lose him or her.

If the efforts are, indeed, collusive, then we can see how a lack of passion appears to keep the relationship together. In the above examples, there appears to be no collusion. However, when the years leading up to the affair are explored deeply, at least some unconscious collusion is evident. Both the above couples were in the stage of having young children which, as it happened, tied the women to the home fires, and concomitantly to a lack of passion. Having lost their once energetic and sexy partners, the men seemed to bristle at this stage of life. It happens in both of the above examples that it was the male partners who had the difficulty tethering the horse of passion to the reality of acceptance. When one or the other partner feels unappreciated and hence unloved—for men or women it may be a reaction to children, or a reaction to their partners' immersion in work—then most couples become vulnerable and that vulnerability is manifested in various ways.

Hope and hopelessness in the countertransference with couples

Countertransference reactions in couple therapy can be more powerful and are certainly more complex than in individual treatment. Therapists have to be aware of the responses evoked by each patient and by the couple as a whole, as they witness and try to understand the partners' often rageful, defensive, and confusing interactions. Unresolved oedipal issues can run rampant in the threesome. The therapist often feels like the parent, at least at first, with two siblings struggling to establish their position of "good one/bad one." Unconscious fantasies or memories of the primal scene may be evoked in the therapist, who is privy to the details of a couple's sexual life. Interestingly, envy, often seen as insidious and destructive, may be particularly virulent in the countertransference in treating couples. West and Schain-West (1997) enumerate many patient qualities of which a therapist can be envious, including wealth, children, family support, the ability to love and be loved. Just having a relationship is sometimes enviable, depending on the therapist's current status—single, recently divorced, or possibly in an unhappy situation.

The therapist's own developmental progress in resolving oedipal, separation, and intimacy issues will, of course, influence an unconscious reaction to the couple's plight. If the therapist overidentifies with a partner's need to separate from a clinging parent before he or she is ready, for example, this can be confusing for one partner and may be seen as support for the other partner, even though it is not intended. One partner may remind the therapist of a parent or sibling; a therapist may be attracted to, or repulsed by one of the partners; or a therapist may feel forced into a "child" role, either because this is the defensive pattern the couple uses in difficult situations or because the therapist is in need of parenting.

Hope and hopelessness are certainly a large part of the couple therapist's conscious and unconscious countertransference. Most therapists consciously hope to be able to help the partners to understand and resolve their problematic issues and ride off into the sunset together—if indeed, that is, what the partners want. Some couples inspire more hope than others.

One of the ways of staying conscious of the hope and hopelessness generated in the countertransference is for the therapist to be acutely aware of each partner's agenda when entering treatment: Do they both want to stay together? Does one partner want to get out and is hoping to accomplish this "gently" by being in therapy? Has one partner brought the other in for treatment, as the other is seen as the cause of all the problems? Are one or both hoping for permission to end the relationship? Although it may be more usual for a therapist to have the countertransference hope that the couple will stay together—provided, of course, that the relationship is not abusive to either partner in any way—couple therapists must stay alert to the possibility that the relationship may not work.

Conclusion

In some ways, analytic couple therapy, by its very nature, democratizes the psychoanalytic situation. The atmosphere is always fluid—and naturally lively and current. As we look at hope and hopelessness in treating couples, we become aware of the reciprocal affect that the people in the room—including the therapist—continuously exert on each other. Because mutuality is highlighted in couple therapy, there can be a kind of contagion operating, where feelings of hope and hopelessness on the part of any one of the three participants influence the other two. This, and the other complexities discussed in this chapter, present the couple therapist with an intriguing challenge.

"One should be able to see things as hopeless and yet be determined to make it otherwise" (F. Scott Fitzgerald).

CHAPTER TEN

Hopelessness in the countertransference

Dhwani Shah

The experience of hopelessness is a frequent visitor to the analytic setting. Freud's (1937c) referring to psychoanalysis as an "impossible profession" (p. 248) became commonplace over time and took some of the sting out of this remarkable aspect of our clinical work. Nonetheless, the struggles of working with our experiences of hopelessness in day-to-day encounters with our patients remain largely unspoken. After all, hopelessness is a difficult and exhausting experience to endure. It has a certain cognitive certainty in the way it feels which can undermine the inherent vitality and exploration in the analytic space. A peculiar deadening feeling emerges and takes hold. The experience of a sinking sensation in one's abdomen or tightness in the pit of one's stomach is common, sometimes accompanied by feeling slightly dizzy or faint. One feels gripped by a sense of there being no chance for growth or change. In contrast to an open and vibrant atmosphere filled with vitality and play (or, an angry arena where battle lines are sharply drawn), the experience of hopelessness is characterized by a sense of rigidity and deadness. Time feels warped and at a standstill; there is an agonizing sense of paralysis of movement and flow, which leaves the analyst feeling trapped and helpless. Human bonds with the patient collapse and the analyst feels absorbed in his own endless rumination of there being no possibility of intimacy or relationship. Distressing negative thoughts often occur, such as "This treatment is going nowhere," or "This is a failure." An atmosphere of doom inhabits the analytic space and can lead to feelings of anxiety and inadequacy.

This is in sharp contrast to what takes place during an ordinary and expectable analytic hour. Under such calm circumstances, there is a constant dynamic interaction between the patient and the analyst with each party emotionally affecting the other. In order for the analytic space to be a place of growth and transformation, the analyst strives to navigate between his experiences of doubt, uncertainty, and confusion to arrive at an understanding of what is happening and in the process help the patient have an in-depth experience of his psychic life. In contemporary analytic theory, there is general agreement that countertransference is an unavoidable and indispensible tool the analyst can use in the service of furthering the analytic process. Such consensus has only gradually evolved, though. Over the course of psychoanalytic theorizing, three perspectives on countertransference have been noticeable: (i) in traditional usage, countertransference was viewed as an obstacle to the analytic process, based on one's own personal history and biases that interfere with free floating attention and unconscious communication between the patient and the analyst (Freud, 1910d); (ii) then, countertransference came to be regarded as a consequence of projective identification of the patient's self or internalized objects (Heimann, 1950; Racker, 1957) and therefore a helpful source for understanding the patient's internal world, and, finally, (iii) countertransference was posited to be a reverie-based method of emotional containment for the patient's unbearable affects and fantasies (Bion, 1963; Oelsner, 2013). In the emotional storm created in the analytic space between our patients and ourselves, we use our reactions as guides in assisting us with our fundamental analytic task: the promotion of psychic development and growth. We do our best to invite into our mind the experiences of conviction and doubt, certainty and confusion, and vitality and deadness to allow for the relational analytic process to take hold. We retain optimism and safeguard our imagination of a patient who is less replete with ego deficits and more free of neurotic inhibitions. Similar to an artist who "sees" the shape and image of what she is about to create, analysts also envision what patients would be like with the lessening of the burden of neurotic misery (Akhtar, 2009; Loewald, 1960).

The collapse of this very analytic vision constitutes the essence of hopelessness. When hopelessness invades the analytic space, what before was seen as possibility and success in imagining a future collapses. In an often rigid and concrete fashion, there feels as if there is no vision or potential for growth. Our analytic vision stumbles and we are left with a pervasive sense of stupor and dead ends with no possibility of creation. This can occur with varying levels of severity and conviction; even the degree of awareness of one's hopelessness can vary. For the sake of conceptual clarity, it may be useful to separate "acute" experiences of hopelessness that occur unexpectedly and then recede out of consciousness from "chronic" forms of hopelessness experienced in situations described as impasses, stalemates, or "negative therapeutic reactions" (Freud, 1923b). These difficult situations often lead to profound struggles and inevitable enactments that can place a heavy burden on the analytic space and disrupt the analyst's equilibrium. These struggles often lead to defensive reactions on the part of the analyst which can, in turn, lead to further disruptions. The aim of this contribution is to bring into focus these difficult experiences and to aid the reader in making use of them to guide treatment and restore analytic vision.

Acute hopelessness

During the moment-to-moment flow of an analytic session, the analyst receives and experiences a flow of associative material, emotional reactions, and wishful impulses as useful guides in aiding the analytic process. Often the analyst is gripped with an emotion or a stream of thought, which on the surface does not have a direct counterpoint in the patient's associative material. However, being responsive to such reactions and observing them carefully can lead to a deeper emotional understanding of a patient's internal conflicts and internalized objects, especially when there is an intensity to our reactions that does not correspond to the clinical situation (Racker, 1957).

At this point, a note of caution is warranted: An analyst's reaction to the patient is actually the amalgam of his own reaction and the patient's associations and behaviors (in their relational coconstructed space) that have led to that reaction. As Renik (2006) notes: "An analyst's perceptions are constantly influenced by a variety of conscious and unconscious idiosyncratic factors, and the analyst can never know, in any given moment, to what degree or entirely in what manner his or her listening is being shaped by highly personal thoughts and feelings of which he or she is unaware" (p. 88).

Concrete explanations for countertransference reactions such as "He put his anger inside of me and made me feel angry" can be helpful when the analyst has been flooded by his emotional reactions to his patient and requires a method of creating an observing space to restore analytic balance and treatment, but these explanations can also be used defensively to avoid more personal and painful fantasies the analyst suffers when difficult situations unconsciously begin to affect the analyst's narcissistic balance. The analyst might then be tempted to believe that his subjective conscious reaction is concretely related to the patient's direct experience. Fink (2007), highlighting this danger, writes:

> The underlying assumption—that the analyst knows herself so well that she knows what part of her reaction to the analysand is subjective and what part of it is objective—is fundamentally flawed; for the analyst continues not to know all of her own motives even after a very lengthy analysis—such is the nature of the unconscious. (p. 187)

Falling into concrete explanations of one's countertransference reactions often comes in the form of an empathic rupture with the patient when the analyst is listening to something new or unexpected which can make him lose his bearings, or when his formulation of a moment in treatment no longer applies to what he is listening to in the session (Faimberg, 2001, 2013; Fink, 2007). Turning to theory-based countertransference explanations can often be a defensive rationalization when the analyst is faced with doubt or the unknown. As Schwaber (2005) notes, we strive "listening to learn what we don't yet know, to linger with a nuance that might not fit our course, that might indeed reveal to us that we were not listening … in this … open ended effort (p. 791).

With this caution in mind, acute experiences of hopelessness in the analyst can be valuable guides in uncovering previously unfelt conflicts and fantasies. One aspect of hopelessness that can enter the analytic space is a profound and sometimes sudden sense of doubt in the analyst's mind—doubt about whether the treatment will work, or if the analyst is even "getting it," that is, understanding what the patient is trying to communicate. The sense of knowing, having insight or meaning, is lost in this moment and a disturbing feeling of confusion invades the analyst's mind. This can occur if the patient's associations do not seem to follow any psychic logic and are vague and incoherent, or the patient's tone of voice and manner of speech convey hopelessness and defeat. In these moments, the analyst's reaction of doubt and confusion might convey an unconscious communication from the patient. Feldman (2009) writes persuasively about such communication of doubt in the moment-to-moment interactions in the analytic space in the analyst. He notes:

> In addition to the inevitable and appropriate doubts about his understanding and his work, the analyst is subjected to conscious and unconscious pressures from the patient, the aim of which seems to be to fill him with uncertainty, confusion and doubt ... it is a means of communicating something important about the nature of the patient's state of mind, his internal objects and their relationships. It may be a way of drawing the analyst into sharing a disturbing state of mind ... on the other hand, the patient may project his own uncertainty into the analyst's mind freeing himself to embrace a state of manic confidence ... finally, the patient may be driven by hatred and envy to attack the analyst's state of mind and derive perverse gratification from this process. (p. 217)

The analyst's capacity to serve emotionally as a container for these unbearable experiences necessitates him to first fully experience them and then "recover" back to his reflective stance to continue the analytic work: "It is important to recognize the extent to which this process reflects elements of the patient's state of mind, and represents the patient's need to have this recognized and experienced by the analyst ... the analyst's capacity to reflect, in due course, on this situation, may enable him to deepen his understanding of the patient" (Feldman, 2009, p. 230).

The acute experience of hopelessness in the analyst can also serve as a signal for the possibility of unfelt loss and mourning on the part of the patient. In a process of "concordant identification" (Racker, 1957), the analyst might experience the patient's unfelt grief over an early loss, as well as possible defenses against the grief. As will be discussed in detail under chronic hopeless countertransferences, the experience of hopelessness can paradoxically be a method of expressing grief, but also warding off the intense pain and helplessness of true mourning, which requires confronting not only the loss of the loved one but the fantasied hopes and dreams that were connected with the longed-for object. Negativity and hopelessness as concrete realities can be clung to as a source of solace and control: "Fascination with the negative preserves the exciting, the perverse, magically omnipotent illusion that one can control what is uncontrollable" (Coen, 2003, p. 465). Woven into the experience of hopelessness is both the expression of the loss and pain it caused as well as a method in which the patient shields himself from the helplessness and pain of the loss.

Clinical vignette: 1

Lamar, a twenty-four-year-old first generation Jamaican American PhD graduate student in art history, sought consultation for chronic symptoms of low energy, low motivation, and difficulty with concentration in the context of his engagement breaking off one year prior. After a two-year engagement to his girlfriend of over seven years, the relationship ended after Lamar learned of his girlfriend's infidelity. Struggling to get through the day and finish his thesis, Lamar denied feeling sad about his loss, noting "I was sad for a while, now I feel just numb to it." After several sessions of hearing his struggles with writing his dissertation thesis described in a dry, emotionally disconnected manner, I struggled to feel emotionally engaged with him and emotionally involved. His content lacked emotional depth; he appeared to be focused on his work, and wanted help with tips on breaking through his writer's block. During one particular moment where he was again describing the details of what he needed to do to complete his thesis chapter, I suddenly felt a surge of hopelessness within me that lasted several seconds. It felt as though there was nothing left to feel, nothing to connect the two of us. In that moment, in a concrete way I felt there was nothing I could do for him—he was lost to me emotionally and I felt like an observer, watching him from a distance, with no possibility of engaging or being with him. After a moment of recovery, I reflected on my reaction. Was this hopeless reaction on my part a way of expressing my anger toward him for disrupting my feeling of needing to be helpful? On further reflection, I remembered that he had mentioned that before the breakup with his fiancée, they would sit and study together in their apartment on their bed, side by side, he introducing her to his favorite artists from Jamaica. Perhaps my sudden emotional reaction reflected his feeling of being excluded and cast aside by her, with no possibility of connection or mutual engagement. It occurred to me at that moment that Lamar's dry, emotionally disconnected manner of relating was also a method of warding off more painful affects of loss and helplessness that felt too unbearable to feel. Exploring Lamar's frozen grief and longing led to a deepening of the treatment and to further fantasies of lost hopes from his difficult childhood transitions to America without a consistent paternal figure and their connection with the sudden loss of his lover.

Chronic hopelessness

In contrast to acute moments of hopelessness, which the analyst can transiently experience and then recover from so as to aid with the analytic process, chronic experiences of hopelessness can cause significant disruptions in the analytic work and can strain the analyst's capacity to remain engaged with the patient. The literature on impasses, negative therapeutic reactions, chronic narcissistic transferences, and "stuck" or "bogged down" analyses all speak to the difficult countertransference experiences the analyst endures in these circumstances. In these difficult moments, the analyst feels trapped in a one-dimensional space where there is no experience of growth or possibility of play—only hopelessness and dead space are permitted. Any positive movement or authentic intimacy is quickly dismissed and defended against by the patient. The message that seems to be omnipresent toward the analyst is "You mean nothing to me, this relationship is nothing." Serious disruptions in the analyst's professional ego ideal (Giovacchini, 1993) can affect one's ability to maintain a therapeutic responsiveness to the patient; such reactive countertransference reactions can become truly difficult to manage. It is only with the passage of time and bearing considerable emotional strain that the analyst can find meaning in such a hopeless atmosphere. He might discern that all this had reflected an immersion in the unconscious roles assigned to him by the patient and find a path forward, from within the patient's worldview, to temporarily stand outside of the stuck pattern and move the analysis forward (Chaplan, 2013).

The chronic hopeless countertransference, although difficult to bear, becomes a valuable tool in understanding the patient's inner conflicts and resistances.

> Relentless, prolonged quality of repetitive, "signature" patterns of interaction in the analyses, sometimes leading to the analyst's feeling at wit's end. Relief occurs only when the analyst grasps something preconscious, just beyond the pair's immediate communication ... the stuckness morphs into something "the same only slightly different," a sign of growth within the heart of the entanglement. (Chaplan, 2013, p. 593)

The analyst strives to make some meaning of this misery and emptiness only to find himself often confused and shut out. Amati-Mehler and Argentieri (1989) eloquently speak this experience:

> With a feeling of weariness, the analyst too analysed her own painful sense of frustration, impotence, exasperation and irritation; the sense of challenge launched by such overt despair and the desire to meet the challenge and to fight the destructiveness of inertia and failure; above all, the authentic sense of compassion for the patient and the wish to understand the sense of this stubborn mechanism. It is only through time and considerable emotional strain that the analyst can find meaning in the hopeless atmosphere. (p. 296)

When reviewing the literature on these hopelessly stuck analytic situations, several themes emerge. A common thread throughout the literature pertains to the secret unspoken and unfelt hopefulness that lies buried in the bitter bosom of the patient's overt hopelessness (Amati-Mehler & Argentieri, 1989). The stereotyped atmosphere of despair paradoxically carries a deep unconscious hope, that what was lost in early (often preverbal) childhood can be regained: "The analysis and the analyst are invested with an unrealistic task, which consists in preserving the illusion that what is past or lost forever can still be provided and restored. The perpetuation of this demand, accompanied by resentment about the lack of its fulfillment, is the extreme defense against the threat of separation" (Amati-Mehler & Argentieri, 1989, p. 302).

The desperate unconscious longing to regain what has been lost cancels "realistic hope" and creates a stuck scenario where the patient and analyst can be bound forever in fantasy. Experiencing genuine hopefulness would mean a catastrophic rupture from this rigid and timeless fantasy of being united with the idealized lost object from childhood. Omnipotent hope and hopelessness are conjoined in these moments:

> The paradox lies in the necessity to have both opposites coexist. There is no alternative intermediary space between how "it was" and how "it should be"; pathological hope cancels realistic hope and gives way to hopelessness. Real chances available in life are dismissed, or rather not recognized, because they do not fit the rigid model that illusion pretends to realize ... In fact ... it seems as if the resentment and the mournful complaint represented the last and unique possible tie with the primary object, and as if giving this up would mean the definite downfall of illusion and the admission that it is really, truly lost. An interminable analysis thus, as we said before, or even an interminable chain of subsequent analyses, can serve to guarantee oneself a perfect accomplice to keep this pathological hope alive. (Amati-Mehler & Argentieri, 1989, p. 302)

In describing these "someday" and "if only" fantasies, Akhtar (1996) notes that the analyst's task is in helping the patient transition from pathological hope to realistic hope, the danger being a worsening of clinging to the "stuck" pattern of hopelessness. Carefully and with considerable patience and tact, the analyst's assistance in identifying and making inordinate hope conscious can lead to a transformation of such fantasies. However, fixed chronic experiences of hopelessness sometimes necessitate a "rupturing" of his hope by the analyst, confirming the irreversibility of the situation (Akhtar, 1996; Amati-Mehler & Argentieri, 1989). Using one's own emotional experience is a valuable tool in this process, as the following case demonstrates.

Clinical vignette: 2

> Beth, a forty-eight-year-old third generation Irish American librarian with two children, began treatment with me after the collapse of her marriage of twenty years due to her husband's frequent violent outbursts and substance abuse. She reported recurrent depressive symptoms, constant anxiety, and chronic difficulties

with recurrent muscular pain throughout her upper body and abdomen which had gone undiagnosed and treated periodically with steroid medications by her rheumatologist. Beth described her past as filled with disappointments and rejections. Beth's mother struggled with psychotic depression throughout her life and died suddenly, isolated and living alone. She felt her mother was distant and critical of her growing up and favored her more attractive younger sister and older brother. Although her father was occasionally experienced as charming and seductive, he was often emotionally absent and had multiple affairs with other women, that confused Beth and left her feeling betrayed. Highly educated and verbal, Beth was eager to begin psychotherapy and readily agreed to an analysis after several months of treatment with some relief of her symptoms. After two months into the analysis, however, Beth's depression, anxiety, and chronic pain returned with full force and filled her with despair after a romantic disappointment with a man she had met online. She described constant unremitting anxiety and pain, and was unable to obtain any relief from medications. Beth filled the analytic hours with descriptions of her suffering and her anger at her ex-husband for abandoning her, as well as her frustration at others whom she felt could not help her. Any attempts to empathically engage Beth or interpret her hurt and frustration left her feeling more alone and misunderstood. She began to feel hopeless about the analytic process and wondered if it was useful at all. What had started as a promising treatment for Beth now felt dead and lifeless to her. I began to feel a deep sense of despair and hopelessness with Beth that was difficult to bear. Time felt frozen and no possibility of growth or change felt possible. A feeling of confusion and unreality took hold of me and I had difficulty understanding what was happening between us. Any moments of genuine reflection or closeness between us quickly eroded into doubts and despair about the process.

After several months of hearing Beth's unremitting agony, a disturbing image of a lifeless corpse in a morgue being beaten over and over again by an anonymous stranger repeatedly entered my mind and stayed with me during these difficult moments. At first thought, I felt the image represented Beth beating me, a dead analyst, over and over again with her hopelessness as an expression of her aggression and envy toward me. Reflecting further, it occurred to me that it was my own anger toward Beth that was being expressed. Perhaps this sadistic fantasy was a way of allowing me some connection with her during moments when I experienced being completely shut out from her, "beating" some life into our relationship. Regardless of what the image meant, I felt it was important to bear these difficult fantasies and to struggle with empathically staying close to her inner experience despite the worsening deadening atmosphere. Several sessions after this event, Beth flatly stated being in analysis was like "beating a dead horse," with no hope for any change. She then associated to loving riding horses when she visited her aunt in Connecticut when she was twelve; there was a feeling of excitement and exhilaration that she lost as an adult. The image of Beth, free and hopeful with excitement resonated with me but then I suddenly remembered my own image of a stranger beating a dead body. Was this image of our relationship comfortable for me? It occurred to me that I was distancing myself from Beth. I was surprised to realize that I felt uncomfortable being close to Beth's exhilaration and excitement and my body language and tone of voice probably reflected this on some level. Perhaps I was experiencing what Beth experienced growing up: Being helpless and confused, without any relatedness except for beating on what was already dead. Perhaps this represented the experience of her mother's psychotic withdrawal. However, on a more unconscious level it also felt as though I was enacting and identifying with the image of her critical and distant mother who felt uncomfortable with closeness with Beth. This realization allowed me to regain my analytic attitude and notice the way in which I colluded with Beth's protection of herself from her longings of intimacy with me. Later in the analysis, this hopelessness was also revealed as a secret wish to having her mother embrace her, never letting her go. Letting go of hopelessness meant letting go of the hope that she could attain some level of intimacy with her mother that she always dreamed of having, and experiencing the psychic terror of self-annihilation and abandonment without her. Being locked in a hopeless struggle with me preserved this fantasy.

Related to the unconscious fantasies of returning to longed-for experiences of primary union is the countertransference experience of time being frozen. In contrast to the expected ebb and flow of time found in a typical analytic encounter, it feels as though time stands still in these moments. The analyst feels caught in an eternal dead space. The defensive aims of this time standstill include the patient's wish to arrest growth, to avoid change, to postpone adulthood, and to preserve archaic rescue fantasies (Akhtar, 1993; Amati-Mehler & Argentieri, 1989; Orgel, 2012; Wurmser, 2012). The experience of frozen time might also be a method of defending against psychic dissolution and trauma (Giovacchini, 1993, Schmithusen, 2012). This central traumatic experience, which the analyst reexperiences in the countertransference, is a representation and a defense against an early traumatic situation where time is arrested in the present to avoid being confronted again with the breakdown which occurred in infancy. The patient wards off this primal terror of annihilation (which is unconsciously a part of his experience) by rendering the analyst an inaccessible dead object which results in his experience of time standstill:

> The phenomenon of time standing still is brought about due to a radical defense. Through this phenomenon, defenses are actively brought into play, which prevents any further development of the catastrophic fear that developed when the child was separated from the maternal object at a time before the ego was consolidated. This fear of reexperiencing a traumatic psychic breakdown derives from a severely traumatic experience which took place in the past at a time when the immature psychic apparatus was overwhelmed and internalized ... This standstill in time is the result of a defense against an underlying, nonsymbolized and as such incomprehensible fear of annihilation or fear of psychic death, and at the same time it is a precise repetition of this earlier relationship of psychic annihilation that takes place in the transference relationship. The standstill in time is an attempt to deny the reality of circular, cyclic, as well as linear time and therefore to negate development.
> (Schmithusen, 2012, p. 70)

Introducing the temporal element into the analysis by discussing the passing of years and the end of things (including in some cases the analysis) can lead to a premature retraumatization of the patient. However, if the analyst's holding functions are firmly in place and if sufficient time for mourning has been allowed, then utilizing this countertransference experience for interpretive purposes can deepen the patient's moorings in the temporal dimension of experience and the reality of linear time.

Reactions to the patient's hopelessness

Reviewing the literature on countertransference reactions to these emotionally challenging clinical scenarios, several common themes emerge. The analyst, feeling the weight of hopelessness and negativity enveloping the analytic space, and for himself difficult to bear, feels an oppressive environment and a need to act or escape. Often these reactions are responses to a disruption of the analyst's sense of self and professional identity or the analytic setting. There is a temporary loss of the observing analytic self, where one's own emotional reactions can be used in the service of deepening the analytic experience for the patient.

Countertransference disturbances usually involve threats to the analyst's professional self-representation, the analyst's mode of operation, and the analytic setting itself (Giovacchini, 1993). A constant bombardment of misery, pessimism, and doubt in the analytic setting feels intrusive and disruptive of the analytic process, even if there are no overt attempts or demands on the patient's part. Unconsciously, the analyst might feel that the patient is not providing the necessary feedback the analyst needs to feel secure in his analytic role, and experiences the patient's hopelessness as an assault on his sense of self and identity. As Giovacchini (1993) notes, "Patients, of course, have no obligation to make their therapists happy or avoid upsetting their narcissistic balance. Nevertheless, analysts are human, and they will react to certain situations regardless of their professional orientation" (p. 162). This painful narcissistic injury can then lead the analyst to defensively protect himself, which can lead to a disruption of the analytic setting. The analyst, unable to bear this injury, feels compelled to either *under-respond* or *over-respond* to his internal feelings of misery and despair.

Under-responsiveness to hopelessness

As described above, intractable narcissistic transferences in patients with melancholia, severe trauma, somatoform disorders, or other narcissistic states can lead to a deadening of the analytic space. The analyst feels bored or pushed aside. The patient's speech and manner of relating creates an effect in the analyst that he is not being related to; instead, the analyst feels as if he is an "excluded observer," shut out from the relating to the patient (Steiner, 2011). In these moments, there is a disembodied quality to the analytic space which may be difficult to tolerate. The analyst is tempted to escape from this experience by withdrawing inward. Daydreaming, sleepiness, frequent glances at the clock, allowing the patient to "just keep talking until time runs out" are emotional tactics aimed at managing the hopeless and deadening atmosphere. They can also be means of expressing hatred toward the patient—an experience that can cause much guilt and anxiety if fully felt. In their classic paper on hate and countertransference, Maltsberger and Buie (1974) describe countertransference hate as a mixture of aversion and malice. They argue that the aversive component of hatred is the fundamentally most dangerous because the aversive impulse tempts the therapist to psychologically abandon the patient. Narcissistic transferences, threats of suicide, and assaults on the analyst's ideal can lead to uncomfortably intense countertransference reactions that are often unconsciously defended against and avoided:

> There is a tendency to daydream about being elsewhere doing something else with someone else. Subjectively, the therapist may be aware of some anxiety and restlessness, or possibly he may find himself drowsy. He may feel bored. While this defense offers little scope for acting out of the unconscious or preconscious hostility, the therapist may well convey his aversion to the patient by yawning, glancing too often and too obviously at his clock, or by other signs of inattention, conveying nonverbally to his patient, "I do not want to be with you." (p. 639)

Another method of avoiding a direct experience of hatred in these difficult clinical circumstances is turning hate against the self and having fantasies of self-devaluation and degradation. Chronic doubt, feelings of worthlessness, and hopelessness in the analyst can serve as "masochistic retreats" away from the patient and cause a direct experience of frustration and hatred toward the patient, which could render the analyst with feelings of unbearable guilt and shame. This turning inward can then be interpreted as a rejection from the patient, which can lead to further defensiveness and acting out.

Over-reactiveness to hopelessness

The analytic attitude of free floating attention to both the patient's transferences and the analyst's own countertransference reactions can be put in jeopardy when the analysis feels like it is in a hopeless quagmire of deadness and doubt. The analyst, overcome with hopelessness and doubt, can feel the temptation to "do something." Often this impulse is not fully felt by the analyst until it is satisfied. One might have certitude in one's convictions which feel hurried, or a certain pressure in one's body to act or perform some task for the patient. Giovacchini (1993) describes this experience well:

> The therapist feels confused and anxious because he does not understand what is going on ... he feels helpless and frustrated and is overcome by an impulse to do something. He struggles, out of his anxiety, to give himself and the patient relief ... the function of interpretation in these difficult circumstances is not to expand understanding ... rather, the interpretation is designed to make the analyst feel better and to halt the patient's protestations and manifestations of psychopathology ... the patient, instead of feeling understood, only senses and receives the anxious parts of the interpretation. (p. 30)

Of historical note, Hinshelwood (2013) argues that this type of countertransference may have occurred in Freud's (1918b) treatment of the Wolf Man: Frustrated by his "obliging apathy," lack of self sufficiency, and passivity, "Freud was provoked to take action on the basis of the emotional state of frustration ... having been provoked, Freud's irritation and impatience led him to become active" (p. 91).

Subjectively, the analyst in the moment of giving the interpretation often feels a firm sense of conviction and certitude; it is only on later reflection that he realizes the defensive nature of the interpretation. Britton and Steiner (1994) refer to this phenomenon as an overvalued idea on the part of the analyst:

> It is recognized that an observation which may at the time be convincing to the analyst, and even perhaps to the patient, is often inaccurate and sometimes mistaken. Among such errors some are determined by the defensive needs of the analyst, and we refer to this type of false insight as an *overvalued idea*. An awareness of the possibility that an insight may be an *overvalued idea* helps to alert the analyst to the need to sustain doubt and to examine subsequent clinical material to evaluate his understanding. At the same time it is clearly important that the analyst interprets with conviction, so that

his capacity to entertain doubt must exist alongside a willingness to commit himself to a point of view which seems right at the time, and yet be willing to relinquish this view if subsequent evidence demands it. The experience of a moment of insight or discovery may give a sense of excitement and achievement to the analyst, but it is our experience that once uttered the interpretation often loses some of its conviction and that the importance of doubt, guilt and other feelings associated with the depressive position are an inevitable part of the experience. (p. 1070)

Paradoxically, unfelt hopelessness by the analyst can lead to defensive certainty in one's therapeutic actions which on retrospect feel forced or one dimensional. Steiner (2011), in his paper, "Helplessness and the Exercise of Power in the Analytic Session," describes this phenomenon as "narcissistic helpfulness." Rapid interpretations given with a degree of certainty and a quickening pace can be a clue that this type of "helpfulness" is operating in the analytic space. The aim of the intervention by the analyst unconsciously is not to deepen the analytic process, but to give the analyst and patient relief from the unbearable experience that is occurring between them, often involving a state of complete helplessness and vulnerability. As Steiner notes:

> My over-activity concealed an inner feeling of helplessness. I could see that I was colluding with the patient's phantasm of omnipotent repair and that I too had been trying to prevent a disaster and restore the patient to reason. It then became possible for me to admit to myself that I could not protect the patient from his acting out, and my feeling of helplessness gave way to sadness … once I accepted my helplessness, I seemed to be able to be more thoughtful. (p. 126)

Steiner goes on to say that narcissistic helpfulness is rarely successful because it ignores the actual needs of the object. It also involves a concrete type of thinking in which the object has to be materially restored, and as a result it betrays omnipotent fantasy rather than genuine reparation. This defensive reaction on the part of the analyst is often experienced in the treatment of trauma survivors, where as a defense against the unbearable feeling of helplessness felt with the patient, the therapist unconsciously attempts to assume the role of the omnipotent rescuer

(Herman, 1992). These temptations also exist in analyzing the patient's pathologically "hopeful" early childhood fantasies of union and symbiosis. There may be an urge to rescue the patient, colluding with the omnipotent fantasy, or actively interpreting the defenses too quickly in an effort to ward off one's own unfelt hopelessness. As Akhtar (1996) notes:

> ... the analyst must be highly vigilant toward his own emotional experience. The informative potential of counter-transference in such cases is considerable. Since the idealization inherent in "someday" and "if only" fantasies is not easily verbalized by the patient, often the analyst has to decipher it through his own feelings. Within transference, the analyst is invested by these patients with the task of preserving an illusion. This puts pressure on the analyst. On the one hand, there is the temptation to actively rescue the patient. On the other hand, there is the allure of quickly showing the patient that his expectations are unrealistic, serve defensive aims. Cloaked in the guise of therapeutic zeal, hasty attempts of this sort often emanate from the analyst's own unresolved narcissism and infantile omnipotence. (p. 743)

The quickening pace of one's experience with the patient and the urge to act are often clues to this process of "narcissistic helpfulness" occurring in the analytic space. There is a concrete zeal and excitement about "figuring it out" or "finally getting to something important" that can be intoxicating because it eliminates the dreadful hopeless atmosphere pervading the relationship. Allowing oneself to recognize the unfelt hopelessness that can feel unbearable to the analyst can pave the path toward a richer and more nuanced perspective.

Clinical vignette: 3

> Judy, a fifty-six-year-old second generation Mexican American school teacher, entered psychoanalytic psychotherapy to treat her longstanding severe depressive symptoms which increased after her husband began questioning their relationship because of a lack of strength and passivity he perceived on Judy's part. She felt these comments "destroyed her" because she was already feeling a profound sense of inadequacy and shame about her inability to return

to work after taking twelve years off to raise their two boys. The victim of sexual abuse by her stepfather, Judy decided to dedicate her life to her children to allow them to feel safe and protected in a way she never felt. As her two boys grew up, she found herself feeling less and less involved in their daily life and finding herself more isolated and alone. This led to a return of painful ruminations of recurrent self-blame and criticism, which she felt she had previously liberated herself from. Judy reported desperately wanting to go back to work and felt it was imperative that we set this as our goal for treatment. As the therapy progressed, Judy felt her symptoms of depression decreased and she felt more able to engage with her husband and her children. Despite this, she felt a profound inhibition to engage in any work. Any effort to help Judy understand her conflicts around returning to teaching would lead to a concrete pattern: She desperately wanted to return to work, but could not bring herself to do it. After one year of treatment, I began to feel a sense of hopelessness about Judy's situation. Despite her reporting decreased guilt and distress, she had made no progress in returning to work and continued to insist it was the most important aspect of her progress. Feeling a sense of urgency about her situation, I found myself eagerly and quickly making interpretations that felt satisfying to me at the moment of speaking them—it was as if I was eagerly trying to solve the puzzle of her obvious conflict over teaching. I began to make genetic interpretations involving her conflicts with competitiveness and power and her difficulty with bearing the loss of safety her current life offered, with an assuredness that felt forced on retrospect. These interpretations led to her feeling more confused and wanting a behavioral solution to her problems: "I wish someone would just push me to do it." Reflecting on this enactment, I realized that I was carrying an unfelt sense of hopelessness that was leading me to be overly active and helpful, playing the role of the omnipotent rescuer. This allowed me to regain a more calm and reflective stance which then allowed a space for a shared feeling of hopelessness that mirrored her early sexual trauma.

This movement to more concrete thinking on the part of the analyst can also be seen in situations where the analyst, desperate to find some relief, begins to formulate in his mind and relate to the patient in a more "practical" and concrete fashion. Problem-solving or other alternatives to the analysis, such as psychopharmacology, take center stage in the analyst's vision of treatment. While it is true that these other modalities of treatment can be incredibly useful and important aspects of treatment and should certainly be taken into consideration, the *impulse* on the part of the analyst to move in this direction in his thinking about the patient should warrant some self reflection. (Of note, the impulse *not* to consider other modalities of treatment is also worthy of reflection, especially when the analysis is at a stalemate.) Giovacchini (1993) notes that in "hopeless" clinical situations, the therapist will try to give something therapeutically helpful to the patient, but the patient cannot accept or use what is being offered at the time. This in turn is felt as a narcissistic blow by the therapist, who by offering medication or a concrete treatment plan can then be cast in the role of omnipotent savior, restoring the therapist's narcissistic supplies: "The therapist's knowledge of and capacity to prescribe drugs is exalted … they [the therapists] can maintain their narcissistic equilibrium as they identity with the powerful, potentially magical, curative effect of the antidepressant drugs" (Giovacchini, 1993, p. 282). This in turn can lead to a withdrawal from the patient's inner life and conflicts and lead to a deadening of the analytic environment.

If analysts cannot feel they can "reach" the patient, or if they feel despite their best efforts their patients are not improving, hopelessness in the countertransference can begin to give way to aggression and sadism. The forbidden delight of analysts resorting to sadomasochistic enactments with patients, both subtle and overt, is a difficult and guilt-provoking reality. It is worth noting several subtle enactments that may take place in this regard. Using language or a tone of speech that conveys criticism of a patient's inner life can inadvertently occur, as well as taking a harsh, overly parental attitude with the patient. While a healthy sense of humor and playfulness often deepen an analysis, using humor in a subtly mocking fashion toward the patient may also be a method of discharging tension and anger.

Concluding remarks

In this contribution, I have described the feelings of hopelessness within the analyst. This often unspoken experience can cause disruptions in the analyst's ability to empathize with and deepen the analytic experience for the patient. I have outlined two distinct experiences of hopelessness in the analyst, namely, acute and chronic hopelessness. After considering the dangers of using one's own emotional reactions in a concrete way toward understanding a patient, I have described the sudden emergence of doubt and loss of meaning in the countertransference experience, and the importance of bearing these states and then "recovering" from them in the service of deepening the analytic process. Following this, I have discussed clinical material where hopelessness in the analyst signaled a defense against mourning in the analysand, the recognition of which led to the recovery of previously unfelt sadness in the patient. I have then considered chronic hopelessness in the analyst with an emphasis on the secret unfelt hope and longing within the patient that is often masked by a pervasive atmosphere of lifelessness and dejection. This has led me to consider the reactions of hopelessness analysts often have, with a distinction of either feeling the need to "over-respond" or "under-respond" to the overwhelming experience of misery, pessimism, and doubt.

To be sure, analysis is certainly not an easy task for either of the parties involved in the endeavor. In order for the analysis to deepen and for psychic change to occur, the unbearable aspects of one's inner experience need to be contended with within the analytic space. The analyst's ability to have the capacity to tolerate and contain what feels unrelenting without defensively "colonizing" the patient with his own perspective or personality is essential (Ferro, 2002). When this can be managed, the experience of hopelessness within the analyst can be a surprisingly fecund space where growth occurs despite the seemingly bleak exterior of the clinical process. Once the concrete and rigid internal experience of hopelessness is ruptured in the analyst, a more textured perspective emerges. Tenacious hopelessness intertwines with clinging to longed-for hopeful reunions. Psychic deadness breathes for new life and a hunger for vitality. Frozen endless time can be glimpsed as a longing for union and timelessness. These experiences are true for both the analyst and analysand, who by engaging in the analytic space risk the emotional storm of intimacy that hopelessness can stand against.

EPILOGUE

EPILOGUE.

CHAPTER ELEVEN

The hopelessness and helplessness dyad: a concluding commentary

Mary Kay O'Neil

My thoughts about *hopelessness* were always linked with the word *helplessness*. At times I was not even sure if this was to be a book about hopelessness or helplessness; the two words became interchangeable and I could not remember which was the theme of the book. It was this cognitive confusion, this inability to separate words that led me to explore the hopelessness-helplessness dyad. I was no longer helpless: I could manage my frustration with the question "Why this word confusion?" By considering the thinking of others—the psychoanalytic literature, the contributors to this volume, and clinical examples—hope of communicating some understanding of the relationship between hopelessness and helplessness emerged.

The intricate relationship between hopelessness and helplessness

Schmale (1964) is the one psychoanalyst who discusses the genesis of helplessness and hopelessness. For him, helplessness reflects a loss of ego autonomy with a feeling of deprivation resulting from the loss of gratification which is desired from an other-than-self object. Hopelessness, on the other hand, is a loss of autonomy with a feeling of despair coming from the individual's awareness of his own inability to provide himself with gratification. Both hopelessness and helplessness are connected differently to the loss of ego autonomy and Schmale connects lack of help from another person to helplessness and self-help to hopelessness. Unlike Schmale, I cannot separate hopelessness and helplessness; they are bound together as an interdependent pair. Help, whether from another person or self-help reduces helplessness and increases hope.

My purposes in this final chapter are to offer my thoughts about the hopelessness and helplessness dyad, synthesize the views on the subject in the thought-provoking chapters by our contributors, and draw on examples from my clinical experience. The chapters in this book traverse three realms—the developmental, the sociocultural, and the clinical—in which hopelessness and its opposite, hope, appear as part of the human experience.

The hopelessness/helplessness dyad (and their opposites hope and help) encompasses other concepts used within psychoanalysis: conscious and unconscious wishes, deprivation, depression, despair, gratification, self, other, relational patterns, autonomy, and I add "opportunity." To begin generally, people seek therapy, analysis, when they feel pain, have no help, and are unable to do anything about it on their own. They can feel anxious, depressed, despairing, deprived, and empty; they come with the hope of being helped by another person as they have been unable to help themselves. The act of seeking help in itself awakens hope; how a person is received by the helper and what is offered provide opportunity. Clearly, hope, help, and opportunity can refer to the external or internal realm or both. Self as in autonomy and other as in relationships are involved. The absence of hope, help, and opportunity involve deprivation, depression, even despair. When applied to treatment these concepts can be simple or straightforward but most often are complicated and intertwined. The straightforward situation is this: A person in pain seeks a therapist, finds one, they "match", help is offered, and the person agrees—takes the opportunity—feels hope, and over time is assisted by the therapist to find ways of helping himself and eventually to separate from the helper—to be autonomous. Hope and the expectation of help are essential for the analyst and analysand to make the therapeutic contract.

The reality of therapy is rarely that simple. Mitchell (1993), in his book *Hope and Dread in Psychoanalysis*, considers the nature of the secret wishes and deep fears that simply being human involves, thereby underlining the complications of elucidating hope, giving and receiving effective help, as well as finding and using opportunity. Opportunity can come from either external or internal sources, it can be present or absent. However, the capacity to *use* opportunity has to do with characteristic relationship patterns and self-image feelings.

As Akhtar points out in his introduction to this book, hope is the sustainer of life but unfortunately can be reduced, even absent so that a person does not want to go on living. Hopelessness is not an easy subject because loss of hope is extremely painful. The dearth of psychoanalytic literature is indicative of the difficulty of dealing with such a painful human experience. This volume, however, does map out the dark terrain of hopelessness. In Akhtar's thorough overview, he traces the psychoanalytic understanding of hope and hopelessness (sparse as it is in the literature). Akhtar teaches well the concepts that apply to hopelessness and goes on to discuss the technical implications of these conceptualizations. He not only prepares the reader for the ensuing chapters but alerts us to the reasons for addressing "hopelessness" in the three realms—developmental, cultural, and clinical. All three must be considered to understand more fully the hopelessness which our patients bring to us and with which they wish to be helped.

A survey of the chapters in this book

Now, let us explore the thoughts of the other contributors to *Hopelessness*. Rather than summarize these, I will focus on ideas in their chapters which struck me as especially important and also attempt to articulate the thoughts evoked in me about the interdependent connection with helplessness. Together the chapters address most or all of the concepts that are related to a sense of hopelessness. Each of these concepts is potentially present throughout the life cycle. Hope and hopelessness, nevertheless, are expressed differentially at each phase of development. That is, at different phases, from infancy through childhood, adolescence, young adulthood, mid-life, and old age, one or more issues (related to developmental tasks) comes to the fore, while others are less important. Although the contributors focus on hopelessness, external or internal helplessness, conscious or unconscious with variations at each developmental phase are always indirectly present. In my view, hopelessness and helplessness act in parallel—they increase or decrease together.

Ann Smolen's (Chapter Two) attunement to infants and children demonstrates how emotional and physical deprivation contributes to a sense of hopelessness. Her moving account of her work with broken children (ranging in age from nine months to eleven years) not only brings the literature alive but adds to the understanding of a child's affective development. Several important thoughts about children's hopelessness emerged: Hopelessness is linked with Spitz's "anaclitic depression," Bowlby's maternal loss, and Winnicott's hope in acting-out. Without hope, there is no will to live and children may die; a good object attachment must first be established in order for its loss to be mourned; and, in agreement with Anna Freud, when children have not been able to develop a secure attachment in infancy, they often feel little or no distress or anxiety when separation or loss of love is threatened. Along with Mitchell, she reminds us that infantile hopes represent a self-healing return to the point of suspended psychological growth. Such hopes do not need to be renounced but reanimated to grow and develop into mature hopes through the maturational process. Hopelessness and helplessness are linked in this first developmental phase—a child has to be nurtured and helped to grow; growth is the infant's and child's life task and cannot be accomplished without help. A child cannot grow by himself and the severely deprived child sometimes dies. As a child is helped to grow, resilience—ability to look after oneself—increases and it is here that characteristic ways of relating become important. Some children have a tendency to passively withdraw while others seek help. These characteristics may be ingrained or associated with the degree of mistrust and fear within the child.

Rose Vasta (Chapter Three) takes us into hopelessness in adolescence. She stresses that the capacity to balance the opposing forces of hope and hopelessness is crucial for ongoing psychological development. For adolescents, this is particularly difficult given their natural shifts in affect, difficulty in dealing with frustration, and uncertainty about their future. Her view is that surviving phase-limited hopelessness is a necessary condition for the development of hope. Of course, adolescents are not as dependent as infants, nor do they need as much help to grow as children. An analytic colleague identified the adolescent task of learning to help self and others with this parental guideline: "Never do for an adolescent what he can do for himself, never do for yourself what he can do for you." Acting-out, gang involvement, and self-destructive behavior to a limited degree can be adaptively defensive against powerlessness, difficulty in tolerating the frustration of waiting time to realize goals and wishes, parental overprotectiveness, and alienation. An adolescent can be determined to fulfill dreams, to become more independent, but without opportunity or the assistance of facilitating circumstances the young person can be helpless to do so. Helplessness ensues when intense unrealizable desire supersedes realistic wishes, when waiting to reach maturity and fulfill future hopes becomes intolerable, when circumstances or relationships are too restricting or do not provide needed structure and security.

Jon Ellman (Chapter Four) moves us into mid-life but cogently questions whether the phase's inevitable life tasks (building relationships, and family, attaining financial stability, confronting loss of youthfulness, loss of parents, becoming the adult, and personalizing death) can be limited to a certain time period. Although these issues usually arise between the ages of thirty and sixty-five, Ellman has treated people in their early twenties and their seventies whose anxieties revolve around mid-life tasks. He is in agreement with Modell (1989) who cautions that human time is cyclical; conflicts recur endlessly and may be worked-through at increasingly high levels of mastery. Whereas in infants and young children, time has little meaning, and in adolescence, waiting for future gratification is frustrating, the mid-life person begins stocktaking—what have I accomplished? The shortening of time and the end of postponing, when accepted, make one realistically hopeful about the rest of one's life. When not accepted, hopelessness and helplessness can ensue. Narcissistic people are especially at risk as inevitable stocktaking confronts them with failures in living up to grandiose ambitions or shifts in self-image and humiliation when they experience loss of physical attractiveness or prowess, damage done to loved ones, or previously avoided emptiness. Ellman demonstrates why hopelessness can arise at mid-life due to the lack of mourning grandiose, therefore unattainable wishes, what has not been accomplished and are now missed, longed-for, or lost. Mourning allows for a more integrated person who plans for what can be realistically accomplished. Although, in childhood and adolescence, mourning is usually relevant only in the face of serious loss, it is integral to accomplishing the tasks of mid-life. Analysis with emphasis on mourning and moving on can reduce helplessness.

Unfortunately, we do not have a chapter on later life and the hopelessness and helplessness that can ensue at this phase. It is, however, possible to assume that mourning, acceptance, and integration continue to be adaptive ways of approaching the good and bad of life experience and the inevitable end of one's life. Additionally, there is good reason to believe that for the last phase of life, analysis can assist older analysands to surmount hopelessness and to continue along their developmental path. Valenstein (2000) notes the increased numbers of older patients seeking help. A group study found that they respond positively to analysis and psychoanalytic psychotherapy. As aging is the final developmental phase of the life cycle, their hopes are limited to understanding the story of their lives with respect to the present and future and making the most of what time is left. Of course, earlier conflicts (oedipal and preoedipal) can be revived in this later phase and as Valenstein asserts these conflicts can be ameliorated sufficiently so that they do not interfere with finding satisfactory solutions for the last phase of life. He illustrates the group's findings by describing the course and outcome of the analysis of two older men. Here are two clinical examples from my experience of work with older patients.

Clinical vignette: 1

> A woman in her eighth decade presented, wanting help around her relationships with her children and the challenge of organizing herself financially. Beneath this phase specific and not uncommon presenting problem was a secret hope—that she could write a book about her courageous second marriage to a prominent man—a marriage for which she had risked rejection by her family and had a child taken from her. She felt helpless about writing her story. Having had an analysis earlier in life, she was able to effectively use a new "piece" of therapy to work on her presenting problems, review her past, and consider the inhibitions and blockages which interfered with her writing. A year or so after her therapy, she published her book.

Clinical vignette: 2

> An older man enters analysis with the hope of relief of chronic depression and of being able to take charge of this phase of his life. His father had died when the patient was preadolescent; many decades later, he continues to feel deprived and hopeless that he will

ever receive longed-for good parenting and be able to identify with a father he barely knew. He comments, "All my life, I have kept trying to find him; I am dying for information about him and I never got it. Nor did I ask; I was too much in shock to be rational about asking." Does he really just want to know his father (warts and all) or is he also secretly hopeful of finding the ideal father as well as parental approval—of catching up developmentally and feeling good about himself? A repetitive dream (in which he is left alone, unable to play golf as well as his friends and be accepted as one of them) reveals this inhibiting secret longing and self-depreciation. The hope is that he can be helped to separate emotionally and find satisfaction in his remaining time less encumbered by the sadness of his father's death.

The next section of the book pertains to the sociocultural realm. It consists of two chapters, namely Eve Holwell's "Literary Depictions of Helplessness" (Chapter Five) and Sylvia Chong's "The Illusion of a Future" (Chapter Six), which bring the reader to the external world and delineate the reciprocal impact on a person's inner world. These thoughtful chapters, which analyze a short story, a novel, and a poem, as well as three movies, are well worth reading. As seen in the literature and cinema examples, hope and hopelessness are, of course, present in and contributed to by circumstances beyond the clinical world. These same circumstances—often dire—can render a person helpless. It behooves psychoanalysts to be aware of a patient's unique reaction to circumstances in the outside world at the various phases of development. As well, these chapters underline that much can be learned about psychoanalysis from other disciplines and vice versa. Having read Ishiguro's (2005) disturbing and perceptive book, *Never Let Me Go*, made into a movie on which Chong chose to comment, I want to add a few additional thoughts.

Wishes and tasks appropriate to the various phases of life are faced in the collapsed life of the young woman Kathy, cloned to "complete" her life prematurely as an organ donor after caring for other predestined donors. Here is a passage from the book which illustrates my view.

> … swaying about slowly in time to the song, holding an imaginary baby [a pillow] to my breast (p. 71) … I just waited for that bit that went: "Baby, baby, never let me go …" And what I'd imagine was a woman who'd been told she couldn't have babies, who'd really,

really wanted them all her life. Then there's a sort of miracle and she has a baby, and she holds this baby very close to her and walks around singing: "Baby, never let me go ..." partly because she's so happy, but also because she's so afraid something will happen, that the baby will get ill or be taken away from her. (p. 70)

Kathy is eleven years old. She has the natural wish for a baby that arises in most preadolescent girls as they approach puberty to become women. At the same time, she wants to be the baby, to be protected and to be the adult who protects the baby from feared danger. One of the few human realizations of the evil done by cloning these children and depriving them of parental caring, growth, and development, is expressed by "Madame" who, in tears, watches this dance. Later, in her twenties, being a "caretaker" before "completing," Kathy becomes aware of her helplessness—her hope, her real wish can never be met—physically, she could not have a baby. In fact, she is deprived of a future that would extend into mid- and later life. Yet, at the end of her condensed life, Kathy does not fall into hopelessness. She comes to accept the good (education, culture, and friends at a special school) and the bad (a shortened life lived only to allow others to live), momentarily hopes, and then mourns all she lost of her life and moves toward her inevitable end. "The fantasy [to see her deceased love 'Tommy' wave to her] never got beyond that—I didn't let it—and though the tears rolled down my face, I wasn't sobbing or out of control. I just waited a bit, and then turned back to the car, to drive off to wherever I was supposed to be." It is as though Kathy briefly experienced being human and moved, however, quickly through the tasks, the hopes, and the emotional ups and downs of each phase of development. Was she in denial of her helplessness? Perhaps, but as Vaillant (1992) asserts, denial can be an adaptive defense in the face of hopeless circumstances about which one is helpless.

The Holwell and Chong chapters show us how literature and cinema allow us to experience vicariously our painful fears of dire hopelessness and helplessness against which we protect ourselves. As Chong points out, in films more than literature we can avoid the depth of human pain. Is it less difficult to see pain in movies than to allow it into our thoughts through written (literature) or spoken (analysis) words? Do we protect ourselves by believing that movies are not real—only movies? Or is a picture worth 1000 words? When we are unable to face the reality of the inevitable pains of life or the devastating pains of gratification failure and when defenses (such as losing ourselves in movies or books) no longer work, we fall into helplessness and must seek help.

The next section of the book brings us back into the consulting room and the various therapeutic modalities—couple therapy, individual psychodynamic psychotherapy, psychoanalysis, each supported by the touchstone of literature and theory but all utilizing understanding of the unconscious at the core of transference and countertransference. Sarah Usher (Chapter Nine), given her long experience of working with couples, underlines the urgency and/or shame at failure with which members of a couple expose their private selves not only to a therapist but also to their partner. Couple work is intensely involving due to the complications of double histories and varying hopes and needs of two individuals, the multiplicity of possible transferences, and countertransference. Usher does not shy away from the countertransference pressures on the analyst of working with three people in the room and realizes the necessity of not overidentifying with one or the other of the couple. Developmental progress in resolving oedipal, separation, and intimacy conflicts can influence the therapist's unconscious reaction to the couple's issues. Hope and hopelessness are consciously and unconsciously present in the transference and countertransference. Yet, hopelessness and helplessness can be differentially present for the individuals and in the relationship. For example, improvement in the relationship can indicate hopefulness, whereas one member of the couple can be struggling and less hopeful about individual growth or the individual(s) may grow but the relationship may not survive.

The intensity of the emotional pressure on the analyst, whether working with individuals or couples, requires that the analyst has external support. For such support (emotional and intellectual) we look to the thinking of others—most often in our literature. Hopelessness is a painful state when present to any degree but despair, which involves losing all hope, all confidence and yielding to the bleakness of one's inner world is desperately painful for both analyst and analysand. Jeanne Bailey (Chapter Seven) provides us with that support—that touchstone. She offers a comprehensive review of the development of our colleagues' understanding and their work with despair, keeping in mind the differences between hopelessness and despair. She states, "Despair is different from hopelessness as it involves fear of unrelenting pain which the individual feels helpless to manage and hopeless to remedy."

Her summary harkens back to my notion that either external or internal opportunity must be present for a person to hope and to Schmale's belief that both come from the loss of ego autonomy. Bailey makes us aware that despair is not always present but enters treatment at times of empathic failures or misreading so that the analyst is not experienced as helpful; that despair can occur at many levels of experience and at any phase of development and most often comes from the analysand's terrible life experiences evoking shock that even arouse despair in the analyst. Helplessness fluctuates in the analyst and analysand in relation to the intensity of the despair.

An analyst's struggle with her own hopelessness and even despair on hearing the analysand's horrible circumstantial gratification failures and inner experience of self-destructive helplessness is courageously articulated by Judi Kobrick's (Chapter Eight) case example of Christian. In fact, "On the Edge of Hopelessness and Despair: An Uncertain Landscape" dovetails Bailey's chapter by providing the case example which brings Bailey's views and the literature clinically alive. Kobrick's use of poetry and her patient sensitivity, her deep caring, and her ability to hold back, to tolerate the possibility of failure and to assist a hopeless man over many years to find his own way of helping himself are movingly exemplary. She did not give in to the desire to avoid the despair and dread experienced by her patient; nor did she try to impose a sense of hope. Although life opportunity and, later, the chance to receive help were there, Christian had to use the help offered in his own way. Leaving the analysis unfinished, sometime later, he hesitantly returned with a gift—his typed autobiography. He could not face the analyst directly but waited outside until invited in. His handwritten note acknowledged "... without the benefit of our discussions over the past years, it would have been much more difficult to accurately write this autobiography, not to mention coming to a meaningful understanding of many of the events which transpired." Despite himself, he seems helped and able to help himself. Kobrick, however, was left with the unanswerable question, "Have I been able to give him some hope in the face of hopelessness?" She expresses her persistent feeling: "Christian seemed to disappear into the ether but always remained present within me, yet I am left with a sense of loss. What was related, lived and imagined seems incomplete."

Analysands use us as they need us and analysts often have to bear not knowing if and how they helped. Dhwani Shah's (Chapter Ten) "Hopelessness in the Countertransference" attempts to bring to the fore feelings of hopelessness that can arise within the analyst. Rather than pushing away hopelessness by trying to be helpful with "over-responsiveness" or failing to admit limitations and being "under-responsive" by withdrawing from horrible experiences and unbearable feelings, Shah demonstrates the use of countertransference. The analyst's experience of hopelessness can be acute or chronic. Yet, in Shah's view, if these states are borne, the "recovering" from them can be used to deepen the analytic process. This last chapter ends on a hopeful note: "The experience of hopelessness ... can be a surprisingly fecund space where growth occurs despite the seemingly bleak exterior of the clinical process. These experiences are true for both the analyst and the analysand, who by engaging in the analytic space risk the emotional storm of intimacy that hopelessness can stand against." John Steiner's 2011 paper, "Helplessness and the Exercise of Power in the Analytic Session" underlines Shah's views. Steiner in his abstract says, "From time to time I was able to recognize and accept my helplessness and relinquish my attempts to reach the patient. These moments of recognition led to a shift of atmosphere in which a feeling of sadness replaced the more familiar confrontational mood. In these sadder moods, the patient felt I was more available and he too seemed more able to contemplate loss" (p. 135).

Another vignette and some concluding thoughts

Before closing, I want to share a few more thoughts about hopelessness and helplessness. In my view, hope for change and the capacity to use help are critically associated with relational patterns developed due to earlier trauma. That is, relationship patterns can interfere with making good use of opportunity. A clinical example follows.

Clinical vignette: 3

> A middle-aged married man and father seeks help. All goes well for some months, the man makes progress, and both the analyst and the analysand seem to agree that help is being given and received. That is, until the analyst inadvertently causes a narcissistic injury by becoming visibly drowsy during one of the sessions. The analyst admits this and is open to discussing it but the man declines the offer to discuss the admitted injury. He leaves therapy suddenly and blames the analyst. The analyst, feeling shocked, guilty, and

helpless, is left to hold the anger and hurt of sudden irretrievable loss.

As a child, this man had experienced sudden parental death due to an unexpected heart attack. He had lost all hope of ever seeing the loved parent again. He was rendered emotionally and physically helpless. The opportunity to mourn the loss with the help of the bereaved other parent was unavailable. Not surprisingly then, he could not treat the analyst any differently than he had treated others in his life. In fact, a characteristic reenactment occurred—he left the analyst as he had left other would-be helpers suddenly and without discussion.

As Bollas (1983) succinctly commented, "Patients may enact fragments of a parent inviting us unconsciously to learn through experience how it felt to be a child of such a parent" (p. 1)—in this case, a beloved parent who left suddenly with no discussion. The emotions of hopelessness and helplessness, in my experience, can be most poignant in the loneliness of the older woman whether alone through choice or never having married, through divorce, or loss of a partner who died. The hope of a new intimate or gratifying relationship in the later phase of life is limited whether through lack of real opportunity or an inner blockage due to unresolved developmental issues (e.g., separation). Does the analyst have to accept the lonely situation of single women as described by two insightful authors: "That sun, that light had faded, and she had faded with them. Now she was as grey as the season itself" (Brookner, 1985, p. 153); or "Life could do nothing for her, beyond giving time for a better preparation for death" (Austen, 1811, p. 15, Chapter 31). Or can these women be helped to establish relationships available later in life through openness to opportunities with the few available men, with children, with other women, younger people, and cultural events or through achieving generativity? Only by further sharing of clinical experience with older people can questions about the reality of hope and hopelessness in the last phase of life be addressed.

To put my views succinctly, *hope* is maintained or revived when it is realistic—possible to realize—when real opportunity (external or internal) is present and appropriate help is available from another person or through self-help. *Hopelessness* ensues when one or more of the hope factors are absent and the person is rendered *helpless*. Hopelessness and helplessness are interdependent and opportunity is the intervening factor.

REFERENCES

Abend, S. (1986). Countertransference. *Psychoanalytic Quarterly*, 55: 563–575.

Abraham, K. (1924). A short study of the development of the libido, viewed in the light of mental disorders. In: *Selected Papers on Psychoanalysis* (pp. 418–501). New York: Brunner/Mazel, 1955.

Akhtar, S. (1991). Three fantasies related to unresolved separation-individuation: A less recognized aspect of severe character pathology. In: S. Akhtar & H. Parens (Eds.), *Beyond the Symbiotic Orbit: Advances in Separation-Individuation Theory* (pp. 261–284). Northvale, NJ: Jason Aronson.

Akhtar, S. (1994). Object constancy and adult psychopathology. *International Journal of Psychoanalysis*, 75: 441–455.

Akhtar, S. (1996). "Someday ..." and "if only ..." fantasies: Pathological optimism and inordinate nostalgia as related forms of idealization. *Journal of the American Psychoanalytic Association*, 44: 723–753.

Akhtar, S. (2000). Mental pain and the cultural ointment of poetry. *International Journal of Psychoanalysis*, 81: 229–243.

Akhtar, S. (2009). *The Damaged Core: Origins, Dynamics, Manifestations, and Treatment*. Lanham, MD: Jason Aronson.

Akhtar, S. (2014a). Psychoanalytic treatment of trauma and the analyst's personality. *Psychoanalytic Inquiry*, 34: 1–10.

Akhtar, S. (2014b). The mental pain of minorities. *British Journal of Psychotherapy*, 30: 136–153.

Altman, L. L. (1977). Some vicissitudes of love. *Journal of the American Psychoanalytic Association*, 25: 35–52.

Alvarez, A. (2001). Comment on Jill Scharff's case. *Psychoanalytic Inquiry*, 21: 489–498.

Amati-Mehler, J., & Argentieri, S. (1989). Hope and hopelessness: A technical problem? *International Journal of Psychoanalysis*, 70: 295–304.

Amour (2012). Directed by M. Haneke, produced by Les Films du Losange.

Angel, A. (1934). Einige Bemerkungen uber den Optimismus. *International Journal of Psychoanalysis*, 20: 191–199.

Antichrist (2009). Directed by L. von Trier, produced by Zentropia Entertainment.

Aron, L. (2000). Self-reflexivity and the therapeutic action of psychoanalysis. *Psychoanalytic Psychology*, 17: 667–689.

Austen, J. (1811). *Sense and Sensibility*. Kindle edition.

Away from Her (2006). Directed by S. Polley, produced by Foundry Films.

Baldwin, J. (1957). *Going to Meet the Man*. New York: First Vintage International Edition, 1995.

Balint, M. (1968). *The Basic Fault*. London: Tavistock.

Balsam, R. H. (2000). The mother within the mother. *Psychoanalytic Quarterly*, 69: 465–492.

Barton, R., & Whitehead, J. (1969). The gaslight phenomenon. *Lancet*, 1: 158–1260.

Baudry, J. -L. (1986a). Ideological effects of the basic apparatus. In: P. Rosen (Ed.), *Narrative, Apparatus, Ideology: A Film Theory Reader* (pp. 286–298). New York: Columbia University Press.

Baudry, J. -L. (1986b). The apparatus: Metapsychological approaches to the impression of reality in the cinema. In: P. Rosen (Ed.), *Narrative, Apparatus, Ideology: A Film Theory Reader* (pp. 299–318). New York: Columbia University Press.

Benedek, T. (1938). Adaptation to reality in early infancy. *Psychoanalysis Quarterly*, 7: 200–214.

Benedek, T. (1956). Toward the biology of the depressive constellation. *Journal of the American Psychoanalytic Association*, 4: 389–427.

Benjamin, J. (2004). Beyond doer and done to: An intersubjective view of thirdness. *Psychoanalytic Quarterly*, 73: 5–46.

Berlant, L. (1988). Poor Eliza. *American Literature*, 70: 635–668.

Bibring, E. (1956). The mechanism of depression. In: P. Greenacre (Ed.), *Affective Disorders: Psychoanalytic Contributions to their Study* (pp. 13–48). Oxford: International Universities Press.

Bion, W. R. (1958). On arrogance. *International Journal of Psychoanalysis, 39*: 144–146.

Bion, W. R. (1959). Attacks on linking. *International Journal of Psychoanalysis, 40*: 308–315.

Bion, W. R. (1962). A theory of thinking. *International Journal of Psychoanalysis, 63*: 4–5.

Bion, W. R. (1963). *Elements of Psycho-Analysis*. London: Heinemann.

Bion, W. R. (1967). Notes on memory and desire. *Psychoanalytic Forum, 2*: 272–273.

Bion, W. R. (1970). *Attention and Interpretation*. London: Tavistock.

Bion, W. R. (1992). *Cogitations*. London: Karnac.

Blindness (2008). Directed by F. Meirelles, produced by Rhombus Media.

Blos, P. (1967). The second individuation process of adolescence. *Psychoanalytic Study of the Child, 22*: 162–186.

Bollas, C. (1983). Expressive use of the countertransference. *Contemporary Psychoanalysis, 19*: 1–33.

Borden, W. (1997). Review of "Containing Rage, Terror, and Despair: An Object Relations Approach to Psychotherapy" by J. Seinfeld. *Psychoanalytic Social Work, 4*: 83–89.

Boris, H. N. (1976). On hope: Its nature and psychotherapy. *International Review of Psycho-Analysis, 3*: 139–150.

Boswell, J. (1791). *The Life of Samuel Johnson: Volume III*. London: George Routledge & Sons, 1851.

Bowlby, J. (1958). The nature of the child's tie to his mother. *International Journal of Psychoanalysis, 39*: 350–373.

Bowlby, J. (1960). Grief and mourning in infancy and early childhood. *Psychoanalytic Study of the Child, 15*: 9–52.

Bowlby, J. (1961). Processes of mourning. *International Journal of Psychoanalysis, 42*: 317–340.

Bowlby, J. (1980). *Attachment and Loss, Volume III: Loss—Sadness and Depression*. New York: Basic Books.

Bradshaw, P. (2010). The Road. *The Guardian*, 7 January.

Breaking the Waves (1996). Directed by L. von Trier, produced by Argus Film Produktie.

Brenner, C. (1975). Affects and psychic conflict. *Psychoanalytic Quarterly, 44*: 5–28.

Britton, R., & Steiner, J. (1994). Interpretation: Selected fact or overvalued idea? *International Journal of Psychoanalysis, 75*: 1069–1078.

Brookner, A. (1985). *Hotel du Lac*. London: Triad/Panther.

Browning, R. (1855). *Men and Women*. Boston, MA: James R. Osgood, 1876.

Busch, F. (1997). Understanding the patient's use of the method of free association: An ego psychological approach. *Journal of the American Psychoanalytic Association*, 45: 407–423.
Butler, J. (1990). *Gender Trouble: Feminism and the Subversion of Identity*. New York: Routledge.
Cantor, D. W. (1982). Divorce: Separation or separation-individuation. *The American Journal of Psychoanalysis*, 42: 307–313.
Cantor, P. A. (2013). The apocalyptic strain in popular culture: The American nightmare becomes the American dream. *The Hedgehog Review*, 15: 23–33.
Casement, P. (1991). *Learning from the Patient*. New York: Guilford.
Cath, S. H. (1980). Suicide in the middle years: Some reflections on the annihilation of self. In: W. H. Norman & T. H. Scaramella (Eds.), *Midlife: Developmental and Clinical Issues* (pp. 53–69). New York: Brunner/Mazel.
Chaplan, R. (2013). How to help get stuck analyses unstuck. *Journal of the American Psychoanalytic Association*, 61: 591–604.
Chasseguet-Smirgel, J. (1984). *Creativity and Perversion*. New York: W. W. Norton.
Cheng, A. A. (2001). *The Melancholy of Race: Psychoanalysis, Assimilation and Hidden Grief*. Oxford: Oxford University Press.
Children of Men (2006). Directed by A. Cuarón, produced by Universal Pictures.
Chopin, K. (1899). *The Awakening*. New York: Penguin, 1984.
Coen, S. J. (2003). The thrall of the negative and how to analyze it. *Journal of the American Psychoanalytic Association*, 51: 465–489.
Colarusso, C. A. (2006). The absence of a future: The effect of past experience and current developmental conflicts on a midlife analysis. *Journal of the American Psychoanalytic Association*, 54: 919–943.
Colarusso, C. A. (2007). Transience during midlife as an adult psychic organizer: The midlife transition and continuum. *Psychoanalytic Study of the Child*, 62: 329–358.
Coleridge, S. T. (1798). The rime of the ancient mariner. In: *The Oxford Book of English Verse*. London: Oxford University Press, 1940.
Constant Gardener, The (2005). Directed by F. Meirelles, produced by Focus Features.
Cooper, S. H. (2011). Introduction: The difficult-to-reach patient and the difficult to find dyad. *Psychoanalytic Dialogues*, 21: 593–595.
Dancer in the Dark (2000). Directed by L. von Trier, produced by Zentropia Entertainment.
Darwin's Nightmare (2004). Directed by H. Sauper, produced by Mille et Une Productions.
Davies, J. M. (2005). Transformations of desire and despair. *Psychoanalytic Dialogues*, 15: 779–805.

Dicks, H. V. (1967). *Marital Tensions: Clinical Studies Towards a Psychological Theory of Interaction*. London: Karnac.
DiGiacomo, F. (2009). Q&A: *The Road* director John Hillcoat on adapting a modern classic. *VanityFair.com*, <http://www.vanityfair.com/online/oscars/2009/11/qa-the-road-director-john-hillcoat-on-adapting-a-modern-classic>. Accessed 25 November 2009.
Dogville (2003). Directed by L. von Trier, produced by Zentropia Entertainment.
Dreamlife of Angels, The (1998). Directed by E. Zonca, produced by Diaphana Films.
Elysium (2013). Directed by F. Lawrence, produced by Tristar Pictures.
Erikson, E. H. (1950). *Childhood and Society*. New York: W. W. Norton, 1963.
Erikson, E. H. (1962). Reality and actuality—an address. *Journal of the American Psychoanalytic Association*, 10: 451–474.
Erikson, E. H. (1964). *Insight and Responsibility*. New York: W. W. Norton.
Erikson, E. H. (1970). Reflection on the dissent of contemporary youth. *International Journal of Psychoanalysis*, 51: 11–22.
Faimberg, H. (2001). *The Telescoping of Generations*. London: Routledge.
Faimberg, H. (2013). "Well, you'd better ask them": The countertransference position at the crossroads. In: R. Oelsner (Ed.), *Transference and Countertransference Today* (pp. 49–66). New York: Routledge.
Fairbairn, W. R. D. (1943). The repression and the return of bad objects. In: *Psychoanalytic Studies of the Personality* (pp. 59–81). London: Routledge & Kegan Paul, 1952.
Feldman, M. (2009). *Doubt, Conviction and the Analytic Process: Selected papers of Michael Feldman*. New York: Routledge.
Ferenczi, S. (1931). Child-analysis in the analysis of adults. *International Journal of Psychoanalysis*, 12: 468–482.
Ferenczi, S. (1933). On the confusion of tongues between adults and the child. In: *Final Contributions to the Problems and Methods of Psychoanalysis* (pp. 155–167). New York: Basic Books, 1955.
Ferro, A. (2002). *In the Analyst's Consulting Room*. New York: Routledge.
Fink, B. (2007). *The Fundamentals of Analytic Technique: A Lacanian Approach for Practitioners*. New York: W. W. Norton.
Fisher, M. (2010). The lonely Road. *Film Quarterly*, 63: 14–17, 16.
Fisher, M. (2012). Precarious dystopias: *The Hunger Games*, *In Time*, and *Never Let Me Go*. *Film Quarterly*, 65: 27–33.
Fonagy, P., Target, M., Gergely, G., & Jurist, E. (2002). *Affect Regulation, Mentalization, and the Development of the Self*. New York: Other Press.
Fredrickson, B. L. (2009). Why choose hope? *www.psychologytoday.com/blog/-positivity/200903/why-choose-hope*. Accessed March 3, 2014.
French, T. (1945). The integration of social behavior. *Psychoanalytic Quarterly*, 14: 149–161.

French, T. M., & Wheeler, D. R. (1963). Hope and repudiation of hope in psycho-analytic therapy. *International Journal of Psychoanalysis*, 44: 304–316.

Freud, A. (1965). *Normality and Pathology in childhood*. New York: International Universities Press.

Freud, S. (1910d). The future prospects of psycho-analytic therapy. S. E., 11: 139–152. London: Hogarth.

Freud, S. (1911b). Formulations on the two principles of mental functioning. S. E., 12: 213–226. London: Hogarth.

Freud, S. (1914c). On narcissism: an introduction. S. E., 14: 67–103. London: Hogarth.

Freud, S. (1915c). Instincts and their vicissitudes. S. E., 14: 117–140. London: Hogarth.

Freud, S. (1915e). The unconscious. S. E., 14: 311–315. London: Hogarth.

Freud, S. (1917b). A childhood recollection from *Dichtung und Wahrheit*. S. E., 17: 145–156. London: Hogarth.

Freud, S. (1917e). Mourning and melancholia. S. E., 14: 237–260. London: Hogarth.

Freud, S. (1918b). From the history of an infantile neurosis. S. E., 17. London: Hogarth.

Freud, S. (1920g). *Beyond the Pleasure Principle*. S. E., 18. London: Hogarth.

Freud, S. (1923b). *The Ego and the Id*. S. E., 19: 6–63. London: Hogarth.

Freud, S. (1927c). *The Future of an Illusion*. S. E., 21: 3–56. London: Hogarth.

Freud, S. (1937c). Analysis terminable and interminable. S. E., 23: 211–253.

Friedman, L. (1969). The therapeutic alliance. *International Journal of Psychoanalysis*, 50: 139–153.

Fruitvale Station (2013). Directed by R. Coogler, produced by Forest Whitaker's Significant Productions.

Gay, P. (1988). *Freud: A Life for our Time*. New York: W. W. Norton.

Gediman, H. (1985). Impostor, inauthenticity, and feeling fraudulent. *Journal of the American Psychoanalytic Association*, 39: 911–936.

Gedo, J. E., & Goldberg, A. (1973). *Models of the Mind*. Chicago, IL: University of Chicago Press.

Gerson, S. (2009). When the third is dead: Memory, mourning, and witnessing in the aftermath of the Holocaust. *International Journal of Psychoanalysis*, 90: 1341–1357.

Ghent, E. (1990). Masochism, submission, surrender: Masochism as a perversion of surrender. *Contemporary Psychoanalysis*, 26: 108–135.

Ghent, E. (2002). Wish, need, drive: Motive in the light of dynamic systems theory and Edelman's selectionist theory. *Psychoanalytic Dialogues*, 12: 768–808.

Giovacchini, P. (1993). *Countertransference Triumphs and Catastrophes*. Northvale, NJ: Jason Aronson.

Glover, E. (1925). Notes on oral character formations. *International Journal of Psychoanalysis, 6*: 131–153.

Goldberg, C. (1989). The shame of Hamlet and Oedipus. *Psychoanalytic Review, 76*: 581–603.

Green, A. (1980). The dead mother. In: A. Weller (Trans.), *Life Narcissism, Death Narcissism* (pp. 185–221). London: Free Association.

Greeson, J. R. (2010). *Our South: Geographic Fantasy and the Rise of National Literature*. Cambridge, MA: Harvard University Press.

Guttman, S. A., Jones, R. L., & Parrish, S. M. (Eds.) (1980). *The Concordance to the Standard Edition of the Complete Psychological Works of Sigmund Freud*. Boston, MA: G. K. Hall.

Happiness (1998). Directed by T. Solondz, produced by Good Machine Films.

Heidegger, M. (1962). *Being and Time*. New York: Harper Perennial Modern Classics, 2008.

Heimann, P. (1950). On counter-transference. *International Journal of Psychoanalysis, 31*: 81–84.

Herman, J. (1992). *Trauma and Recovery: The Aftermath of Violence from Domestic Abuse to Political Terror*. New York: Basic Books, 1997.

Hinshelwood, R. D. (2013). Freud's countertransference? Reviewing the case histories with modern ideas of transference and countertransference. In: R. Oelsner (Ed.), *Transference and Countertransference Today* (pp. 88–105). New York: Routledge.

Hoffman, I. (1992). Some practical implications of a social constructivist view of the psychoanalytic situation. *Psychoanalytic Dialogues, 2*: 287–304.

Hornaday, A. (2009). "The Road": Been there, done this post-apocalyptic reckoning. *Washington Post*, 25 November.

Horney, K. (1967). *Feminine Psychology*. New York: W. W. Norton.

Hotel Rwanda (2004). Directed by T. George, produced by United Artists.

Ishiguro, K. (2005). *Never Let Me Go*. Toronto, Canada: Vintage Canada Edition.

Jack and Jill (2011). Directed by D. Dugan, produced by Columbia Pictures.

Jacobson, E. (1943). Depression—the oedipus conflict in the development of depressive mechanisms. *Psychoanalytic Quarterly, 12*: 541–560.

Jameson, F. (1982). Progress versus utopia: Or, can we imagine the future? *Science Fiction Studies, 9*: 147–158.

Jaques, E. (1965). Death and the mid-life crisis. *International Journal of Psychoanalysis, 46*: 502–514.

Jenkins, M. (2010). In a dystopian Britain, teens grope toward a future. *NPR.com*, <http://www.npr.org/templates/story/story.php?storyId=129838461>. Accessed 14 September 2010.

Jones, E. (1955). *The Life and Work of Sigmund Freud, Vol. II*. New York: Basic Books.

Joseph, B. (1982). Addiction to near-death. *International Journal of Psychoanalysis, 63*: 449–456.

Joseph, B. (1983). On understanding and not understanding: Some technical issues. *International Journal of Psychoanalysis, 65*: 291–298.

Kafka, F. (1915). *The Metamorphosis*. New York: Tribeca, 2010.

Keats, J. (1882). *The Complete Poems*. New York: Penguin, 1988.

Kelman, H. (1945). Neurotic pessimism. *Psychoanalytic Review, 32*: 419–448.

Kernberg, O. F. (1980). *Internal World and External Reality*. Northvale, NJ: Jason Aronson.

Khan, M. M. R. (1966). Phobic and counterphobic mechanisms and separation anxiety in schizoid character formation. In: *The Privacy of the Self* (pp. 69–81). New York: International Universities Press, 1974.

Killingmo, B. (1989). Conflict and deficit: Implications for technique. *International Journal of Psychoanalysis, 70*: 65–79.

Klein, M. (1935). A contribution to the psychogenesis of manic depressive states. In: *Love, Guilt and Reparation and Other Works—1921–1945* (pp. 262–289). New York: Free Press, 1975.

Klein, M. (1957). Envy and gratitude. In: *Envy and Gratitude and Other Works—1946–1963* (pp. 176–235). New York: Free Press, 1975.

Laing, R. D. (1960). *The Divided Self: An Existential Study in Sanity and Madness*. London: Penguin.

Laplanche, J. (1976). *Life and Death in Psychoanalysis*. J. Mehlman (Trans.). Baltimore, MD: Johns Hopkins University Press.

Lax, R. F. (2008). Becoming really old: The indignities. *Psychoanalytic Quarterly, 77*: 835–857.

Leaving Las Vegas (1995). Directed by M. Figgis, produced by Lumiere Pictures.

Life is Beautiful (1997). Directed by R. Benigni, produced by Cecchi Gori Group Tiger Cinematografica.

Loewald, H. (1960). On the therapeutic action of psychoanalysis. *Journal of the American Psychoanalytic Association, 41*: 16–33.

Loewald, H. (1962). Internalization, separation, mourning, and the superego. *Psychoanalytic Quarterly, 31*: 483–504.

Loewald, H. (1979). The waning of the Oedipus complex. In: *Papers on Psychoanalysis* (pp. 384–404). New Haven, CT: Yale University Press, 1980.

Lowenstein, R. (1990). Frontiers of adult development in theory and practice. In: R. A. Nemiroff & C. A. Colarusso (Eds.), *New Dimensions in Adult Development* (pp. 97–129). New York: Basic Books.

Mahler, M. S. (1968). *On Human Symbiosis and the Vicissitudes of Individuation*. New York: International Universities Press.

Mahler, M. S., Pine, F., & Bergman, A. (1975). *The Psychological Birth of the Human Infant: Symbiosis and Individuation*. New York: Basic Books.

Maltsberger, J., & Buie, D. (1974). Countertransference hate in the treatment of suicidal patients. *Archives of General Psychiatry, 30*: 625–633.

McGowan, T. (2003). Looking for the gaze: Lacanian film theory and its vicissitudes. *Cinema Journal, 42*: 27–47.

Melancholia (2011). Directed by L. von Trier, produced by Zentropia Entertainment.

Menninger, K. (1959). *A Psychoanalyst's World*. New York: Viking.

Metz, C. (1977). *The Imaginary Signifier: Psychoanalysis and the Cinema*. C. Britton, A. Williams, B. Brewster, & A. Guzzetti (Trans.). Bloomington, IN: Indiana University Press.

Michels, R., & Auchincloss, E. L. (1989). The impact of middle age on ambitions and ideals. In: J. M. Oldman & R. S. Liebert (Eds.), *The Middle Years: New Psychoanalytic Perspectives* (pp. 40–57). New Haven, CT: Yale University Press.

Miller, F. N. (1985). Hopelessness: A narcissistic resistance. *Modern Psychoanalysis, 10*: 65–79.

Mitchell, S. A. (1988). *Relational Concepts in Psychoanalysis: An Integration*. Cambridge, MA: Harvard University Press.

Mitchell, S. A. (1993). *Hope and Dread in Psychoanalysis*. New York: Basic Books.

Mitchell, S. A. (1997). *Influence and Autonomy in Psychoanalysis*. Hillsdale, NJ: Analytic Press.

Mitchell, S. A. (2002). *Can Love Last? The Fate of Romance over Time*. New York: W. W. Norton.

Modell, A. H. (1965). On having the right to a life: An aspect of the superego's development. *International Journal of Psychoanalysis, 46*: 323–331.

Modell, A. H. (1984). Self preservation and the preservation of the self. *The Annual of Psychoanalysis, 12*: 69–86.

Modell, A. H. (1989). Object relations theory: Psychic aliveness in the middle years. In: J. M. Oldman & R. S. Liebert (Eds.), *The Middle Years: New Psychoanalytic Perspectives* (pp. 17–26). New Haven, CT: Yale University Press.

Mulvey, L. (1986). Visual pleasure and narrative cinema. In: P. Rosen (Ed.), *Narrative, Apparatus, Ideology: A Film Theory Reader* (pp. 198–209). New York: Columbia University Press.

Never Let Me Go (2010). Directed by M. Romanek, produced by DNA Films.
Oblivion (2013). Directed by J. Kosinski, produced by Universal Pictures.
Oelsner, R. (2013). Introduction. In: R. Oelsner (Ed.), *Transference and Countertransference Today* (pp. 1–17). New York: Routledge.
Orgel, S. (2012). On negative therapeutic reaction. In: L. Wurmser & H. Jarass (Eds.), *Nothing Good is Allowed to Stand: An Integrative View of the Negative Therapeutic Reaction* (pp. 57–66). New York: Routledge.
Ornstein, A. (1974). The dread to repeat and the new beginning: A contribution to the psychoanalysis of the narcissistic personality disorders. *The Annual of Psychoanalysis, 2*: 231–248.
Ossos (1997). Directed by P. Costa, produced by Madragoa Filmes.
Penley, C. (1989). *The Future of an Illusion: Film, Feminism, and Psychoanalysis*. Minneapolis, MN: University of Minnesota Press.
Perry, S. W. (1989). The phantom self of middle age. In: J. M. Oldman & R. S. Liebert (Eds.), *The Middle Years: New Psychoanalytic Perspectives* (pp. 71–98). New Haven, CT: Yale University Press.
Pianist, The (2002). Directed by R. Polanski, produced by R. P. Productions.
Potamianou, A. (1992). *Un bouclier dans l'economie des etats l'espoir*. Paris: Presses Universitaires de France.
Quinodoz, J. (2008). *Listening to Hanna Segal*. London: Routledge.
Racker, H. (1957). The meanings and uses of countertransference. *Psychoanalytic Quarterly, 26*: 303–357.
Rank, O. (1945). *Will Therapy*. New York: W. W. Norton, 1978.
Rapaport, D. (1960). The structure of psychoanalytic theory. *Psychological Issues, 6*: 39–72.
Rapold, N. (2011). Melancholia. When worlds collide: Lars von Trier's new film ends with a bang. *Film Comment*, September/October.
Reich, W. (1949). *Character Analysis*. V. R. Carfagno (Trans.). New York: Farrar, Straus and Giroux, 1972.
Renik, O. (2006). *Practical Psychoanalysis for Therapists and Patients*. New York: Other Press.
Requiem for a Dream (2000). Directed by D. Aronofsky, produced by Artisan Entertainment.
Revolutionary Road (2008). Directed by S. Mendes, produced by Dreamworks.
Rizzuto, A. (2004). Paradoxical words and hope in psychoanalysis. *Psychoanalytic Psychology, 21*: 203–213.
Road, The (2009). Directed by J. Hillcoat, produced by Dimension Films.
Robbins, B. (2007). Cruelty is bad: Banality and proximity in "Never Let Me Go". *NOVEL: A Forum on Fiction, 40*: 289–302.

Rosenfeld, H. (1971). Contributions to the psychopathology of psychotic patients. The importance of projective identification in the ego structure and object relations of the psychotic patient. In: P. Doucet & C. Laurin (Eds.), *Problems of Psychosis* (pp. 117–137). London: Routledge.

Safran, J. D. (1999). Faith, despair, will, and the paradox of acceptance. *Contemporary Psychoanalysis, 35*: 5–23.

Schmale, A. H., Jr. (1964). A genetic view of affects with special reference to the genesis of helplessness and hopelessness. *Psychoanalytic Study of the Child, 19*: 287–310.

Schmithusen, G. (2012). "Time that no one can count, always begins anew": Thoughts concerning the function and meaning of the so-called negative therapeutic reaction from the perspective of time standing still. In: L. Wurmser & H. Jarass (Eds.), *Nothing Good is Allowed to Stand: An Integrative View of the Negative Therapeutic Reaction* (pp. 67–96). New York: Routledge.

Schwaber, E. A. (2005). The struggle to listen: Continuing reflections, lingering paradoxes, and some thoughts on the recovery of memory. *Journal of the American Psychoanalytic Association, 53*: 789–810.

Scott, A. O. (2011). Bride's mind is on another planet. *New York Times*, 10 November.

Searles, H. F. (1977). The development of mature hope in the patient-therapist relationship. In: *Countertransference and Related Subjects: Selected Papers* (pp. 479–502). New York: International Universities Press, 1979.

Semel, V. (1990). Confrontations with hopelessness: Psychoanalytic treatment of the older woman. *Modern Psychoanalysis, 12*: 215–224.

Settlage, C. F. (1994). On the contribution of separation-individuation theory to psychoanalysis; developmental process, pathogenesis, therapeutic process, and technique. In: S. Kramer & S. Akhtar (Eds.), *Mahler and Kohut: Perspectives on Development, Psychopathology, and Technique* (pp. 17–52). Northvale, NJ: Jason Aronson.

Sharkey, B. (2011). Lars von Treir's "Melancholia" is—gasp—hopeful. *Los Angeles Times*, 11 November.

Silver Linings Playbook (2012). Directed by D. O. Russell, produced by The Weinstein Group.

Sixsmith, M. (2009). *The Lost Child of Philomena Lee*. London: Macmillan.

Slochower, H. (1984). Hope beyond hopelessness. *American Imago, 41*: 237–243.

Slochower, J. (2008). Into the whirlwind: Discussion of paper by Nina Farhi. *Contemporary Psychoanalysis, 44*: 41–49.

Smolen, A. G. (2009). The analyst at work—boys only! No mothers allowed. *International Journal of Psychoanalysis, 90*: 1–11.

Sontag, S. (1966). The imagination of disaster. In: *Against Interpretation: And Other Essays* (pp. 144–158). New York: Picador.

Spitz, R. (1946). Anaclitic depression: An inquiry into the genesis of psychiatric conditions in early childhood. *Psychoanalytic Study of the Child, 2*: 313–342.

Spitz, R. (1960). Discussion of Dr. John Bowlby's paper (Grief and mourning in infancy). *Psychoanalytic Study of the Child, 15*: 85–94.

Spitz, R. (1965). *The First Year of Life. A Psychoanalytic Study of Normal and Deviant Development of Object Relations*. New York: International Universities Press.

Steiner, J. (1984). Some reflections on the analysis of transference: A Kleinian view. *Psychoanalytic Inquiry, 4*: 443–463.

Steiner, J. (1987). The interplay between pathological organizations and the paranoid-schizoid and depressive positions. *International Journal of Psychoanalysis, 68*: 69–80.

Steiner, J. (1993). *Psychic Retreats: Pathological Organizations of the Personality in Psychotic Neurotic and Borderline Patients*. London: Routledge.

Steiner, J. (2011). Helplessness and the exercise of power in the analytic session. *International Journal of Psychoanalysis, 92*: 135–147.

Stekel, W. (1933). Sadism masochism: The psychology of hatred and cruelty. *Psychoanalytic Review, 20*: 114–120.

Stern, D. B. (2010). *Partners in Thought: Working with Unformulated Experience, Dissociation, and Enactment*. New York: Routledge.

Stern, D. B., Stern, D. N., Sander, L. W., Nahum, J. P., Harrison, A. M., Lyons-Ruth, K., Morgan, A. C., Bruschweilerstern, N., & Tronick, E. Z. (1998). Non-interpretive mechanisms in psychoanalytic therapy: The "something more" than interpretation. *International Journal of Psychoanalysis, 79*: 903–921.

Stowe, H. B. (1852). *Uncle Tom's Cabin*. New York: Dover, 2005.

Strenger, C. (2009). Pairing down life to the essentials: An epicurean psychodynamics of midlife change. *Psychoanalytic Psychology, 26*: 246–258.

Symington, J., & Symington, N. (1996). *The Clinical Thinking of Wilfred Bion*. London: Routledge.

Symonds, M. (1968). Disadvantaged children growing in a climate of hopelessness and despair. *American Journal of Psychoanalysis, 28*: 15–22.

Terms of Endearment (1983). Directed by J. Brooks, produced by Paramount Pictures.

Tolpin, M. (2007). The divided self: Shifting an intrapsychic balance the forward edge of a kinship transference: To bleed like everyone else. *Psychoanalytic Inquiry, 27*: 50–65.

Tolpin, M. (2009). A new direction for psychoanalysis: In search of a transference of health. *International Journal of Psychoanalytic Self Psychology, 4S*: 31–43.

Tolstoy, L. (1877). *Anna Karenina*. New York: Modern Library Classics, 2000.
Tougas, C. T. (1999). How rejection of essences expresses despair. *Journal of Analytic Psychology*, 44: 309–329.
Unforgiven (1992). Directed by C. Eastwood, produced by Warner Brothers.
Usher, S. F. (2008). *What is This Thing Called Love? A Guide to Psychoanalytic Psychotherapy with Couples*. Hove, UK: Routledge.
Vaillant, G. (1992). *Ego Mechanisms of Defense: A Guide for Clinicians and Researchers*. Washington, DC: American Psychiatric Press.
Valenstein, A. (2000). The older patient in psychoanalysis. *Journal of the American Psychoanalytic Association*, 48: 1563–1589.
Varvin, S., & Volkan, V. (Eds.) (2005). *Violence or Dialogue?: Psychoanalytic Insights on Terror and Terrorism*. London: International Psychoanalytic Association.
Volkan, V. (1999). Psychoanalysis and diplomacy: I. Individual and large group identity. *Journal of Applied Psychoanalytic Studies*, 1: 29–45.
Volkan, V. (2004). *Blind Trust: Large Groups and Their Leaders in Times of Crises and Terror*. Charlottesville, VA: Pitchstone.
Volkan, V. (2006). *Killing in the Name of Identity: A Study of Bloody Conflicts*. Charlottesville, VA: Pitchstone.
Voltaire (1759). *Candide*. R. Pierson (Trans.). New York: Oxford University Press, 1955.
von Trier, L. (2011). I am a Nazi … I understand Hitler. *Huffington Post: Entertainment*, 18 May.
Wagonfeld, S., & Emde, R. N. (1982). Anaclitic depression—a follow-up from infancy to puberty. *Psychoanalytic Study of the Child*, 37: 67–94.
West, J. J., & Schain-West, J. (1997). Envy in the countertransference. In: M. F. Solomon, & J. P. Siegel (Eds.), *Countertransference in Couples Therapy* (pp. 126–135). New York: W. W. Norton.
Wexler, L. (2000). *Tender Violence: Domestic Visions in an Age of U.S. Imperialism*. Chapel Hill, NC: University of North Carolina Press.
Wild Bunch, The (1969). Directed by S. Peckinpah, produced by Warner Brothers/Seven Arts.
Williams, L. (1991). Film bodies: Gender, genre, and excess. *Film Quarterly*, 44: 2–13.
Winnicott, D. W. (1941). The observation of infants in a set situation. *International Journal of Psychoanalysis*, 22: 229–249.
Winnicott, D. W. (1956). The antisocial tendency. In: *Collected Papers: Through Paediatrics to Psychoanalysis* (pp. 306–316). New York: Basic Books, 1958.
Winnicott, D. W. (1960). String: A technique of communication. *Journal of Child Psychology and Psychiatry*, 1: 49–52.
Winnicott, D. W. (1963). Morals and education. In: *The Maturational Processes and the Facilitating Environment* (pp. 93–105). New York: International Universities Press.

Winnicott, D. W. (1965). *The Maturational Process and the Facilitating Environment*. London: Hogarth.
Winnicott, D. W. (1971). *Therapeutic Consultations in Child Psychiatry*. New York: Basic Books.
Winnicott, D. W. (1974). Fear of breakdown. *International Review of Psycho-Analysis*, 1: 103–107.
Winnicott, D. W. (1987). *Babies and Their Mothers*. New York: Addison-Wesley.
Winnicott, D. W. (1996). *Thinking About Children*. Reading, MA: Addison-Wesley.
Wolverine, The (2013). Directed by J. Mangold, produced by Twentieth Century Fox.
World War Z (2013). Directed by M. Forster, produced by Paramount Pictures.
Wrestler, The (2008). Directed by D. Aronofsky, produced by Wild Bunch Pictures.
Wurmser, L. (2012). Negative therapeutic reaction and the compulsion to disappoint the other. In: L. Wurmser & H. Jarass (Eds.), *Nothing Good is Allowed to Stand: An Integrative View of the Negative Therapeutic Reaction* (pp. 27–56). New York: Routledge.
Zetzel, E. (1965). On the capacity to bear depression. In: *The Capacity for Emotional Growth* (pp. 82–114). New York: International Universities Press, 1970.
Žižek, S. (1997). *The Plague of Fantasies*. London: Verso.

INDEX

Abend, S. 150
Abraham, K. 4, 141
acute hopelessness 183
adolescent
    and countertransference 55
    and desire 47–55
    and hope 44–47
    personality 48–49
Akhtar, S. 6, 13, 98, 153, 182, 189, 192, 197, 205
Altman, L. L. 177
Alvarez, A. 144
Alzheimer's disease 122
Amati-Mehler, J. 6, 11–12, 15, 70, 188, 192
anaclitic depression 24–25, 206
Angel, A. 5–6
Anna Karenina 85
Antichrist 116
Argentieri, S. 6, 11–12, 15, 70, 188, 192

Aron, L. 148
Auchincloss, E. L. 64
Austen, J. 214
The Awakening 86, 90, 99–100, 102, 105

Baldwin, J. 86, 94, 98, 101–102
    story 98
Balint, M. 141
Balsam, R. H. 97
Barton, R. 16
Baudry, J. -L. 129, 131
Benedek, T. 129, 131
Benjamin, J. 159
Bergman, A. 7
Berlant, L. 136
Bibring, E. 136
Bion, W. R. 19, 43, 45–46, 48, 50, 55, 70, 144, 158, 182
Blos, P. 44
Bollas, C. 214
Borden, W. 143

INDEX

Boris, H. N. 8, 19, 23, 25, 43, 47–48, 64, 67
    theory 25
Boswell, J. 60
Bowlby, J. 9, 25, 142, 206
Bradshaw, P. 120
Brenner, C. 141
Britton, R. 195
Brookner, A. 214
Browning, R. 214
Bruschweilerstern, N. 150
Buie, D. 194
Busch, F. 150
Butler, J. 128, 150

Can Love Last? 178
Cantor, D. W. 169
Cantor, P. A. 117
Casement, P. 5
case study
    Anita 32–33
    Beth 189–191
    Bob 175–177
    Boris 8
    Carol 169–172
    Doug 173–175
    Edna 91–94
    Georgie 26–28
    Helen 38–41
    Janice 175–177
    Judy 197–198
    Kathy, H. 125–128
    Lamar 186–187
    Lizzie 30–32
    Miller 16
    Mr. G. 65–67
    Mr. L. 67–73
    Ms. T. 74–79
    Nathan 169–172
    Pamela 166–169
    Rose 28–30
    Sara 33
    Tom 166–169

Cath, S. H. 61
Chaplan, R. 187–188
Chasseguet-Smirgel, J. 8
Cheng, A. A. 134
Childe Roland to the Dark Tower Came 86, 105
    Roland's journey 86–90, 99–100, 102
Chopin, K. 86, 90, 103
chronic disease 122
chronic doubt 194
chronic hopelessness 9, 11–12, 14, 183, 185, 187–189, 199–200, 213
chronic state of mourning 25
chronic state of depression from abuse 152
chronic unrealistic hope of a magical event (*Wunderglauben*) 5
Coen, S. J. 186
Cogitations 48
cognitive disturbances 49
Colarusso, C. A. 58–59, 81
Coleridge, S. T. 81
"confident expectation" 4, 10, 141
Cooper, S. H. 158
countertransference 212
    disturbances 193
    reactions 178, 184
couple therapy 166
creativity 51

Dancer in the Dark 116
Davies, J. M. 149, 151
depressive position 11, 54, 61, 143–145, 196
desire 47
    clinical implications 49–55
    countertransference implications 55
despair 63–64, 139–142, 144–152, 188, 211–212
    and literature 85, 87–89, 105, 109

Dicks, H. V. 177
DiGiacomo, F. 117
"Dogme 95" movement 115
Dogville 116
"dream factory" 107, 134
drugs 53

eating disorder 49
Elysium 108
Emde, R. N. 24
Erikson, E. H. 4, 25, 44, 57, 61

Faimberg, H. 184
Fairbairn, W. R. D. 143
false self 53, 142, 146
Feldman, M. 185
Ferenczi, S. 141, 148
Ferro, A. 200
Fink, B. 184
Fisher, M. 119, 126, 131
Fonagy, P. 155
Fredrickson, B. L. 63
French, T. 4
French, T. M. 4
Freud, A. 34, 206
Freud, S. 4, 11, 19, 47, 97, 107, 109, 115, 129, 141–142, 181–183, 195
Friedman, L. 16
Fruitvale Station 108
The Future of an Illusion 110

Gay, P. 19
Gediman, H. 7
Gedo, J. E. 15
Gergely, G. 155
Gerson, S. 156
Ghent, E. 155
"Gilded Age" 115
Giovacchini, P. 187, 192–193, 195, 199
Glover, E. 4
Goldberg, A. 15
Goldberg, C. 15, 142
good self 146

Green, A. 16
Greeson, J. R. 136
Guttman, S. A. 9

Harrison, A. M. 150
Heidegger, M. 134
Heimann, P. 182
Herman, J. 197
"heroic" interventions 9
Hinshelwood, R. D. 195
Hoffman, I. 19
"Hollywood film" 108, 135
hope 48
    "classical" and British independent positive perspective 5
    normal and pathological 4–8
    "nuisance value" 5
    pathological 6
    positive aspects of 4
    psychoanalytic literature on 8–9
    technical implications 13–17
    "unconscious hope" 5
Hope and Dread in Psychoanalysis 204
Hope Beyond the Void 143
hopelessness 10, 63, 85, 87, 139, 181, 203, 205
    acute 183
    adaptive perspectives 99
    chronic 187
    desire and its special relationship to 47
    examination of the vicissitudes 45
    film theory 128–134
    importance 44–45
    over-reactiveness to 194–197
    survival of 116–122
hopelessness and midlife
    caveats 58–60
    dilemmas of 60–63
hopelessness in childhood
    psychoanalytic treatments 26–41
    survey of literature 24–26

232   INDEX

Hornaday, A. 117, 120
Horney, K. 142, 168

"imperturbable optimism" 4
Ishiguro, K. 123–124, 126, 209

Jacobson, E. 145
Jameson, F. 116–117
Jaques, E. 57–58, 60–64
   contribution of 64
Jenkins, M. 127
Jones, E. 9, 19
Jones, R. L. 9
Joseph, B. 143–144
Jurist, E. 155

Kafka, F. 85
Keats, J. 103, 105
Kelman, H. 9–10
Kernberg, O. F. 64
Khan, M. M. R. 5
Killingmo, B. 14–15
Klein, M. 11, 43, 53–54, 143
Kleinian 60, 81

Laing, R. D. 142
Laplanche, J. 130
Lax, R. F. 18
LeBrun, Robert 91
"libido reservoir" 147
literary genres 86
Loewald, H. 16, 19, 150, 168, 182
Los Angeles Times 116
Lowenstein, R. 16, 19, 150, 168, 182
Lyons-Ruth, K. 150

Mahler, M. S. 7, 25, 172
Maltsberger, J. 194
McGowan, T. 136
Melancholia 64, 109, 111–113, 116, 119, 122, 128, 130
Menninger, K. 4

"Mental Pain and the Cultural Ointment of Poetry" 153
Metamorphosis 85
Metz, C. 129
Michels, R. 64
midlife crisis 57–59, 62, 80
Miller, F. N. 11, 16
Mitchell, S. A. 17, 25–26, 41–42, 59, 63, 148, 157–158, 163, 204, 206
"mobile integrative energy" 147
Modell, A. H. 59, 145, 172, 207
"moments of meeting" 150
Morgan, A. C. 150
Mulvey, L. 129, 136

Nahum, J. P. 150
Never Let Me Go 109, 122, 124, 133
New York Times 116
"nuisance value" 5

Oblivion 108
Oelsner, R. 182
Orgel, S. 192
Ornstein, A. 141, 147

Pandora's Box xvii, 25, 128
"paranoid position" 11
Parrish, S. M. 9
Penley, C. 110, 117, 131
Perry, S. W. 59
Pine, F. 7
Potamianou, A. 6
psychic process 100
psychoanalysis and film studies 110
psychoanalytic literature on hope 8–9
psychoanalytic technique 149

Quinodoz, J. 53

Racker, H. 182–183, 185
Radio-Reloj 64

INDEX

Rank, O. 148
Rapaport, D. 97
Rapold, N. 97, 113
realistic hope 54
Reich, W. 100
Renik, O. 183
Rizzuto, A. 44
The Road 109, 117–119, 121–122, 128, 130–131, 133
Robbins, B. 126
Romanek, Mark 123
Rosenfeld, H. 144

Safran, J. D. 147–151
Sander, L. W. 150
Schain-West, J. 179
Schmale, A. H. 10–11, 100, 203–204, 212
Schmithusen, G. 192
Schwaber, E. A. 184
Scott, A. O. 116
Searles, H. F. 6, 17
Semel, V. 18
Settlage, C. F. 169
Sharkey, B. 116
Silver Linings Playbook 111
Sixsmith, M. 153
Slochower, H. 18, 147
Smolen, A. G. 26, 206
Sonny's Blues 86, 94, 99, 102, 105
  the story 94–97
  themes 97–103
Sontag, S. 111
Spitz, R. 9, 24–25, 206
Steel Magnolia 123
Steiner, J. 49, 74, 143–144, 193, 195–196, 213
Stekel, W. 142
Stern, D. B. 150, 156
Stern, D. N. 150
Stowe, H. B. 133
Strenger, C. 62

Symington, J. 53
Symington, N. 53
Symonds, M. 18, 99

Target, M. 155
Terms of Endearment 123
Tolpin, M. 145–146, 150–151
Tolstoy, L. 85
Tougas, C. T. 142
Tristan 115–116
Tristan und Isolde 113–114
Tronick, E. Z. 150

Unforgiven 119
Usher, S. F. 165, 211

Vaillant, G. 210
Valenstein, A. 208
Varvin, S. 18
Vasta, Rose 206
Volkan, V. 18
Voltaire 19
von Trier, L. 111, 113, 115–116, 130, 136

Wagonfeld, S. 24
Webster's Dictionary 156
West, J. J. 179
Wexler, L. 136
Wheeler, D. R. 4
Whitehead, J. 16
The Wild Bunch 119
Williams, L. 123
Winnicott, D. W. 4–5, 25–26, 35, 43, 51–53, 55, 141, 149, 155, 206
The Wolverine 108
World War Z 108
Wunderglauben 5
Wurmser, L. 192

Zetzel, E. 142, 149
Žižek, S. 132–133